Best Hikes Cleveland

Best Hikes Cleveland

The Greatest Views, Wildlife, and Forest Strolls

Second Edition

Joe Baur

FALCONGUIDES

GUILFORD, CONNECTICUT

FALCONGUIDES®

An imprint of The Rowman & Littlefield Publishing Group, Inc.
4501 Forbes Blvd., Ste. 200
Lanham, MD 20706
www.rowman.com

Falcon and FalconGuides are registered trademarks and Make Adventure Your Story is a trademark of The Rowman & Littlefield Publishing Group, Inc.

Distributed by NATIONAL BOOK NETWORK

Copyright © 2019 The Rowman & Littlefield Publishing Group, Inc.

Photos by the author unless otherwise noted
Maps by The Rowman & Littlefield Publishing Group, Inc.

British Library Cataloguing-in-Publication Information available

Library of Congress Cataloging-in-Publication Data available

ISBN 978-1-4930-3867-1 (paperback)
ISBN 978-1-4930-3868-8 (e-book)

∞™ The paper used in this publication meets the minimum requirements of American National Standard for Information Sciences—Permanence of Paper for Printed Library Materials, ANSI / NISO Z39.48-1992.

Printed in the United States of America

The author and The Rowman & Littlefield Publishing Group, Inc., assume no liability for accidents happening to, or injuries sustained by, readers who engage in the activities described in this book.

Contents

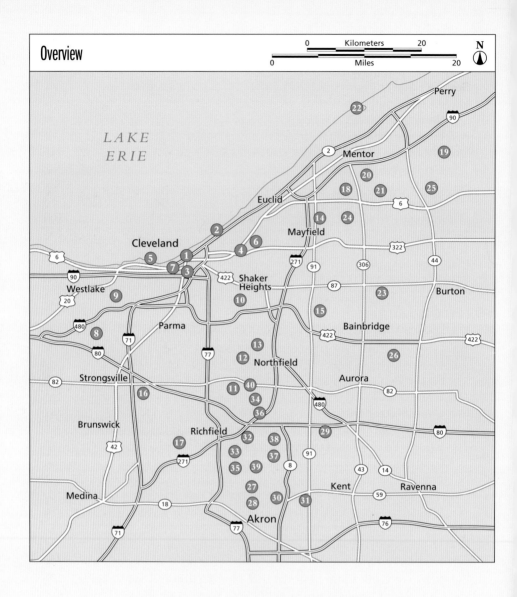

0 Kilometers 20
0 Miles 20

N

LAKE
ERIE

Perry

Mentor

Euclid

Cleveland

Mayfield

Westlake

Shaker
Heights

Parma

Bainbridge

Burton

Strongsville

Northfield

Aurora

Brunswick

Richfield

Kent

Ravenna

Medina

Akron

Acknowledgments

I'm going to do the right thing and first thank my wife, Melanie. Her constant and uplifting support was instrumental and invaluable in the writing of this book. I say this truthfully and without hope of scoring points (although it certainly doesn't hurt); I couldn't have written this book without her encouragement, joining me on the trails more often than not.

Rob Andrukat, my former downtown neighbor and occasional photographer, was kind enough to lend his camera to a few of the photographs throughout this book. Jarret Boroway, Eric Greene, and Victor Granger were also kind enough to join me on hikes, not to mention they no doubt provided Melanie a much-needed break from being trapped in the forest with me.

I would also like to thank Elizabeth Boltuc of the Northeast Ohio Hiking Club for sharing her favorite hikes early on in the planning process of this book, and Larry Grewe of the Buckeye Trail Association, a key player in mapping out our grand finale hike along the Buckeye Trail.

I can't possibly continue without thanking my family. This includes anyone reading this who shares DNA with me or happened to be so lucky to marry into the family.

I'll also be eternally grateful to Marjorie Thomas of Cleveland Metroparks; Andy Avram and Pat Morse of Lake Metroparks; Sandy Ward, Dottie Drockton, and Diane Valen of Geauga Parks District; Vicki McDonald and Cait Anastis at the Holden Arboretum; Tim Hite of Metro Parks, Serving Summit County; Kathie Pohl at the City of Mentor; Kara O'Donnell at the City of Cleveland Heights; Linda Nahrstedt at the City of Stow; and Mary Pat Doorley, Lynette Sprague-Falk, and Rebecca Jones of Cuyahoga Valley National Park for assisting in reviewing the hikes for accuracy. Our park systems are invaluable assets to the region and make Cleveland a truly special place to live.

AllTrails is an app I discovered in preparation for this book. I can't articulate how helpful the app and the AllTrails staff have been. All of the hikes were planned and recorded using their software. I'd also like to acknowledge Swiss Gear for the Alpine Peak Tent used on the Buckeye Trail hike and Nikon for the camera used in all photography except for shots from Rob.

Finally, I thank you, dear reader, because if you're reading this, you most likely humored me and bought the book. Good choice! I know you'll enjoy what our beloved Emerald Necklace has to offer.

Introduction

Let's get it out of the way. Cleveland is no longer the "Mistake on the Lake." Case in point—Johnny Carson no longer hosts *The Tonight Show,* Dennis "Boy Mayor" Kucinich is no longer at City Hall, and the Cuyahoga River has been fire-free since 1969.

No, Cleveland might not be what comes to mind when you think of a place with great hiking. But it should be. There's a reason our parks system has been dubbed the Emerald Necklace. Cuyahoga Valley National Park and the surrounding Cleveland, Lake, Geauga, and Summit County parks decorate our incredible region with a constantly changing tapestry that can make any hiker fall in love with nature all over again.

Erie Street Cemetery's 19th-century Gothic gateway greets you off East 9th Street across from the ballpark. Veterans from the Revolutionary through Spanish-American wars are buried here.

Boardwalks such as these will occasionally (ultimately rarely) pop up throughout this book.

This book came about because Cleveland is, unfortunately, often excluded. People know about us for all the wrong reasons, namely sports misery. But there is more to this city, this region, than sports and the latest headline from someone who parachuted in for the week.

While in Chicago for a wedding, I noticed a selection of local books that included a *Best Hikes Near Chicago*. Curious as to whether a Cleveland book existed, I scribbled a note and vowed to do the necessary research when I returned home. Sure enough, Falcon had published no such book. Other hiking guides exist for the Cleveland area, but none with an emphasis on urban hikes. As young professionals, families, and empty nesters alike continue to refill American cities, I thought it important to offer readers a hiking experience with the heart of the city being covered. Living in downtown Cleveland, I knew what neighborhoods were crying out for an urban hike and which hikes to include outside of the city that wouldn't prove much of a drive. That's what this book is—a hiking guide from the heart of the Forest City.

The trails offered in this book are as diverse as you'd find in areas more generally thought of as hiking towns. There are no mountains, but we have plenty of rolling hills, waterfalls, ravines, easy limestone trail, and rugged backpacking terrain to cover. By the end, you'll know why we Clevelanders lovingly refer to our humble abode on the shores of Lake Erie as the best location in the nation.

Weather

Cleveland experiences all four seasons. In fact, area residents take sadistic pride in the region's ability to welcome all four seasons in a single week. Generally speaking, hikers can expect a little of everything in Cleveland. Summers are generally pleasant, but hot spells can certainly overcome the region. But these are easily avoided with morning or evening hikes. Hikers are welcome to use their smartphones to monitor the weather, but Northeast Ohio is an unpredictable beast. More than a few of these hikes were completed under very wet "0 percent chance of rain" conditions. Suffice it to say, it doesn't hurt to keep an eye on the clouds. Fall brings hikers out of the woodwork (no pun intended) to admire the changing colors. Expect crisp mornings and evenings. Afternoons, too, can be quite chilly if under the cover of trees. Come winter, hikers will usually see plenty of snow accumulation, though climate change has made what was once predictable completely unpredictable. Case in point, 2011–2012 (when the first edition of this book was published) saw one of Cleveland's least snowy winters on record. The winter of 2016–2017 managed to beat that record by several inches. Finally, expect plenty of muddy hiking in the rainy Cleveland spring. But it's worth it to see the flowers coming out to bloom. Some might not enjoy our constantly changing weather or our often-incorrect weather forecasts; but look on the bright side: hikers can experience all forty hikes in drastically different conditions, offering an entirely different experience. Not bad.

Flora and Fauna

Flora

Variety is the key word for the best hikes near Cleveland. The Cuyahoga Valley is composed of approximately 80 percent mixed-mesophytic forest with oaks, maples, and beeches filling in around the Emerald Necklace. Thousands of plant species populate the area with bluebells, bloodroot, and spring beauty decorating the forest in spring and goldenrod popping up in the summer. Cuyahoga Valley National Park alone has twenty-one state-listed rare plant species. These include grasses, sedges, shrubs, and wildflowers. Pines and spruces also populate the trails in addition to the occasional man-made addition. Of course, a place like the Holden Arboretum will offer the best bang for your flora buck. In all, the Greater Cleveland area offers an incredible mosaic of nature's work for hikers to enjoy.

Fauna

Forests, rivers, streams, ravines, and wetlands naturally draw plenty of fauna to the region for nourishment and shelter. White-tailed deer is perhaps most noticeably abundant in the region with chipmunks, squirrels, and rabbits rounding out the mammal population. In select areas hikers can find the rare garden or water snake lurking about. Untold amounts of different bird species call Northeast Ohio's parks home

Holden Arboretum has perhaps the greatest variety of trails within one hike in this book.

with 280 alone in the tiny Cleveland Lakefront Nature Preserve. Suffice it to say, many of the parks listed in this book are worthy of a birding pilgrimage.

Wilderness Restrictions/Regulations

Urban hikes take place entirely within the city limits of Cleveland, but Cleveland Lakefront Nature Preserve, Edgewater, Forest Hill, and the Lake View Cemetery portion of the Little Italy hike have their own respective management systems. Cleveland Metroparks and Cuyahoga Valley National Park manage a majority of the remaining hikes with Metro Parks, Serving Summit County, Geauga Parks District, and Lake Metroparks covering some of the rest. The cities of Mentor, Hudson, and Stow each manage one of their own hikes within this book. In all, these are impressively run organizations with excellent facilities. Cleveland Metroparks, in fact, recently took over control of Edgewater from the state with overwhelming popular support. Simply put, Northeast Ohioans love their parks.

Camping is limited within these parks, though there are possibilities. Hikers would be smart to consult with the respective park system before pitching a tent. The Stanford House, part of the Buckeye Trail overnight hike (Hike 40), is a favorite stopping ground.

All hikes except Holden Arboretum are free to the public. The Buckeye Trail, too, is free, but reserving a space at the Stanford House does cost.

Overall, the parks are very welcoming of all, and any existing rules or regulations will not get in the way of enjoying the hikes.

Getting Around Cleveland

Area Codes

The Cleveland and Cuyahoga County area code is 216. The Lake and Geauga County area codes are 440, and 330 covers Summit County.

Roads

The best hikes selected in this book are no more than a 45-minute drive with many closer. Urbanites and tourists who tend to stay downtown will be pleased to know that the urban hikes are especially accessible by foot, bike, or public transit. Most other hikes will require a car. I-90 and OH 2 are used for eastern hikes and I-77 for southern hikes. The latter occasionally combines with I-480 to travel slightly southeast.

By Air

Cleveland-Hopkins International Airport (CLE) is accessible via I-71, 12 miles away from downtown Cleveland. The Greater Cleveland Regional Transportation Authority serves the airport, connecting visitors to downtown by rail without any transfers.

By Rail

Cleveland is served by AMTRAK and the Greater Cleveland Regional Transit Authority.

By Bus

Greyhound and Megabus are stationed in the downtown area. Nearby travelers in the Greater Akron area can use Metro.

Visitor Information

For general Information on Cleveland, visit Destination Cleveland, www.thisis cleveland.com.

How to Use This Guide

Take a close enough look, and you'll find that this guide contains just about everything you'll ever need to choose, plan for, enjoy, and survive a hike near Cleveland. Stuffed with useful Cleveland-area information, *Best Hikes Cleveland* features forty mapped and cued hikes. Here's an outline of the book's major components:

Each section begins with an **introduction to the region,** in which you're given a look at the lay of the land. Each hike then starts with a short **summary** of the hike's highlights. These quick overviews give you a taste of the hiking adventures to follow. You'll learn about the trail terrain and what surprises each route has to offer.

Following the overview you'll find the **hike specs:** quick, nitty-gritty details of the hike. Most are self-explanatory, but here are some details on others:

Distance: The total distance of the recommended route—one-way for loop hikes, the round-trip on an out-and-back or lollipop hike, point-to-point for a shuttle. Options are additional.

Approximate hiking time: The average time it will take to cover the route. It is based on the total distance, elevation gain, and condition and difficulty of the trail. Your fitness level will also affect your time.

Difficulty: Each hike has been assigned a level of difficulty. The rating system was developed from several sources and personal experience. These levels are meant to be a guideline only, and hikes may prove easier or harder for different people depending on ability and physical fitness.

Trail surface: General information about what to expect underfoot.

Best season: General information on the best time of year to hike.

Other trail users: Such as horseback riders, mountain bikers, inline skaters, and so on.

Canine compatibility: Know the trail regulations before you take your dog hiking with you. Dogs are not allowed on several trails in this book.

Land status: National forest, county open space, national park wilderness, and so forth.

Fees and permits: Whether you need to carry any money with you for park entrance fees and permits.

Schedule: When the route is open to the public and when it is restricted or closed.

Maps: This is a list of other maps to supplement the maps in this book. USGS maps are the best source for accurate topographical information, but the local park map may show more recent trails. Use both.

Trail contacts: This is the location, phone number, and website URL for the local land manager(s) in charge of all the trails within the selected hike. Before you head out, get trail access information, or contact the land manager after your visit if you see problems with trail erosion, damage, or misuse.

The **Finding the Trailhead** section gives you dependable driving directions to where you'll want to park. **The Hike** is the meat of the chapter. Detailed and honest, it's a carefully researched impression of the trail. It also often includes lots of area history, both natural and human. Under **Miles and Directions,** mileage cues identify all turns and trail name changes, as well as points of interest. **Options** are also given for many hikes to make your journey shorter or longer depending on the amount of time you have. The **Hike Information** section provides information on local events and attractions, restaurants, hiking tours, and hiking organizations.

Don't feel restricted to the routes and trails that are mapped here. Be adventurous and use this guide as a platform to discover new routes for yourself. One of the simplest ways to begin this is to just turn the map upside down and hike any route in reverse. The change in perspective is often fantastic, and the hike should feel quite different. With this in mind, it'll be like getting two distinctly different hikes on each map. For your own purposes, you may wish to copy the route directions onto a small

Geologists will love Metro Parks's Gorge Trail with some of the more fascinating rock formations in the region.

sheet of paper to help you while hiking, or photocopy the map and cue sheet to take with you. Otherwise, just slip the whole book in your backpack and take it all with you. Enjoy your time in the outdoors and remember to pack out what you pack in.

How to Use The Maps

Overview map: This map shows the location of each hike in the area by hike number.

Route map: This is your primary guide to each hike. It shows all of the accessible roads and trails, points of interest, water, landmarks, and geographical features. It also distinguishes trails from roads, and paved roads from unpaved roads. The selected route is highlighted, and directional arrows point the way.

Map Legend

Transportation

═〈70〉═	Freeway/Interstate Highway
═⦅422⦆═	US Highway
═⦅82⦆═	State Highway
════════	County/Paved/Improved Road
═ ═ ═ ═	Unpaved Road
╾┼─┼─┼╼	Railroad

Trails

▬ ▬ ▬ ▬	Selected Route
─ ─ ─ ─	Trail
→	Direction of Route

Water Features

⬭	Body of Water
⩴	Swamp/Marsh
⌇	River or Creek
⌒	Spring
⩘	Waterfall

Symbols

⦅20⦆	Trailhead
■	Building/Point of Interest
🅿	Parking
🚻	Restroom
👁	Scenic View/Overlook
❓	Visitor Center/Information
⛺	Picnic Area
⛄	Campground
●─●	Gate
⌣	Bridge
⌒	Cave
⛵	Boat Launch
○	Towns and Cities

Land Management

▭▭	National Park
▭	State/Local Park

Trail Finder

Hike No.	Hike Name	Best Hikes for Waterfalls	Best Hikes for Great Views	Best Hikes for Children	Best Hikes for Dogs	Best Hikes for Stream Lovers	Best Hikes for Lake Lovers	Best Hikes for Nature Lovers	Best Hikes for History Lovers
1	Downtown Hike		•						•
2	Cleveland Lakefront Nature Preserve Lollipop Trail		•					•	
3	Tremont Trek		•	•					•
4	Little Italy to Lake View Cemetery Lollipop Trail		•						•
5	Edgewater Park Trail, Lakefront Reservation		•	•	•		•		
6	Forest Hill Loop Trail			•					•
7	Ohio City Loop Trail			•					•
8	West Channel Pond to Mount Pleasant to Fort Hill Circuit Trail, Rocky River South Reservation		•	•		•		•	
9	Cottonwood to Mastick Woods to Bridle Trails, Rocky River North Reservation				•	•		•	
10	Iron Springs to North Ravine Trail, Garfield Park Reservation			•	•				
11	Hemlock to Deer Lick Cave Loop Trail, Brecksville Reservation			•	•	•		•	
12	Sagamore Creek Loop Trail, Bedford Reservation		•			•		•	

Hike No.	Hike Name	Best Hikes for Waterfalls	Best Hikes for Great Views	Best Hikes for Children	Best Hikes for Dogs	Best Hikes for Stream Lovers	Best Hikes for Lake Lovers	Best Hikes for Nature Lovers	Best Hikes for History Lovers
13	Hemlock to Bridle to Egbert to Buckeye Loop Trail, Bedford Reservation		●			●		●	
14	Sylvan to Castle Valley to Bridle Trail, North Chagrin Reservation				●			●	
15	Look About Lodge to Bridle/Buckeye to Sulphur Springs to Squaw Rock Trails, South Chagrin Reservation			●		●		●	
16	Sugar Bush Trail to Royalview Loop, Mill Stream Run Reservation			●	●			●	
17	Hinckley Lake to Buckeye Trail to Whipp's Ledges Loop Trail, Hinckley Reservation		●	●			●	●	●
18	Chapin Forest Reservation Trails		●	●	●				
19	Girdled Road Reservation Loop Trails			●	●			●	
20	Gorge to Bridle/Buckeye Trail, Penitentiary Glen Reservation	●		●					
21	Holden Arboretum		●		●			●	
22	Mentor Lagoons Nature Preserve Loop Trails		●	●	●		●		

Hike No.	Hike Name	Best Hikes for Waterfalls	Best Hikes for Great Views	Best Hikes for Children	Best Hikes for Dogs	Best Hikes for Stream Lovers	Best Hikes for Lake Lovers	Best Hikes for Nature Lovers	Best Hikes for History Lovers
23	Bridle to Ansel's Cave to Trout Lily Trails, The West Woods			•	•			•	
24	McIntosh to Harvest Loop Trail, Orchard Hills Park		•	•	•				
25	Big Creek Circuit Trails			•	•	•			
26	Whitetail to Lake to Beechnut Trails, Beartown Lakes Reservation			•	•		•		
27	Adam Run Loop Trail, Hampton Hills Metro Park			•	•	•		•	
28	Dogwood to Mingo Trail Loop, Sand Run Metro Park					•		•	
29	Hudson Springs Park Loop Trail		•	•	•		•		
30	Gorge Trail, Gorge Metro Park	•	•	•		•		•	
31	Adell Durbin Park & Arboretum			•					
32	Tree Farm Loop Trail, Cuyahoga Valley National Park		•	•	•		•		

Hike No.	Hike Name	Best Hikes for Waterfalls	Best Hikes for Great Views	Best Hikes for Children	Best Hikes for Dogs	Best Hikes for Stream Lovers	Best Hikes for Lake Lovers	Best Hikes for Nature Lovers	Best Hikes for History Lovers
33	Oak Hill to Plateau Trail, Cuyahoga Valley National Park			●	●			●	
34	Red Lock to Old Carriage Trail, Cuyahoga Valley National Park			●		●			●
35	Riding Run to Perkins Bridle Trails and Furnace Run Trail, Cuyahoga Valley National Park					●		●	
36	Stanford to Brandywine Gorge Trail, Cuyahoga Valley National Park	●	●	●		●		●	●
37	Cross Country to Lake to Salt Run Trail, Virginia Kendall Unit			●	●	●		●	
38	Ledges Area Hike, Virginia Kendall Unit			●				●	
39	Wetmore to Dickerson Run to Langes Run Trail, Cuyahoga Valley National Park			●	●			●	
40	Buckeye Trail to Peninsula Cuyahoga Valley Scenic Railroad Station	●	●			●		●	●

Urban Cleveland

These hikes are all within the City of Cleveland, but offer a mix of neighborhood and park hikes. You'll traverse through some of the city's most historic neighborhoods, including Downtown, a world-class Little Italy, blue-collar turning hipster Tremont, and the bustling streets of Ohio City—home of the world famous West Side Market. Farther out, but still conveniently in the city, you'll find Edgewater Park along the shining shores of Lake Erie, the short but sweet Cleveland Lakefront Nature Preserve, and Forest Hill where Mr. Monopoly John D. Rockefeller used to call home.

The redesigned Public Square as seen from the Terminal Tower Observation Deck
CLEVELAND PUBLIC SQUARE

1 Downtown Hike

See the heart of Northeast Ohio in almost 6 miles worth of urban hiking through Cleveland's Downtown neighborhood. Statues, public art, and historic buildings line the streets as you pass through Public Square, the East Fourth District, the renowned Playhouse Square Theatre District, Cleveland State University, scenic Voinovich Park, and the Warehouse District, finishing just past Settler's Landing where founder Moses Cleaveland and his crew first set foot in 1796.

Start: At the northern quadrant of Public Square at the Tom L. Johnson statue
Distance: 5.7 miles
Approximate hiking time: 2 hours
Difficulty: Easy
Trail surface: Paved sidewalks
Best season: Year-round
Other trail users: Bicycles
Canine compatibility: Dogs permitted
Land status: Public

Fees and permits: None
Schedule: Open 24 hours a day, 7 days a week
Maps: www.thisiscleveland.com
Trail contacts: This Is Cleveland; (216) 875-6680; www.thisiscleveland.com
Finding the trailhead: From Tower City Center, walk to the northern quadrant of Public Square to the Tom L. Johnson statue. GPS: N 41 29' 59.604" / W 81 41' 40.3224"

The Hike

Downtown Cleveland can hardly be properly encapsulated in one hike or one chapter, but we'll give it a shot.

You'll begin your nearly 6-mile urban hike in front of the Tom L. Johnson statue on Public Square. The square itself is where city founder Moses Cleaveland (no, that's not a typo) declared the birthplace of a new American city. The aforementioned Johnson is widely considered to be this city's greatest mayor in history. Naturally, it's the start of one of the best hikes in this book.

Heading east past the square, you'll quickly come to the Fountain of Eternal Life, a memorial to Clevelanders who served in World War II. From there you'll move onward to East 6th Street to connect to Euclid Avenue, Cleveland's main street, to reach the heart of Downtown's entertainment and nightlife—the East Fourth District. This is a pedestrians-only thoroughfare featuring some of the best restaurants in the city.

After hiking through, you'll continue east toward East 9th Street for a hike through the historic and leafy Erie Street Cemetery. Here, you're greeted with a beautiful gothic stone façade just across the street from where the Cleveland Indians play ball.

When you come through the cemetery, you'll turn back north to hike through the Playhouse Square Theatre District. City boosters would be quick to mention that this is the largest theater complex outside of New York City. Comparisons aside, it's simply a gem of Cleveland history that thankfully avoided the wrecking ball in the 1970s.

An aerial view of Cleveland's redesigned Public Square DESTINATION CLEVELAND

As you continue east, you'll walk through the largely revitalized campus of Cleveland State University, once a haven for crime but thanks to the university's efforts now a welcomed neighbor of Downtown Cleveland.

Your next sight after hiking west along the northern portion of Cleveland State is Perk Plaza, an urban park nestled in the corner of East 12th and Chester Avenue. Come on a summer Wednesday afternoon for live music and food trucks as far as the eye can see.

Next you'll wind your way up north on East 9th for over 0.5 mile, past *the* Rock & Roll Hall of Fame to reach Voinovich Park. Named after a former mayor of Cleveland, governor, and senator whose popularity rivals that of Tom L. Johnson, the park offers some of the best views of Lake Erie and the Cleveland skyline. Coincidentally, it also happens to be home to the city's annual Pride parade.

When finished at the park, you'll backtrack briefly on East 9th toward Lakeside Avenue where you'll hike southwest past the city's government buildings and the Free Stamp—a public piece of art Clevelanders find themselves divided on. Nevertheless, it's there for you to either admire or laugh at.

Just past Fort Huntington Park's statue of a triumphant Jesse Owens, a Cleveland native, you'll enter the city's Warehouse District. If you enjoy cacophonous club music with intoxicated individuals stumbling about through the late hours of the

A statue of Moses Cleaveland

night, this is the place to be. But in the daytime, it's a lovely slice of walkable urbanism in the heart of the city. You'll hike through this tiny Downtown neighborhood en route to the Flats—a neighborhood that used to be what the Warehouse District is today. After losing business just up the street to the Warehouse District, the Flats suffered from a couple of decades of neglect. Now revitalization efforts are well under

MOSES CLEAVELAND

You might be wondering why the city's namesake is continually spelled "Cleaveland" and not "Cleveland." Surely this is an oversight or some sort of humorously reoccurring typo, yes?

Actually, the Revolutionary War veteran, politician, and surveyor from Connecticut did indeed spell his name with an extra "a." It's the city itself that is technically spelled wrong.

Explanations vary for the name change from Cleaveland to Cleveland, but the most popular tale revolves around the city's first newspaper, the *Cleveland Advertiser,* launched in 1830. The paper's editor allegedly found his paper headline too long for the space allowed and decided to remove a letter to fit the city name onto the newspaper. Seeing the city spelled "Cleveland" in the city's lone newspaper, residents came to accept that as the correct spelling.

Another, perhaps more likely scenario, is that Moses Cleaveland's surveying party simply misspelled the name of their future town on a map. Either way, Moses Cleaveland retired to his home in Connecticut after founding the city, never to return again. So chances are, his posthumous feelings haven't been hurt too badly.

way. But regardless of its state, it's worth hiking through to the banks of the Cuyahoga River to Settler's Landing Park. As the name indicates, this is where Moses Cleaveland and his surveying party first landed in what we now know as the City of Cleveland.

Your hike drawing to an end, you'll climb uphill away from the Cuyahoga River after you're finished admiring the "crooked river" for its comeback from flammable hazard to a picturesque waterway.

Now on your final leg on Superior Avenue, you'll hike east back toward where you started on Public Square. Just as you finish, you'll get a better look at the wonderfully ornate Terminal Tower sitting atop Tower City Center on your right. It's a beautiful way to end this scenic urban hike through one of the country's most underappreciated downtowns.

Miles and Directions

0.0 Start at the northern quadrant of Public Square in front of the Tom L. Johnson statue. From here, hike northeast on Rockwell Avenue.

0.1 Bear left (north) to take the diagonal path onto the Cleveland Mall toward the Fountain of Eternal Life. You're going to hike around the fountain clockwise, ending the loop by taking the southern path back to Rockwell Avenue. From here, continue hiking northeast toward East 6th Street.

0.3 Turn right (south) down East 6th Street, past the Cleveland Public Library en route to Euclid Avenue.

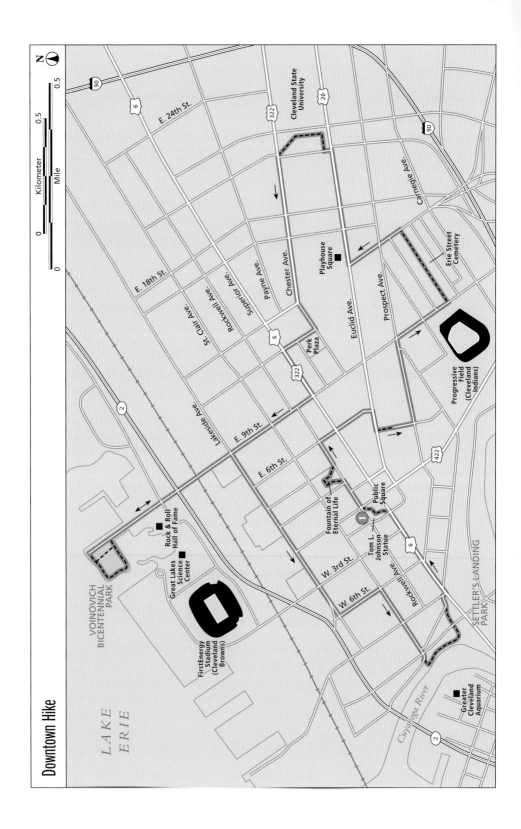

Downtown Hike

LAKE ERIE

VOINOVICH BICENTENNIAL PARK

FirstEnergy Stadium (Cleveland Browns)

Rock & Roll Hall of Fame

Great Lakes Science Center

Greater Cleveland Aquarium

Cuyahoga River

SETTLER'S LANDING PARK

W. 6th St.

W. 3rd St.

Rockwell Ave.

Tom L. Johnson Statue

Public Square

Fountain of Eternal Life

E. 6th St.

E. 9th St.

Lakeside Ave.

St. Clair Ave.

Rockwell Ave.

Superior Ave.

Payne Ave.

Chester Ave.

Perk Plaza

E. 18th St.

E. 24th St.

Euclid Ave.

Prospect Ave.

Carnegie Ave.

Erie Street Cemetery

Playhouse Square

Cleveland State University

Progressive Field (Cleveland Indians)

N

Kilometer

Mile

0   0.5

0   0.5

0.5 Turn right (west) onto Euclid Avenue toward East 4th Street. At East 4th you'll be in front of the historic Cleveland Arcade. Cross the street heading south down East 4th—a pedestrians-only thoroughfare.

0.7 Hike through East 4th to Prospect Avenue where you'll turn left (east) for approximately 0.2 mile.

0.9 Turn right (southeast) on East 9th.

1.1 Turn left (northeast) to hike through the gates of the Erie Street Cemetery. The entire cemetery is approximately 0.2 mile long to the opposite end where it opens up to East 14th Street.

1.3 Take a sharp left (northwest) onto East 14th Street toward the Playhouse Square Theatre District. You'll hike past Prospect Avenue en route to Euclid Avenue.

1.5 Turn right (east) onto Euclid Avenue to hike through the Playhouse Square Theatre District and the Cleveland State University Campus.

1.9 Turn left (north) onto East 22nd Street toward Chester Avenue.

2.0 From here you'll turn left (west) onto Chester Avenue past a softball field, tennis courts, and the old Greyhound Station on your way to Perk Plaza on East 12th Street.

2.5 Turn right (northwest) to hike through Perk Plaza.

2.6 Just a block past the northern end of Perk Plaza, you'll turn left (southwest) onto Superior Avenue to hike toward East 9th Street.

2.8 Turn right (northwest) onto East 9th Street toward the Rock & Roll Hall of Fame and Voinovich Park. This will be an approximately 0.7 mile hike to the park where the trail comes to a dead-end.

3.5 Arrive at Voinovich Park on the shores of Lake Erie with the Rock & Roll Hall of Fame just south. Hike the park counter-clockwise. When you're finished, hike back south on East 9th Street.

4.2 Turn right (southwest) onto Lakeside Avenue to hike past the Free Stamp, government buildings, and the northern end of the Cleveland Mall.

4.7 Turn left (southeast) onto West 6th Street past Bob Golic's Sports Bar and Grille for a couple of blocks.

4.9 Take a right (southwest) to hike onto St. Clair Avenue.

5.0 At W. 9th and St. Clair, you'll come to a steep downhill. Hike down here into the Flats neighborhood of Cleveland, toward the Cuyahoga River. Continue straight at the bottom of the hill, cross the train tracks, and arrive at the banks of the Cuyahoga River.

5.1 Turn left (southeast) to hike along the banks of the river, also known as Settler's Landing Park.

5.3 Take a sharp left (north) onto Settler's Landing Walkway, and take the first right (east) uphill onto Superior Avenue. You will take this for the remaining 0.4 mile back to where you started in front of the Tom L. Johnson statue on Public Square.

5.7 Arrive back at the statue on Public Square to end your hike.

Hike Information

Local Information

Destination Cleveland; (216) 875-6680; www.thisiscleveland.com

Restaurants

Chinato; (216) 298-9080; www.chinatocleveland.com
Chocolate Bar; (216) 622-2626; www.originalchocolatebar.com
Cowell & Hubbard; (216) 479-0555; www.cowellhubbard.com
The Greenhouse Tavern; (216) 443-0551; www.thegreenhousetavern.com
Johnny's Downtown; (216) 623-0055; www.johnnyscleveland.com
La Strada; (216) 861-3663; www.lastradacleveland.com
Lola; (216) 621-5652; www.lolabistro.com
Nauti Mermaid; (216) 771-6175; thenautimermaid.com
Pickwick & Frolic; (216) 241-7425; www.pickwickandfrolic.com
Sushi 86; (216) 621-8686; www.sushi86.com
Teahouse Noodles; (216) 623-9139; www.teahousenoodlescleveland.com
Zocalo; (216) 781-0420; www.zocalocleveland.com

Hike Tours

Cleveland Hiking Club; www.clevelandhikingclub.org
Cleveland Metroparks; (216) 635-3200; www.clevelandmetroparks.com
NEOHiking; www.meetup.com/NEOHiking
Take a Hike Tours; www.clevelandgatewaydistrict.com

GREEN TIP
Littering is especially noticeable on urban hikes.
If you see someone throwing trash on the sidewalk,
muster up some courage and ask the person not to.

2 Cleveland Lakefront Nature Preserve Lollipop Trail

Ornithologists, prepare to change your shorts. This urban nature preserve has over 280 bird species in addition to diverse plant and mammal populations. Add the scenic overlook promising a beautiful juxtaposition of the city's modern skyline and traditional manufacturing industry for a hike that's more than a worthy addition to any Cleveland hiker's itinerary.

Start: At the northwestern corner of the parking lot in front of the nature center on mulch trail
Distance: 1.3 miles
Approximate hiking time: 30 minutes
Difficulty: Easy
Trail surface: Mix of mulch, dirt, and grassy trail
Best season: Year-round
Other trail users: None
Canine compatibility: Sorry, no dogs allowed
Land status: Public
Fees and permits: None
Schedule: Open daylight hours year-round

Maps: Port of Cleveland; (216) 241-8004; www.portofcleveland.com
Trail contacts: Port of Cleveland; (216) 241-8004; www.portofcleveland.com
Finding the trailhead: From Cleveland, take OH 2 East toward I-90 for approximately 1.7 miles when it will merge with I-90 East. Continue for another 2 miles and take exit 177 for Martin Luther King Junior Drive. Turn left onto Martin Luther King Junior Drive and continue onto Lake Shore Boulevard. The parking lot will be on the left. GPS: N 41 32' 30.2922" / W 81 37' 45.3576"

The Hike

What makes a brisk 1.3-mile hike qualify to be one of the forty best hikes near a major city like Cleveland? An overlook and scenery you won't soon forget.

The Cleveland Lakefront Nature Preserve rightly describes itself as a unique urban wildlife haven on Lake Erie. While you might naturally think 1.3 miles of man-made trails will be moderately interesting at best, the preserve's lollipop loop actually (and surprisingly) yields a substantial amount of diversity and wilderness you wouldn't expect to find within eyesight of the city.

You begin in front of the Lakefront Metroparks Office, hiking on the mulch trail-head that begins at the northwestern corner of the parking lot. This trail will quickly wind behind the nature center, reaching a metal gate within the first 0.1 mile. Here you can log your name and arrival, an opportunity you will not find at any other trail within this book.

Continuing through the gate, you'll quickly find yourself immersed in natural surroundings more reminiscent of a backcountry escape than an urban trek. More than 280 species of birds, twenty-nine species of butterflies, sixteen species of mammals (red fox, coyote, mink, and deer), two species of reptiles, twenty-six plant species, and nine species of trees and shrubs have been identified over time by various

View from the overlook of Cleveland's skyline with a hint of the city's Rust Belt history joining in

researchers. It seems worth noting again that, yes, this is indeed just 5 miles away from the city center. The preserve is easily one of the more unexpected gems in a city full of surprises to travelers and locals alike.

Grassy trails take up a majority of the first out-and-back leg that you'll traverse again upon your return. Before long (this is an incredibly short hike, after all), you'll arrive back onto mulch-covered trail that amasses to a small hill at the fork in the trail. Ahead lies the loop of the Cleveland Lakefront Nature Preserve, which can be conquered in either direction. For the purposes of the book, we're heading counter-clockwise by following the mulch trail northeast back onto mixed trail. This will quickly wind into a straight, northwestern shot toward Lake Erie where you'll turn left to hike along the coast.

This area, covered in high grasses and the sounds of chatterbox birds, will lead to the overlook junction. This is another brief, out-and-back hike to the western corner of the nature preserve and the main reason you're doing this hike to begin with. Follow signs for the overlook where you'll be treated to amazing, panoramic views of the Cleveland skyline and Lake Erie. Even better for history and Rust Belt nerds is the noteworthy presence of an old factory standing proudly south as if it's trying to join the skyline (though in reality the building is actually northeast of the city). For urbanites, this might be the best overlook in the book.

When you're finished standing in awe, you'll finish your loop by returning to the overlook junction (again, we're talking spitting distance) and turning right to head back to your mulch-covered junction where you started the loop. From here, simply repeat the stick portion of the lollipop to wind back to the gate behind the nature center where you'll be just 0.1 mile from finishing your hike.

In all, you might be a skeptic at first glimpse considering the trail's meager distance. Perhaps you might want to combine the lollipop with another hike in this book for a more sufficient day's worth of hiking, but there's little doubt you'll understand just why this truly is one of the forty best hikes near Cleveland by the end.

Miles and Directions

0.0 Start at the northwestern corner of the parking lot. You'll see a trail marker at the mulch-covered trailhead with the Lakefront Nature Preserve logo. Hike on this trail, winding north around the Nature Center building toward a small gate.

0.1 Arrive at a small gate next to an equally small Lakefront Nature Preserve station equipped with a book where hikers such as you can log their arrival. Hike through the gate and follow the trail east.

0.3 You'll be guided onto a gravel driveway, hiking north. Shortly after that, you'll come to a red arrow that will put you back onto mulch trail just like what you started on at the beginning of the hike. Follow this trail back into the woods.

0.4 Now you're at the beginning of the loop portion of the trail, standing in the middle of a mulch-covered circle. We're going to hike the trail counter-clockwise, so turn right (northeast) to hike back into the woods.

CLEVELAND LAKEFRONT NATURE PRESERVE

This peninsula comprises approximately 88 man-made acres that over time have become a haven for some of the most diverse species of migratory birds, butterflies, and animals in the region. Formerly known as Dike 14, the Port Authority of Cleveland opened this unique piece of urban green space to the public in February of 2012.

The US Army Corps of Engineers are responsible for how the land mass has taken shape. They began working on the area in the late 1970s using sediment dredged from the Cuyahoga River. The Army Corps placed the sediment in this area from 1979 to 1999 to preserve the width and depth of the Cuyahoga River's ship channel used to move goods and raw materials.

Following the closure of the area as a dumping ground to sediment, nature began to take over, resulting in a diverse habitat full of plant and animal life that had the public calling for redevelopment of the site as a nature preserve for hiking and bird-watching. Today the preserve has come full circle as a stalwart example of the city's commitment to improving sustainability throughout the region.

0.7 Turn right to hike east toward the overlook, a very short out-and-back link that offers tremendous, panoramic views of the Cleveland skyline and Lake Erie. Return to this junction when you're finished at the overlook, and continue the hike east back toward where you started the loop.

0.9 Return to the mulch hill where you started the loop. From here, backtrack for the remainder of the hike to where you started the Cleveland Lakefront Nature Preserve Lollipop Trail.

1.3 Arrive back at the trailhead to end your hike.

Hike Information

Local Information

Destination Cleveland; (216) 875-6680; www.thisiscleveland.com

3 Tremont Trek

Hike a Cleveland neighborhood actually worthy of the overused descriptor "historic." Eastern European churches and Victorian-style homes line the streets of this traditionally working class neighborhood turned hipster haven with a vibrant scene of restaurants and shops. A scenic overlook of the city skyline (just over a mile away as the crow flies) is the icing on the cake, helping urban hikers to understand why this is one of Cleveland's fastest-growing neighborhoods.

Start: At the Lincoln Park gazebo
Distance: 4.4 miles
Approximate hiking time: 1.5 hours
Difficulty: Easy
Trail surface: Paved sidewalks
Best season: Year-round
Other trail users: Public
Canine compatibility: Yes
Land status: Public
Fees and permits: None
Schedule: None
Maps: Tremont West; (216) 575-0920; www.tremontwest.org
Trail contacts: Tremont West; (216) 575-0920; www.tremontwest.org

Finding the trailhead: From Cleveland head west on Superior Avenue over the Detroit-Superior Bridge. After the bridge, the street will turn into Detroit Avenue. Take the first left onto West 25th Street. In 0.5 mile, turn left onto Lorain Avenue and take the second right onto West 20th Street for just 0.1 mile. Turn left onto Abbey Avenue for 0.4 mile. Take the West 14th Street ramp on the right to Fairfield Avenue. Continue straight to drive south on West 14th Street. Arrive at Lincoln Park in approximately 0.3 mile and look for street parking. GPS: N 41 38' 43.3632" / W 81 41' 25.1268"

The Hike

You'll begin your Tremont Trek at a modest gazebo in the heart of Lincoln Park, a large green space lined with historic churches and Victorian-style homes. First you'll hike northwest toward Kenilworth Avenue, where you'll turn left for a brief excursion down Scranton Road. Here you'll find some of the more modest working-class homes of the neighborhood, ending at Tremont Taphouse—a gastropub favorite across the city.

Returning to Lincoln Park (but at the southwestern corner), you'll begin hiking south for a mini-loop of sorts that takes you through some of the more historic homes of the neighborhood. The only unfortunate reality of this hike is the extent the neighborhood has been carved by the interstate system. But it's easy to see that this traditionally tough as nails neighborhood is fighting on to preserve its rightful place as one of Cleveland's unique and vibrant neighborhoods.

Tourists will be most excited to pass the *A Christmas Story* House & Museum on the northbound leg of this loop. Though this house was only used for the exterior, the interior has been redesigned like the home seen in the famous holiday film and

Clevelanders enjoy a "Taste of Tremont" at the annual summer festival.

serves as a museum for fanatics of the flick. A sign in the traditional *A Christmas Story* font will welcome you outside, but you'll truly know you have arrived when you see the "frag-e-lee" leg lamp sitting in the window place.

When finished marveling at movie history, continue north back toward Lincoln Park where you'll begin your hike through the neighborhood's trendy shops and restaurants on Professor Avenue. Fight the temptation to stop at Edison's Pizza Pub or Scoops. (You can and will come back later.)

Professor Avenue will take you north away from the commanding St. Theodosius Russian Orthodox Cathedral—another Tremont staple with a movie connection (Robert De Niro's *The Deer Hunter*) that some might mistake as an artifact stolen from Moscow itself. Nope, you're still in Cleveland.

Hiking north, you'll soon wind onto University Road where a scenic overlook of the Cleveland skyline awaits in front of some of the neighborhood's newer, more posh residences. Though the skyline overlook at the Cleveland Lakefront Nature Preserve (Hike 2) is more than a worthy addition, this overlook offers a closer peek at the city skyline, standing just over a mile from the city center as the crow flies. Note that you will leave this overlook envious of the homeowners surrounding you. Few sights are as welcoming to wake up to in the region as this.

TREMONT IN A NUTSHELL

Like most neighborhoods of the City of Cleveland and the region itself, this area traces its roots back to early Native American inhabitants who used the land as a hunting ground. The neighborhood was first incorporated back in 1836 as part of the vibrant town of Ohio City (separate from Cleveland at the time). The City of Cleveland later annexed Tremont as a neighborhood in 1867. But until the early 20th century, the neighborhood was actually known as "University Heights" and "Lincoln Heights." It wasn't until 1910 when the neighborhood received its current name after the local Tremont Elementary School.

The late 19th century saw the neighborhood become a home for Eastern European, Irish, Greek, and German immigrants who have largely shaped the aesthetic of the neighborhood into what it is today—evident in the plethora of churches of various denominations surrounding Lincoln Park. Christian or not, it's worth visiting the neighborhood on the Orthodox date of Good Friday to see followers of the respective Orthodox churches come out in the middle of their ceremonies to embrace one another in a beautiful, candle-lit march.

Besides the neighborhood's Eastern European influence, it's also hard to miss the street signs reflecting academia, like "Professor," "Literary," "University," and "College." This harkens back to the short-lived Cleveland University, the first institution of higher education in the city, which survived only one year of operation due to clashes between faculty and trustees and graduated just eleven students in its brief existence. And thanks to these remaining influences in culture and architecture, the neighborhood has blossomed into one of Cleveland's trendiest and fastest-growing neighborhoods.

After rightly fighting the urge to steal one of the nearby homes, you'll wind back south through some of the more historic homes of the neighborhood featuring uphill green lawns. You'll then find your way back to Starkweather Avenue at a familiar junction from earlier in the urban hike, ending back at the Lincoln Park gazebo where you started.

Miles and Directions

0.0 Start at the gazebo in the middle of the Tremont neighborhood's Lincoln Park. Take the northwestern trail to hike in the same direction toward Kenilworth Avenue.

0.1 Turn left (west) onto Kenilworth Avenue to hike underneath the interstate toward Scranton Road.

0.3 At Scranton Road, turn left (south) to hike a couple of blocks.

0.4 In front of the Tremont Taphouse you'll turn left (east) onto Starkweather Avenue, hiking once again underneath the interstate toward West 14th Street.

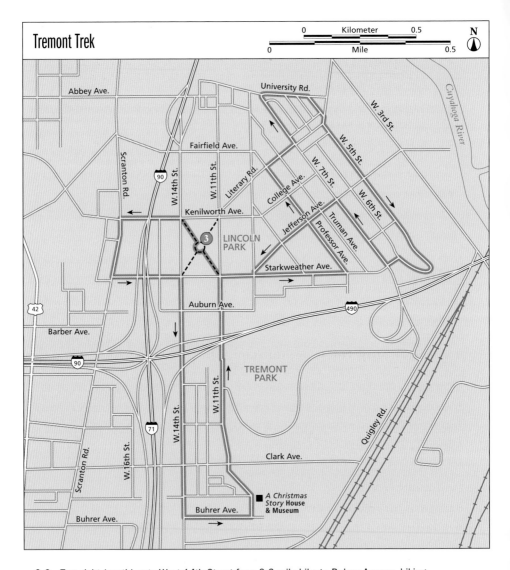

0.6 Turn right (south) onto West 14th Street for a 0.6-mile hike to Buhrer Avenue, hiking underneath I-490 in the process.

1.3 At Buhrer Avenue, turn left (east).

1.4 Take another left (north) onto West 11th Street where you'll soon pass the *A Christmas Story* house. The street will then bend northwest, and you'll continue hiking north on West 11th.

1.9 The road may seem like it's come to a neighborhood dead-end. But you'll continue hiking north and find an old pedestrian bridge that crosses over I-490. The road will continue on the other side where you'll resume hiking north until Starkweather Avenue.

2.1 Turn right (east) onto Starkweather Avenue for approximately 0.4 mile.

2.5 At Professor Avenue, take a sharp left (northwest).

2.8 Turn right (northeast) onto Literary Road. In a little less than 0.1 mile, you'll take another left (northwest) onto West 7th Street. Hike on this street until it dead-ends.

3.1 At University Road you'll turn right (east) to approach a scenic overlook of the Cleveland skyline on your left. When finished at the overlook, continue east until West 5th Street where you'll turn right (southeast).

3.7 Turn right (southwest) onto Marquardt Avenue for a couple of blocks. Then turn right again (northwest) onto West 7th Street.

3.8 At Jefferson Avenue turn left (southwest), hiking toward Starkweather Avenue.

4.2 Turn right (west) onto Starkweather Avenue. You'll see Lincoln Park again just a block away. Take the first diagonal path on your right into the park, hiking northwest.

4.4 Finish your hike at the Lincoln Park gazebo.

Hike Information

Local Information

Destination; (216) 875-6680; www.thisiscleveland.com
Tremont West; (216) 575-0920; www.tremontwest.org

Local Events / Attractions

A Christmas Story **House & Museum;** (216) 298-4919; www.achristmasstory house.com
Ale Fest; www.clevescene.com
Arts in August; www.tremontwest.org
Taste of Tremont; www.tasteoftremont.com
Tremont Arts & Cultural Festival; www.tremontwest.org
Tremont Farmers' Market; www.tremontfarmersmarket.com

Restaurants

Bac Asian American Bistro & Bar; (216) 938-8960; www.bactremont.com
Barrio Tremont; (216) 999-7714; www.barriotremont
Dante; (216) 274-1200; www.restaurantdante.us
Edison's Pub; (216) 522-0006; www.edisonspub.com
Fahrenheit; (216) 781-8858; www.fahrenheittremont.com
Grumpy's Café; (216) 241-5025; www.grumpys-cafe.com
Lucky's Café; (216) 622-7773; www.luckyscafe.com
Parallax; (216) 583-9999; www.parallaxtremont.com
The South Side; (216) 937-2288; www.southsidecleveland.com
Tremont Taphouse; (216) 298-4451; www.tremonttaphouse.com
Ty Fun; (216) 664-1000; www.tyfunthaibistro.com

4 Little Italy to Lake View Cemetery Lollipop Trail

Lake View Cemetery offers hikers an outdoor museum of Cleveland history in a garden-like setting. Enjoy a brisk hike through Cleveland's historic Little Italy neighborhood en route to the cemetery loop, where you'll pass the eternal resting homes of John D. Rockefeller, Eliot Ness, and President James A. Garfield. As ever, be respectful.

Start: At the future home of Mayfield Rapid Station on Mayfield Avenue in Little Italy

Distance: 4 miles

Approximate hiking time: 90 minutes

Difficulty: Easy

Trail surface: Paved

Best season: Year-round

Other trail users: Public

Canine compatibility: Public

Land status: Public

Fees and permits: None

Schedule: Opens at 7:30 a.m., closes at 5:30 p.m.

Maps: Cleveland Heights Historical Society; www.chhistory.org

Trail contacts: Cleveland Heights Historical Society; www.chhistory.org

Finding the trailhead: From Downtown Cleveland, walk to the Tower City Rapid Station. Take the Red Line east toward Stokes/Windermere to the Euclid-E. 120th Rapid Station. Hike south from the Rapid Station just one block to arrive at Mayfield Avenue, and start your hike. GPS: N 41 30' 31.215" / W 81 36' 0.4536"

The Hike

We've all heard of monopoly man John D. Rockefeller, President James A. Garfield, and Eliot Ness of "The Untouchables" fame. Though all three led very different lives, they have one eternal thing in common. They're resting in peace at Cleveland's historic Lake View Cemetery.

Nestled in Cleveland's East Side Little Italy neighborhood between the inner-ring suburbs of East Cleveland and Cleveland Heights, Lake View Cemetery is the permanent home for 100,000-plus souls and counting. Locals rightfully call it an outdoor museum with treasures inside, such as the James A. Garfield Monument and Wade Memorial Chapel.

You'll begin this hike at the Little Italy/University Circle Rapid Station on Mayfield Avenue. Besides offering the opportunity to ditch your car for the day, starting here also gives you an excuse to take in Cleveland's cherished Little Italy neighborhood. On a typical afternoon you'll hear music from Italian favorites like Dean Martin blaring outside the many restaurants, shops, and churches.

As you hike through Little Italy, you'll start hiking uphill alongside Lake View Cemetery. Just over 0.5 mile from the start, you'll come to the entrance and begin your loop inside the cemetery.

The James A. Garfield Monument in the background honors the 20th US president. The tower is 180 feet high and offers a "Forest City" view of the Cleveland skyline.

Inside sits 285 acres modeled after the great garden cemeteries of Victorian England and France. The cemetery was originally developed in a rural arboretum setting to integrate landscapes with sculptures and architecture honoring those who have passed. You'll get a hefty sampling as you hike around the cemetery's outermost loop. It's worth noting that there is no officially sanctioned trail here like what you might find at a metro park. Instead you'll find small, winding streets typical of any cemetery. But the history and beauty of this cemetery make it well worth your time when hiking in Cleveland.

As you're hiking, you may feel like you're in a garden rather than a cemetery. That's because the original designers in 1869 followed a growing movement to make cemeteries more romantic and comforting to loved ones left behind. Winding roads along rolling hills and decorated water elements are designed to soothe those grieving and give the setting the essence of a park for passersby. For those hiking, it truly offers a scenic tour of Cleveland history.

Toward the end of your loop around the cemetery, you'll come to the Wade Memorial Chapel. Built in 1901, the chapel was constructed in honor of Jeptha Wade,

JAMES A. GARFIELD MONUMENT

The James A. Garfield Monument began construction in 1885, four years after the 20th president met his untimely end at the hands of Charles J. Guiteau. Architect George Keller designed the 180-foot-tall monument combining Romanesque, Gothic, and Byzantine styles with Berea Sandstone. Dedicated in 1890, the memorial is open to the public from April 1 through November 19 from 9 a.m. to 4 p.m.

Five terra cotta panels by Casper Bubel adorn the exterior of the balcony with more than 110 figures (all life size) depicting Garfield's life and death. Within these panels you'll see Garfield as a teacher, a major general in the Union army, and taking the oath of office.

The Memorial Hall inside features meticulously designed gold mosaics with colored marble and stained glass windows surrounded by red granite columns. The windowpanes represent the thirteen original colonies plus Ohio. The centerpiece of the room is without a doubt the 12-foot-tall marble statue of Garfield constructed by native Ohioan and sculptor Alexander Doyle.

But the highlight of the memorial sits just sixty-four steps ahead from the lobby to the outdoor balcony, where on a clear day you can take in 40 miles of the Lake Erie shore enveloping the Downtown Cleveland skyline. It's arguably the most beautiful view you'll ever find in a cemetery.

who was a Cleveland industrialist and president of the cemetery association that founded Lake View Cemetery. Not a bad postmortem present for the boss!

Continuing east back toward the entrance, you'll start to see the James A. Garfield Monument peeking out from the plethora of mature oak trees. It's a fitting end to your loop around one of Cleveland's greatest resting souls.

Back at the cemetery's entrance on Mayfield Avenue, now is the perfect time to backtrack to the heart of Cleveland's Little Italy neighborhood where you can refuel however many calories burned in the 4-mile hike at any number of stomach-filling establishments, such as Presti's Bakery or La Dolce Vita. But in all honesty, you can blindfold yourself, spin around five times, throw a rock, and follow wherever it lands. Chances are, you won't be disappointed.

Miles and Directions

0.0 You'll begin at the ground level of the Little Italy-University Circle Rapid Station, right in the heart of Cleveland's Little Italy neighborhood, and hike east along Mayfield Road toward the entrance of Lake View Cemetery. You'll continue on this road—which includes a steep uphill climb just outside the main strip—until you reach the cemetery's entrance.

Little Italy to Lake View Cemetery Lollipop Trail

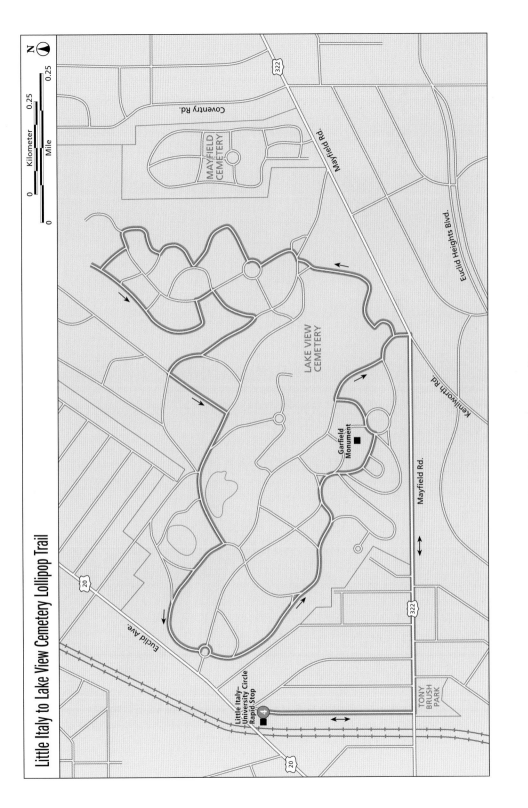

0.6 Turn left (north) through the entrance of Lake View Cemetery away from Mayfield Road. You'll then keep to the right, hiking northwest on paved road.

0.9 Approach another junction where you'll want to stay to the right, hiking northeast. Shortly after that, you'll turn left (northeast) to hike up to what looks like a small traffic circle.

1.0 At the circle, turn right (east) and take the first right to continue hiking east. You'll continue to follow this path as it winds north.

1.2 Again, stay to the right (east) to continue hiking the outer loop of the cemetery's paved paths.

1.3 Turn right (east) for another path that will wind north before ushering you back west, all in under 0.1 mile. When you come to your next junction just before 1.4 miles, you'll turn right (north) and then another quick left (southwest). Continue hiking this path southwest as it winds back into another path where you'll turn right (south) at around 1.7 miles. You'll then take another quick right (west).

1.8 You'll approach a fork where you'll want to take a sharp right to hike north.

1.9 Turn right (north) and then take the first left to hike southwest.

2.1 Turn right again (west) to hike toward Wade Memorial Chapel. You'll stay on this path, ignoring one turn on your right, until you reach the chapel.

2.3 Arrive at Wade Memorial Chapel. From here, turn right (north) until you reach another small, paved circle.

2.6 Continue straight (west) to take the path that runs parallel to East 123rd Street. The path will then bend south.

2.8 Stay to the right (southeast) at fork in the trail. You'll start following signs for the Garfield Monument.

3.0 Turn left (northeast) and continue hiking toward Garfield Monument, which should be in plain sight by now.

3.1 Arrive at Garfield Monument. From here, continue to hike alongside the monument as the path winds northeast.

3.3 Turn right (east) to hike back to the Lake View Cemetery entrance where you started the lollipop loop. You'll then backtrack to the Mayfield Rapid Station, hiking west.

4.0 End hike at the Mayfield Rapid Station.

Hike Information

Local Information
Destination; (216) 875-6680; www.thisiscleveland.com

Restaurants
La Dolce Vita; (216) 721-8155; www.ladolcevitacleveland.com
Presti's Bakery; (216) 421-3060; www.prestisbakery.com

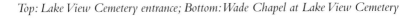

Top: Lake View Cemetery entrance; Bottom: Wade Chapel at Lake View Cemetery

5 Edgewater Park Trail, Lakefront Reservation

This brisk hike will take you by the busy Edgewater Yacht Club and through Edgewater Beach and the surrounding park area. Mostly paved trails guide you through the hike, offering scenic views of Lake Erie and the Cleveland skyline at nearly every turn.

Start: At the northernmost parking lot west of the Edgewater Yacht Club

Distance: 2.6 miles

Approximate hiking time: 45 minutes

Difficulty: Easy with one steep hill on paved trail

Trail surface: Mostly paved with a small section of dirt trail

Best season: Year-round

Other trail users: Motorized vehicles prohibited

Canine compatibility: Dogs permitted on 8-foot leash

Land status: Public

Fees and permits: None

Schedule: 6 a.m.–1 p.m. daily

Maps: Cleveland Metroparks; (216) 635-3200; www.clevelandmetroparks.com

Trail contacts: Cleveland Metroparks; (216) 635-3200; www.clevelandmetroparks.com

Finding the trailhead: From Cleveland, drive west on OH 2 toward Lakewood. Take the Edgewater Park/Whiskey Island exit in just under 3 miles. Turn right from the off-ramp into Edgewater Park and follow alongside the western end of the Edgewater Yacht Club until the road dead-ends into the northern parking lot. GPS: N 41 29' 30.7602" / W 81 44' 14.55"

The Hike

You'll find you can pick up the paved trail along the southern edge of the northernmost parking lot at Edgewater Park. There's no definitive trailhead here, but it's obvious this is where you'll need to start your hike. Hop on the paved trail and hike west away from the city, which you couldn't miss even on Lake Erie's foggiest of days.

The trail will wrap to the south alongside and onto Edgewater Beach, easily the most popular beachfront in the City of Cleveland for residents and visitors alike to bask in the sun or even play some ultimate Frisbee on an adjacent grass field. Though not exactly the largest beachfront in the region, you'll find Clevelanders flocking to this area as soon as the rays of the sun sneak past our typically cloudy city. This is a city that truly appreciates its sunshine.

As you hike west through the beach, you may notice a brand-new pedestrian pathway that burrows underneath the highway (actively being redesigned into a pedestrian and cycling-friendly boulevard) to the Detroit-Shoreway neighborhood at West 76th Street. If you're here on a summer day, you can always take a detour to the Battery Park Development to play some volleyball. You'll know you're there because of the giant Battery Park sign on an old smokestack for a former battery manufacturing facility converted to a wine bar. If only more dead industrial giants were reused for serving delicious alcohol, the world would be a better place.

The Cleveland skyline from Edgewater Park shows just how close the city is from the shores of Lake Erie.

Passing through Edgewater Beach, you'll begin hiking uphill on pavement for your only steep climb of the hike. This will take you to another grassy area with picnic pavilions where families and friends come to grill. But just past the first pavilion, you'll find a dirt trail on your right that heads downhill and closer to the beach. This will seem like the kind of trail you're used to in more remote regions of Northeast Ohio as opposed to a city neighborhood. Turn around at any point for a great look at Lake Erie and even the city skyline. But for the best look at the city on the hike, continue west until you come to a small, unmarked parking lot.

Continue following the paved trail and you'll soon wrap back around to hike east through another more established parking lot. Now as you're hiking east through the grassy area you ignored earlier to hike downhill, you'll see an amazing view of the city skyline. Few things are actually worthy of sharing on social media, but this view is one of those things.

Soon you'll return to hike the steep hill again. But what goes up, must come down, making the easterly hike a breeze. Now you could simply follow the trail all the way back to the parking lot, but we went ahead and kept hiking eastward after the beach, alongside the highway and just south of the largest of the Edgewater Park

EDGEWATER PARK: FROM BLIGHT TO BRIGHT

Edgewater Park has changed ownership several times, finally landing in the hands of Cleveland Metroparks in 2013 following years of disrepair and public outcry demanding the kind of beachfront Clevelanders deserve. Almost overnight the park improved and it has quickly returned to its rightful place as one of Cleveland's greatest parks. But it's just one chapter in the lakefront's history.

The last decade of the 19th century saw continued growth for the Forest City, and residents needed a place for outdoor recreation. In 1894 the City of Cleveland purchased the land we now know as Edgewater Park, opening the following year. But when the city's fortunes began to reverse for the worse (Hint: The 70s and late 20th century in general weren't so kind to the region), the park became mired in pollution and security problems. That's why the takeover by Cleveland Metroparks has been unanimously welcomed.

Today, Edgewater Park's 146 acres of land, overlooking 6,000 feet of Lake Erie shoreline, are yet another shining example of how this city keeps on fighting.

parking lots. This will take you around the lot and toward the yacht club where you'll turn back north to finish the hike at the northernmost parking lot where you started.

Miles and Directions

0.0 Start on the paved trail on the southern end of the parking lot, hiking west.

0.2 Continue following the trail south through Edgewater Beach. As you pass a parking lot on your left (east), the trail will begin to wind to the west.

0.3 Stay straight (west) to hike across Edgewater Beach.

0.4 Begin a steep, uphill climb that takes you to a picnic area of the park. Continue on this trail, hiking west.

0.7 Turn right (north) to take a new trail into the woods and down closer to the beach as it quickly wraps to the left (west).

1.0 You'll arrive at a small, unmarked parking lot that visitors use for a view of the Cleveland skyline. Take a U-turn around the trees to your left (south) and take the first right to hike southwest toward West Boulevard.

1.1 Arrive at West Boulevard and Edgewater Drive and take a sharp left (northeast) past a sign for Edgewater Park. Continue on this trail past another parking lot.

1.4 Turn left (north) to hike toward the lake. The trail will quickly turn to the right to run parallel to the lake, hiking east.

1.6 Arrive back where you first left this trail to go downhill toward the beach. Continue east, hiking downhill this time and again through the beach.

Edgewater Park Trail, Lakefront Reservation

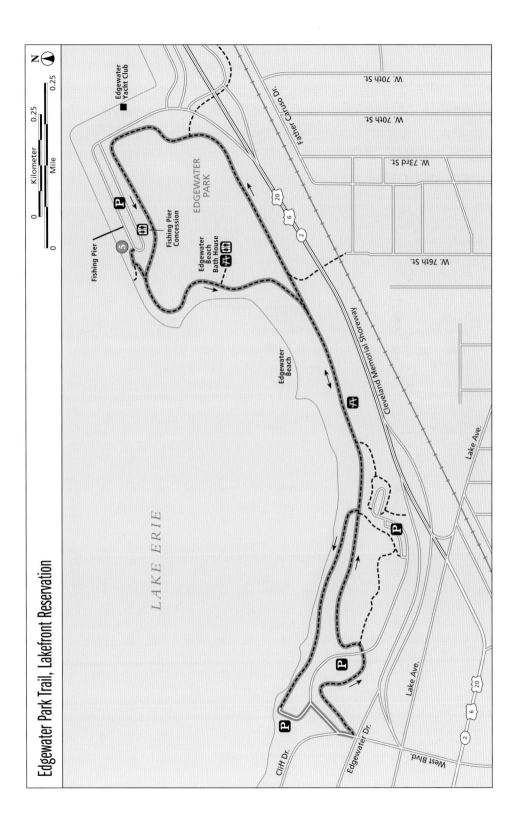

LAKE ERIE

Edgewater Yacht Club

N

Kilometer
0   0.25   0.25

0   Mile   0.25

Fishing Pier

Fishing Pier Concession

EDGEWATER PARK

Edgewater Beach Bath House

Edgewater Beach

Father Caruso Dr.

W. 70th St.

W. 70th St.

W. 73rd St.

W. 76th St.

Cleveland Memorial Shoreway

Lake Ave.

Lake Ave.

West Blvd.

Edgewater Dr.

Cliff Dr.

20 6 2

20 6 2

1.9 Stay straight (east) to hike away from the beach, alongside the highway and toward the Edgewater Yacht Club. You'll follow this trail all the way back to where you started your hike.

2.6 End your hike.

Hike Information

Local Information

Destination; (216) 875-6680; www.thisiscleveland.com

Hike Tours

Cleveland Hiking Club; www.clevelandhikingclub.org
Cleveland Metroparks; (216) 635-3200; www.clevelandmetroparks.com
NEOHiking; www.meetup.com/NEOHiking

GREEN TIP
If you're driving to or from the trailhead, don't let any passenger throw garbage out the window. Keep a small bag in the car that you can empty properly at home.

6 Forest Hill Loop Trail

There's a reason famous industrialist John D. Rockefeller selected this area as his summer retreat in the late 19th century. Beautiful hardwood trees, such as sugar maple and beech, line the sides of the park's numerous ravines. What begins as a seemingly uneventful stroll through a modern day park quickly becomes enveloped in years of untamed growth. Though this was once a well-manicured center of relaxation for the affluent, Forest Hill has since become overgrown with diverse vegetation that makes for excellent hiking territory.

Start: At the Lee Road parking lot in Cleveland Heights
Distance: 3.5 miles
Approximate hiking time: 1.5 hours
Difficulty: Easy with only a handful of inclines and declines
Trail surface: Mostly paved and occasionally graveled trails
Best season: Year-round, especially beautiful with fall colors
Other trail users: Mountain bikers
Canine compatibility: Dogs not permitted
Land status: Public
Fees and permits: None
Schedule: N/A

Maps: City of Cleveland Heights; www.cleveland heights.com
Trail contacts: City of Cleveland Heights; (216) 691-7373
Finding the trailhead: From downtown Cleveland, drive east on Euclid Avenue for 1 mile. Turn left onto East 30th Street and go 0.6 mile. Turn right onto Superior Avenue East and go for 4.3 miles until Euclid Avenue. Turn left onto Euclid Avenue for a hot second before turning right onto Forest Hills Boulevard for just under a mile. Turn right onto Lee Boulevard for 0.3 mile, and the destination will be on the right. GPS: N 41 31' 10.7826" / W 81 34' 19.8978"

The Hike

John D. Rockefeller, the man who made monopoly popular before the board game, sold his Forest Hill estate to his son John D. Rockefeller Jr. in 1923. In 1938, Rockefeller Jr. donated 266 acres of his 700-acre estate to the neighboring inner-ring suburbs of East Cleveland and Cleveland Heights to be used as a public park. Landscape architect A. D. Taylor designed Forest Hill Park to be an urban oasis for surrounding Clevelanders. Exactly 60 years later, the park was listed on the National Register of Historic Places. Today, you'll find a mixture of what you'd expect to find in a modern American park with surprisingly remote areas with impressive vegetation.

You'll enter from the Cleveland Heights side of the park off Lee Road. As soon as you enter you'll find paved trails circling the parking lot. In reality you can hop on the trail at any point, so long as you start hiking north around the four softball fields in the middle. If you come on a summer day, you just might see all four fields in Little League action.

Wildflowers are blooming out from under the ruins of John D. Rockefeller's former summer retreat.

Hiking north on the paved trail, you'll continue working your way around the fields, passing restrooms and tennis courts along the way. Now hiking west, you'll start to move away from the fields and through the tall grasses of the Great Meadow en route to a turnaround. This is the site of the Rockefellers' former residence. It started as a resort, and the family later turned it into their summer home away from their mansion on Euclid Avenue's Millionaires' Row. The house sat at the top of a tall sledding hill.

Continuing to follow the paved trail, you'll soon cross Forest Hills Boulevard to reach a small lake Rockefeller had constructed. If you come at the wrong time, you might have some geese *bombs* to avoid as you circumvent the body of water. Otherwise, it's a calming presence in the middle of a busy park.

Once around the lake, you'll continue hiking west toward more remote portions of the park. Sounds of your natural surroundings will begin to fade away, unless you're visiting in the middle of marching band practice on a weekday afternoon. Though not as peaceful, it's fun in an interesting kind of way to hike with a drumline soundtrack.

Soon you'll come to a junction that takes you down a somewhat steep hill (still paved), dumping you out behind a nearby apartment high-rise in East Cleveland. This

John D. Rockefeller's summer home once stood near here. Unfortunately, the home has since been lost to a fire.

will lead back across Forest Hills Boulevard, taking you to the most remote corners of the park.

On the other side of the street, you'll hike east through somewhat dense woods along dilapidated concrete trails. Not long after you'll find yourself alongside a small creek with what looks to be manufacturing ruins surrounding the waterway. Just around the corner you'll find the trail continues uphill—back to civilization, as it were.

The softball fields again in sight, you could easily end your hike here. Instead, you'll begin to find the blue blazes of the Buckeye Trail on nearby trees. Bet you weren't expecting that!

Follow the blazes into the southeastern corner of Forest Hill Park for your last leg. This small half-loop takes you down by Monticello Boulevard before you hike north alongside Lee Road, which happens to be what you drove in on. Before you know it, you're back at the parking lot to end your hike.

In all, it's a surprising amount of diversity in 3.5 miles of hiking. Children playing in parks, remote trails in dense woodland. And to think one man used to own all of this. Thankfully, it's now for us all to enjoy.

Dirt trail in Forest Hill

Miles and Directions

0.0 Start hiking north on the paved path that connects to the northern corner of the parking lot.

0.1 Arrive at a junction with restrooms nearby. Turn left (west) away from Lee Road and the tennis courts.

0.2 Continue hiking west through a four-way junction, passing softball fields along the way. Soon you'll come to a dead end where you'll turn left to continue on the paved trail south.

0.3 Turn right (west) away from the softball fields toward a more remote portion of the park with trees lining your hike on the left.

0.4 Keep to the left, hiking west toward a half-loop that winds north and back east.

0.7 Continue hiking east past a bridge on your left that goes over Forest Hills Boulevard.

0.9 Stay to the left, hiking northeast briefly before a junction where you'll turn left (north) to cross Forest Hills Boulevard toward the lake in the East Cleveland portion of the park. Shortly after crossing, you'll want to follow the path to the right, hiking east. This will take you around the lake. Continue on this path, hiking counter-clockwise around the water until you reach the northwestern corner.

1.5 Now at the northwestern corner of the lake, turn right (west) to hike away from the lake and into forested area.

1.7 You'll see the bridge over Forest Hills Boulevard you ignored earlier, except now you're on the opposite side. Continue ignoring it and follow the trail as it winds north.

1.8 Turn left (west) to hike downhill on a gentle slope.

2.0 Pass a small connector trail to the nearby apartment high-rise on your right to continue hiking southwest toward Forest Hills Boulevard. When you get to the street, watch for traffic and cross hiking south. Continue on the other side toward a parking lot. Cut through the northern end of the parking lot, hiking east to pass a small playground on your right. You'll follow this trail as it bends southeast before continuing due east onto gravel trail when you enter a more dense area of the woods.

2.7 Ignore a small footpath that looks to be a trail on your right. Instead, continue to the left to hike east. You'll soon come to old, dilapidated debris in a small creek. Hike past this and follow the trail, bending to the left to hike northeast uphill. At the top of the hill, continue following the flat, paved trail as it winds east, closer to the entrance of the park.

2.9 Turn right (east) to take the trail into the southeastern portion of the woods. If you miss this turn, you'll soon end up back in the parking lot where you started.

3.0 Now on dirt trail, you'll begin to see the blue blazes of the Buckeye Trail. Soon you'll come to another junction. A left turn (north) will take you right back into the parking lot, so we're going to turn right (south) to complete this half-loop into the woods.

3.2 Stay to the left as you hike alongside Monticello Boulevard to continue on your final leg north.

3.3 The trail turns left (west) back into the parking lot where you began. You can technically end here or continue following the paved trail around the southwestern corner of the parking lot where you'll take a sharp right (northeast) to come back to where you started.

3.5 End your hike at the northern end of the parking lot where you began.

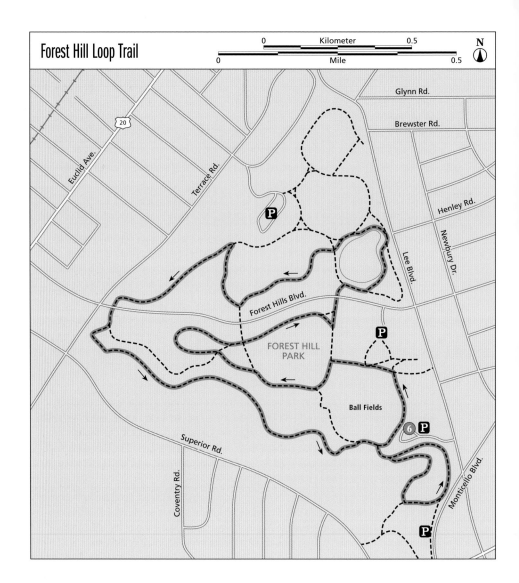

Hike Information

Local Information

Destination; (216) 875-6680; www.thisiscleveland.com

Other Resources

Cleveland Heights Historical Society; www.chhistory.org
Forest Hill; (216) 932-8952; www.fhho.org

7 Ohio City Loop Trail

Tour the history and ongoing revitalization of arguably Cleveland's trendiest and liveliest neighborhood equipped with a century-old market district anchored by the venerable West Side Market, restaurants and breweries that hint at the neighborhood's pre-Prohibition past, and grand Victorian-style homes lining the residential streets of Ohio City.

Start: At the West 25th-Ohio City Rapid Station
Distance: 3 miles
Approximate hiking time: 1 hour
Difficulty: Easy neighborhood hike
Trail surface: Paved sidewalks with just one path through Fairview Park
Best season: Year-round
Other trail users: Public
Canine compatibility: Dogs allowed
Land status: Public
Fees and permits: None

Schedule: None
Maps: Ohio City Inc.; (216) 781-3222; www.ohiocity.org
Trail contacts: Ohio City Inc.; (216) 781-3222; www.ohiocity.org
Finding the trailhead: Walk to the Tower City Rapid in Downtown Cleveland and take the Red Line west one stop to the West 25th-Ohio City Rapid Station where you will start your hike. GPS: N 41 29' 5.0136" / W 81 42' 5.583"

The Hike

Ohio City is perhaps Cleveland's most vibrant neighborhood, even beating Downtown with its anchor institution the West Side Market drawing shoppers and hungry Clevelanders alike by the thousands. Luckily, you'll see it just a few blocks ahead when you start your hike from the West 25th–Ohio City Rapid Station.

Hiking past this venerable piece of Cleveland history, you'll turn up West 25th Street to hike past the vibrant bars, restaurants, and handful of shops that make Ohio City Cleveland's ultimate neighborhood comeback story. Passing the Ohio Savings Bank building and the Old Angle Tavern—the place to be for any and all soccer matches or good old-fashioned Irish drinking, you'll hike down Bridge Avenue to make your way to the residential heart of the nearly 200-year-old neighborhood decorated with Victorian-style homes that will tempt you to end your hike early in order to sign a lease. Continuing down Bridge, you'll soon pass the birthplace of John Heisman—an innovative football coach better known today for a certain trophy awarded to college football's best. A plaque in the front yard from the Ohio Historical Society signifies the home. Some historians believe Heisman was actually born a few blocks west.

The Bridge leg of your hike will actually trickle into the adjacent Detroit-Shoreway neighborhood very briefly as you turn up West 45th Street to Franklin Boulevard where you'll return to the Ohio City borders. The main reason we headed this far out west (besides a residential tour through the leafy neighborhood) was so

Fresh off its centennial celebration, Cleveland's West Side Market continues to be an Ohio City staple and foodie draw across the world.

you can hike past the allegedly haunted Franklin Castle on your eastern return at West 44th Street and Franklin. The stony, historic building is four stories high with more than twenty rooms inside and is the most haunted house in the state (you know, if you believe in that sort of thing). Why is it haunted? Glad you asked.

German immigrant Hannes Tiedemann had the home built in 1881. Things were presumably peachy for 10 years until his 15-year-old daughter succumbed to diabetes. Soon, the house claimed another life—Tiedemann's mother. To be fair, she was elderly at the time, so it's hardly that spooky. Then again, three more children died in the Tiedemann household, leading to speculation in the neighborhood that there may have been even more deaths not being reported. These ongoing rumors fueled by speculation of sexual impropriety led to the haunted Franklin Castle story we know today. Perhaps we'll soon know more of the house's haunted standing, as alterations are under way to convert the building into a family home.

Moving on to far less creepy matters, your scenic urban hike continues east toward the gorgeous Stone Gables B&B at Franklin and West 38th Street. You'll turn down the latter past one of the neighborhood's more impressive urban farms as you make your way to Fairview Park. Hike onto the paved path that cuts through the park west to east alongside the urban farm. Depending on the weather, you might see a softball game going on or kids playing on the playground before you reach the opposite end at West 32nd Street, where you'll turn back up to rejoin Franklin and continue hiking east.

At tiny Franklin Circle you'll turn right down Fulton Road to pass the stunning and visually dominant Franklin Circle Christian Church. President James A. Garfield once served as a pastor here.

Farther down the road you'll pass some of the newer residential developments in the neighborhood, nicely juxtaposed with the charming old houses and a handful of new restaurants before reaching Carroll Avenue across from Carnegie West Public Library. You'll use Carroll to reach a sidewalk that cuts through the Saint Ignatius High School campus at West 30th Street. Hiking south, you'll no doubt be tormented with envious thoughts unless you're one of the few who somehow managed to attend an even more awe-inspiring high school campus in an urban surrounding. Unlikely.

Now on the final leg of your hike, you'll finish by hiking east along Lorain Avenue, past the revitalized Market Square Park and toward the rapid station you started at—its complex red exterior now in sight. Back at the station, this is the difficult part where you're supposed to leave the neighborhood. But if you decide to stick around

WEST SIDE MARKET

Though just passing its centennial celebration, the history of the West Side Market dates back even further when Ohio City was its own township and a rival of the City of Cleveland.

In 1840, 22 years after the city's founding, two prominent businessmen and former mayors, Josiah Barber and Richard Lord, donated land at Lorain Avenue and Pearl Street (today's West 25th Street) to the City of Cleveland on the condition it be used as a marketplace. The West Side Market would not open for another 72 years as the Pearl Market (formerly located on today's Market Square Park) continued to serve its residents, even after Cleveland annexed Ohio City in 1854.

After decades of growth, the Pearl Market proved too small and a new market was commissioned by the city to be built across the street. The end result, as you can still see today, was a magnificent public market space with yellow-brick interior and room for 100 indoor stalls and 85 outdoor produce stalls. The venerable West Side Market has remained a Cleveland and an international foodie staple ever since.

Ohio City Loop Trail

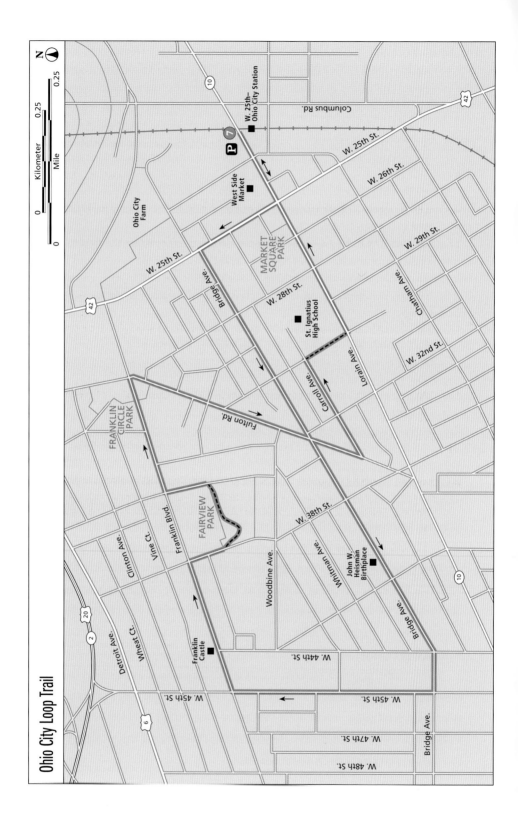

N

0   0.25
Kilometer

0   0.25
Mile

W. 25th–
Ohio City Station

Columbus Rd.

P 7

West Side Market

W. 25th St.

W. 26th St.

Ohio City Farm

W. 25th St.

W. 29th St.

MARKET SQUARE PARK

W. 28th St.

Chatham Ave.

St. Ignatius High School

Bridge Ave.

W. 32nd St.

Lorain Ave.

Carroll Ave.

FRANKLIN CIRCLE PARK

Fulton Rd.

FAIRVIEW PARK

Franklin Blvd.

Clinton Ave.

Vine Ct.

Woodbine Ave.

W. 38th St.

Whitman Ave.

John W. Heisman Birthplace

Detroit Ave.

Wheat Ct.

Franklin Castle

W. 45th St.

W. 44th St.

W. 45th St.

W. 47th St.

W. 48th St.

Bridge Ave.

Bridge Ave.

to peruse the nearby West Side Market or perhaps take in a Brother's Burrito from Ohio City Burrito on 25th (you'll hate Chipotle afterward), no sane person would blame you.

Miles and Directions

0.0 Start at the West 25th–Ohio City Rapid Station and turn left (southwest) to hike on Lorain Avenue toward West 25th Street.

0.1 Turn right (northwest) on West 25th Street, hiking past the West Side Market and Market Square Park.

0.2 At Bridge Avenue, turn left (southwest) to hike through the historic heart of the neighborhood for almost 0.8 mile.

1.0 Stay straight on Bridge Avenue (west) for one block then turn right (north) onto West 45th Street. Continue hiking on this street for 0.3 mile.

1.3 Turn right (east) onto Franklin Boulevard until West 38th Street.

1.5 At West 38th Street in front of Stone Gables B&B, turn right (south) to hike toward Fairview Park.

1.6 Turn left (east) into Fairview Park onto a paved path. You'll keep to your left to continue hiking through the park on the northernmost path until you reach West 32nd Street.

1.7 Turn left (north) onto West 32nd Street for about 0.1 mile when you'll return to Franklin Boulevard.

1.8 Take a right (east) onto Franklin, hiking to Franklin Circle at Fulton Road and Franklin Boulevard.

2.0 Turn right (south) onto Fulton Road for about 0.4 mile.

2.4 With the Carnegie West Public Library on your right, turn left (northeast) onto Carroll Avenue.

2.6 Turn right (southeast) onto West 30th Street to hike through the Saint Ignatius High School campus for just one block to Lorain Avenue. You'll then turn left (northeast) onto Lorain Avenue to hike back to the West 25th–Ohio City Rapid station, which should be within sight at this point.

3.0 Arrive back at the West 25th–Ohio City Rapid Station to end your hike.

Hike Information

Local Information

Ohio City Inc.; (216) 781-3222; www.ohiocity.org
Destination Cleveland; (216) 875-6680; www.thisiscleveland.com

Cleveland Metroparks

These hikes fall into the Cleveland Metroparks system that surrounds the Greater Cleveland area, primarily in Cuyahoga County. Cleveland Metroparks deserves credit for delivering to Clevelanders what Emerald Necklace founder William "Mr. Metropolitan Park" Stinchcomb envisioned in the early 20th century. Rocky River Reservation, both North and South, offer some of the system's most popular trails over generally easy terrain. Rivaling the Rocky River Reservation in popularity are the Chagrin reservations on the East Side with sprawling trails that can take you away from civilization and into seclusion. Bedford offers some of the longest trail possibilities and you can find rock climbing out in Medina County's Hinckley Reservation.

You'll find a little bit of everything at the Rocky River Reservations. Here a local fishes in the Rocky River. Behind him there's a group playing through on the golf course.

8 West Channel Pond to Mount Pleasant to Fort Hill Circuit Trail, Rocky River South Reservation

It's hard to believe this seemingly remote beauty is actually spitting distance from Cleveland Hopkins International Airport. The occasional airplane roaring by serves as the only reminder. Otherwise, prepare to find yourself enveloped by wetlands, the adjacent Rocky River, and old oak forest. This hilly trail will leave some catching their breath after steep climbs that lead to picturesque views of the wetlands and river, 100 feet below. Whatever your athletic prowess, the top of Fort Hill is an idyllic spot for a picnic with a significant other.

Start: Trailhead is the only one available at the Rocky River Nature Center parking lot.
Distance: 3.1-mile circuit
Approximate hiking time: 1 hour
Difficulty: Moderate due to steep hills
Trail surface: Forested trail, stairs, paved path
Best season: Year-round
Other trail users: Bicycles, horses, and motorized vehicles prohibited
Canine compatibility: Dogs permitted on 8-foot leash
Land status: Public
Fees and permits: None
Schedule: 6 a.m.–11 p.m. daily

Maps: www.clevelandmetroparks.com
Trail contacts: Rocky River Nature Center; (440) 734-6660
Finding the trailhead: Drive on I-71 heading south from Cleveland for about 10 miles. Slight left onto Berea Freeway (signs for OH 237 S/Airport/Berea/I-480 W/Toledo). Take exit 238 for I-480 west from Cleveland toward Toledo. Continue for about 2.5 miles. Take exit 7 for Clague Road. Turn left onto Clague Road, right onto Mastick Road, and take the first left onto Shepard Lane. Parking lot will be on right after less than a mile. GPS: N 41 24' 32.9862" / W 81 52' 55.8912"

The Hike

Like most hikes in and around Cleveland, the trailhead kiosk conveniently greets you right outside your car next to the parking lot—easy to find, easy to get started. No matter the season, you'll find Clevelanders young and old out enjoying this southern portion of Rocky River Reservation, known for massive shale cliffs unlike anything strangers to the Buckeye State would expect to find near the shores of Lake Erie. Wetlands and wildlife are also in abundance along this leg of the Rocky River in North Olmsted, Ohio. Don't be surprised if you find some white-tailed deer prancing about during your hike. Feel free to give Bambi a wave, but keep your distance. These are wild animals, after all.

You'll begin your hike working your way toward the Mount Pleasant Loop Trail by way of the West Channel Pond Loop Trail. As you get started, you'll pass by the Rocky River Nature Center. If you're one of those special individuals who never

A man heads up the Fort Hill steps. COURTESY OF THE CLEVELAND METROPOLITAN PARKS DISTRICT

FORT HILL STAIRS

Many Clevelanders know about the 135 stairs that take you 100 feet above the river to Fort Hill. The history of the hill, however, might not be as well known.

On the triangular eastern end of Fort Hill lie earthworks, which were once thought to protect a fort occupied by Whittlesey Tradition Native Americans around AD 1000 to 1640. The triple line of trenches and embankments can still be seen today, although they are greatly eroded. Using evidence from recent archaeological excavations, some scientists now believe the earthworks are much older and may have been built to identify an area of Fort Hill used for rituals of some kind. Cleveland Metroparks asks hikers to stay on the marked trail to protect this valuable cultural and historic feature. Besides, nobody wants to go down as the dullard who trounced centuries-old Native American history, so it's best to do as instructed.

Many geologic forces played a part in shaping Fort Hill and indirectly shaping Cedar Point Valley's cultural history. Those who get their kicks from geology and history are welcome to learn more about Cedar Point Valley at the Rocky River Nature Center.

grew out of the childhood habit of refusing to use the restroom before getting in the car, then feel free to hit the restrooms before you get started. If running water causes you problems, then hiking alongside the Rocky River is no place to test your bladder control.

Once you pass the nature center, you'll briefly join the West Channel Pond Loop Trail, signified by a blue sign with a bird. Look for the entrance to the Mount Pleasant Loop on your right (north). Cleveland Metroparks does an excellent job marking their trails, so you can't miss it, not to mention you have this thoroughly researched, informative, and enlightening guide in your hands (pat on my shoulder).

Mount Pleasant itself is a lollipop trail. Walking along the handle of the lollipop is a breeze—the perfect warm-up for the uphill climb at the beginning of the loop. Meantime, take care crossing Shepard Lane (early on in the Mount Pleasant portion), and enjoy yourself as you quickly escape from the sounds of civilization, though the easygoing joyride ends as you come to the end of the handle with the North Olmsted Waste Water Treatment Facility in plain sight, due north. Here, you'll take a sharp right up the switchback to begin your Mount Pleasant climb. Working your way east along the loop, you'll be treated to your first glimpse of the Rocky River, 100 feet or so below you.

Continue along the loop, back down the lollipop handle to where you entered Mount Pleasant. Again, you'll briefly hop back on West Channel to the mouth of the Fort Hill Loop Trail on your left (south). Although you could've turned back after finishing Mount Pleasant, the hike around Fort Hill is worth it for the 135-stair climb to the top of the hill that'll leave you puffing for air whether you're an Olympic athlete or an animated Mr. Potato Head. Your reward is a gorgeous, panoramic view of an even more powerful Rocky River that will silence any cynic of the Midwest. Take a moment to enjoy the sights before descending back down toward the parking lot where you will end your hike.

Miles and Directions

0.0 Start at the lone trailhead connected to the parking lot. You'll see a map of Rocky River Reservation and a white maple leaf on an orange sign indicating the beginning of the Woodland Loop Trail. Walk up the paved road.

0.7 Continue along the path past the Rocky River Nature Center.

0.9 Turn right (north) onto West Channel Pond Loop Trail and continue toward Mount Pleasant Loop Trail.

1.2 You'll approach a fork in the road. Keep right (north) to begin the Mount Pleasant Loop Trail. **Option:** Stay to the left (west) to continue on the Woodland Loop Trail.

1.3 The trail quickly comes to a road, Shepard Lane. Cross the road and continue the trail directly across the street.

1.4 Here you'll take a switchback on the right (south) to begin your first climb up a hill. At the top, you'll come to another fork in the road. Stay right (south) for the duration of the loop until you return to this split in the trail.

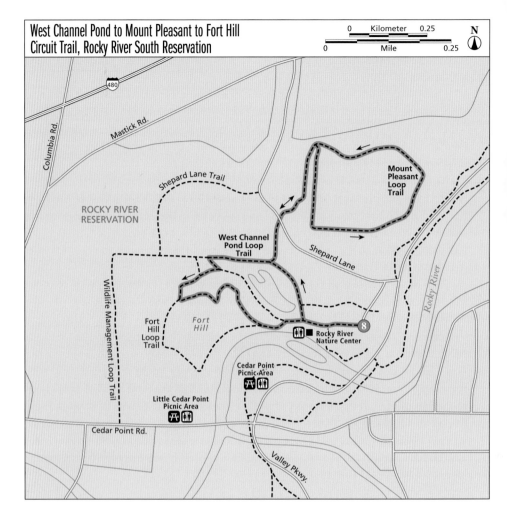

2.1 You're back at the split from mile 1.4. Head back down (north) the hill and take the sharp left (south), repeating a small portion of the Mount Pleasant Loop Trail.

2.2 Cross Shepard Lane again to continue along the trail.

2.3 You'll approach the fork from earlier where you began the Mount Pleasant Loop Trail. This time, turn right (west) to continue the West Channel Pond Loop Trail from earlier. **Bailout:** Turn left (east) to hike the portion of West Channel Pond Loop you hiked earlier toward the Woodland Loop Trail and head back to the trailhead.

2.5 Turn left (south) to begin the Fort Hill Loop Trail. Shortly thereafter, you'll come to another split. Stay to the (right) to continue along the Fort Hill Loop Trail. **Option:** Turn left (east) to rejoin the West Channel Pond Loop Trail on a portion you haven't hiked yet, and head back toward the beginning of the loop, close to the parking lot trailhead.

2.6 Take the stairs on the left (east) to climb atop Fort Hill.

2.8 On left (north), enjoy the overlook of the Rocky River Reservation wetlands before continuing along the trail.

2.9 Another overlook comes quickly, this time on right (south) of Rocky River, 100 feet below. Continue down a long set of steep steps (east) toward the bottom of Fort Hill.

3.0 At the bottom, keep right (east) to head back toward Rocky River Nature Center. You'll soon pass the center once more where you can stop for a restroom break before returning to the trailhead.

3.1 Arrive back at the trailhead.

Hike Information

Local Information

Destination Cleveland; (216) 875-6680; www.thisiscleveland.com

Local Events / Attractions

Birds of Prey Weekend (February), **Cedar Valley Settlers Celebration & Music Festival** (September)

Hike Tours

Cleveland Hiking Club; www.clevelandhikingclub.org
Cleveland Metroparks; (216) 635-3200; www.clevelandmetroparks.com.
NEOHiking; www.meetup.com/NEOHiking

Fall offers some of the best views of the Rocky River. But you can't go wrong in any season.

9 Cottonwood to Mastick Woods to Bridle Trails, Rocky River North Reservation

The Rocky River will flow steadily beside you throughout this long yet relatively flat hike. Massive shale cliffs give the reservation much of its character with willows, sycamores, and cottonwood trees sprinkled throughout the forests, floodplains, meadows, and wetlands. Wildlife consists of a variety of bird species that will draw ornithologists. But more likely to cross your path is the white-tailed deer, one of Northeast Ohio's more ubiquitous mammals.

Start: At the Cottonwood Loop Trailhead
Distance: 7 miles
Approximate hiking time: 2.5 hours
Difficulty: Moderate due to length
Trail surface: Paved, mostly crushed gravel and flat dirt paths
Best season: Year-round
Other trail users: Bicycles; horses on Bridle Trail portion only; motorized vehicles prohibited
Canine compatibility: Dogs permitted on 8-foot leash
Land status: Public
Fees and permits: None

Schedule: 6 a.m.–11 p.m. daily
Maps: www.clevelandmetroparks.com
Trail contacts: (440) 734-6660
Finding the trailhead: Drive on I-71 heading south from Cleveland for about 8 miles. Take exit 238 toward Toledo to merge onto I-480 W. In about 1 mile, take exit 9 and turn left onto Grayton Road. In less than a mile turn left again onto Puritas Avenue. At the bottom of the hill, turn left onto Valley Parkway. Cottonwood Picnic Area will be on your left. GPS: N 41 25' 57.3564" / W 81 50' 55.2696"

The Hike

A glimpse at the Rocky River Reservation map might lead one to believe there's not much in the way of a long hike. The Cottonwood and Mastick Woods Loop trails are both brief excursions under a mile. Head north on the All Purpose Trail and you'll find just a couple more short hikes.

Though the brevity of these hikes might be a turnoff for some, you simply cannot skip this area. To do so would be a disservice to the architects of Cleveland Metroparks, William Stinchcomb and Harold Groth. In fact, it was on this 3.8-acre parcel of land that the foundation of the Emerald Necklace was set. Purchased in April 1919 for $195, this was the first land purchased for what is now known as Cleveland Metroparks. With this in mind, it would be sacrilege not to give due respect to this important region in Cleveland hiking. Luckily, the long and winding Bridle Trail is reason enough to visit Rocky River Reservation.

You'll begin at the Cottonwood Loop Trailhead where the Bridle Trail intersects. As noted, Cottonwood Loop Trail is a short jaunt around a floodplain forest known for its late spring wildflowers. While you very easily could stick to the Bridle Trail, it's worth taking on this loop before heading out on your main trek. The wide dirt

Bluebells blossom alongside the Rocky River.

paths, beautiful greenery, and pleasant sounds of the river trickling past will surprise you. When you're finished, you'll come back to the crushed gravel of the Bridle Trail, which you'll take north shortly before coming to the Mastick Woods Loop Trail.

This is another brief loop you're welcome to skip if you want to get going onto the more scenic portions of the Bridle Trail. But you're here, so why not take a look?

Mastick Woods takes you on a 0.4-mile paved half-loop around park pavilions and playground equipment. On a busy day, it's nice taking this on to embrace your inner-child as kids run around in the sparkling sun.

When you're reconnected with the Bridle Trail, you'll continue north on a relatively un-noteworthy trail, hiking alongside the All Purpose Trail until you reach Puritas Avenue. You'll hike across the bridge here toward a City of Cleveland sign welcoming you into the city. It's a surprising reminder that what was long ago considered a refuge from urban life is actually still pretty much in the city.

After crossing the bridge, you'll have to cross Puritas Avenue itself to hike north on the Bridle Trail. Be careful crossing the street here. This cannot be emphasized enough. Despite having the right-of-way and a giant yellow crossing sign, cars

The Rocky River Reservation Courtesy of Cleveland Metroparks / Kyle Lanzer

continue to speed through seemingly oblivious to the damage they can cause to the human body. This is the only frustration you'll experience on this hike, thankfully.

Hiking north on the Bridle Trail, you'll pass the Mastick Woods Golf Course on your right with the Rocky River flowing by on your left. You may find golfers or fly fishermen, perhaps even both. It's just another example of how diverse this particular reservation is.

After passing the golf course, the trail will become seemingly more remote. You'll come across dirt trail, exposed roots, and occasionally jagged terrain that will leave you wondering if you're still actually on the Bridle Trail. Indeed you are.

As you can see on the map, the Bridle Trail on both ends of your hike comes to a small loop not unlike a suburban cul-de-sac you'll use to turn around. You'll simply backtrack to the Puritas Avenue intersection where you have the option of ending your hike early by continuing your backtrack to the parking lot, or you can continue south past the Rocky River Stables. If you're lucky, you might find some blooming bluebells here in the spring.

Like the northern leg, this too comes to a turnaround loop that you'll use to backtrack to Puritas Avenue and back to the trailhead to finish your hike.

WILLIAM STINCHCOMB

A memorial to Cleveland Metroparks' founder and first director, William Stinchcomb, sits just north up the road from this hike. Many in Cleveland put Stinchcomb and his work on par with that of city founder Moses Cleaveland, which speaks to the importance this man has played in the region.

Mr. Metropolitan Park believed urbanites needed occasional refuge in nature to live a healthy life, which not coincidentally is where many believe Stinchcomb found himself to be most at peace. Thanks to his work and leadership in making Cleveland Metroparks a reality, today's Clevelanders are lucky enough to be graced by one of the most impressive park systems in the country, rivaling Boston's own U-shaped Emerald Necklace, which is said to have served as inspiration to Stinchcomb. Visit Rocky River Reservation today and you'll find Clevelanders running, cycling, and hiking throughout the reservation just as Stinchcomb envisioned.

Laying out his vision, Stinchcomb once said, "We must have these great outdoor rest places close to a great industrial city such as this is, and as working days grow shorter we must find healthful ways of filling leisure time." Most would agree it's not premature to euphorically pronounce, "Mission Accomplished."

In the end, you'll realize this is a hike where the map deceives you. Glimpsing the map will have you believe this is nothing but boring old Bridle Trail with plenty of backtracking. Though there is some backtracking, the hike is hardly boring with plenty of nature to keep your senses invigorated, including the Rocky River itself flowing steadily beside you throughout a majority of your hike.

Miles and Directions

0.0 Start at the southern end of the parking lot. You'll come to a trail post marking the Cottonwood Loop and Bridle Trails. Continue south for the Cottonwood Loop Trail.

0.1 You'll approach a junction at the Rocky River. Turn right (west) to hike alongside the river toward another junction. In about 500 feet, you'll again turn right (north) to hike back out of the woods toward the parking lot where you'll reconnect with the Bridle Trail.

0.3 Hike back onto the Bridle Trail, bearing right (east) toward the 0.4-mile Mastick Woods Loop Trail.

0.5 Stay to the right at the parking lot where you'll pick up the paved Mastick Woods Loop Trail, hiking around the park grills and playground equipment.

0.7 You'll come back to the parking lot where you'll want to turn left (west). Almost immediately you'll turn right (north) at the driveway to hike back onto the Bridle Trail toward Puritas Avenue.

A former road returns to nature as a trail.

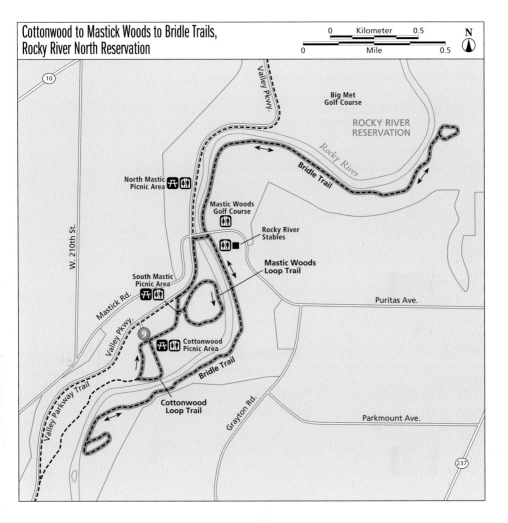

0   Kilometer   0.5

0   Mile   0.5

N

10

Valley Pkwy.

Big Met
Golf Course

ROCKY RIVER
RESERVATION

Rocky River

Bridle Trail

North Mastic
Picnic Area

Mastic Woods
Golf Course

Rocky River
Stables

W. 210th St.

Mastic Woods
Loop Trail

South Mastic
Picnic Area

Puritas Ave.

Mastick Rd.

Valley Pkwy.

9

Cottonwood
Picnic Area

Valley Parkway Trail

Bridle Trail

Cottonwood
Loop Trail

Grayton Rd.

Parkmount Ave.

237

0.9 After hiking alongside Valley Parkway, you'll be pushed onto the Puritas Avenue sidewalk. Turn right (east) to hike toward a Bridle Trail crossing sign on the other end of the bridge. Here you'll turn left (north) to hike the northern portion of the Bridle Trail alongside Rocky River. Continue until you reach the turnaround loop at the northernmost point.

2.1 Stay to the left heading northwest to complete the mini-lollipop.

2.3 You'll return to the beginning of the loop. Continue hiking south over familiar territory back to Puritas Avenue.

3.8 Return to Puritas Avenue, cross the street, and continue hiking south past the stables to continue on the Bridle Trail.

4.6 Keep to the right at the southern loop to continue south. You'll turn left in about 500 or so feet to continue winding back to this junction. When you return, hike back up north to Puritas Avenue.

6.5 Return to Puritas Avenue, turn left (west) to again cross the Rocky River and reconnect with another familiar portion of the Bridle Trail. Hike this for 0.5 mile back to the parking lot.

7.0 Arrive at the parking lot to finish your Bridle Trail–heavy hike.

Hike Information

Local Information

Destination Cleveland; (216) 875-6680; www.thisiscleveland.com

Hike Tours

Cleveland Hiking Club; www.clevelandhikingclub.org
Cleveland Metroparks; (216) 635-3200; www.clevelandmetroparks.com
NEOHiking; www.meetup.com/NEOHiking

Other Resources

Cleveland Historical; www.clevelandhistorical.org

GREEN TIP
Consider the packaging of any products you bring with you. It's best to properly dispose of packaging at home before you hike. If you're on the trail, pack it out with you.

10 Iron Springs to North Ravine Trail, Garfield Park Reservation

From Garfield Park Nature Center, this hike offers a peek into the Cleveland of yesteryear with about a mile of the hike on a former trolley route that connected Garfield Heights to Cleveland in the earlier part of the 19th century. To get here, you'll wind your way through beautiful forested, grassy, and all-purpose trails alongside a calm yet scenic stream.

Start: At the Garfield Park Nature Center
Distance: 2.7 miles
Approximate hiking time: 1 hour
Difficulty: Easy
Trail surface: Mostly old, paved trail and occasional forested and all-purpose sections
Best season: Year-round
Other trail users: Public
Canine compatibility: Dogs permitted on 8-foot leash
Land status: Public
Fees and permits: None
Schedule: 6 a.m.–1 p.m. daily
Maps: www.clevelandmetroparks.com

Trail contacts: Garfield Park Nature Center; www.clevelandmetroparks.com; (216) 341-3152
Finding the trailhead: Drive on I-77 heading south from Cleveland for about 7 miles. Take exit 156 to merge onto I-480 driving east toward Youngstown. Take exit 23, OH 14/Broadway Avenue exit. In 1 mile turn right onto Broadway Avenue. In 1 more mile turn left into Garfield Park Reservation, then take an immediate left. Garfield Park Nature Center will be on your left. GPS: N 41 25' 57.5466" / W 81 36' 19.3494"

The Hike

Though tucked away inside the old suburb of Garfield Heights, the park is deeply connected to the history of Cleveland and is spitting distance away from one of the city's most historic (and sadly) most troubled neighborhoods, Slavic Village. The neighborhood is dubiously known around financial circles as the epicenter of the 2008 housing collapse.

Turning to much happier thoughts, the history of Garfield Park dates back to 1894 when the City of Cleveland purchased three farms 0.5 mile south of the city limits for a new south side park. Much of the original stonework remains, a byproduct of 1930s New Deal projects. You'll see and hike over a beautiful stone bridge toward the end of the hike, just down the road from the parking lot.

This is perhaps one of Cleveland Metroparks' easiest yet most important hikes. Either before or after your hike, it's worth peeking into Garfield Park Nature Center for some historical context.

You'll spend a majority of today's hike on the Iron Springs Loop Trail—1.2 miles of paved, yet gritty trail. What makes this trail significant is that it follows portions of an old trolley route that used to connect the area to Downtown Cleveland. At first

The Garfield Park Nature Center features exhibits on the history and wildlife of the area.

you might be confused as to whether or not you're really supposed to be hiking on paved trail. But like an epiphany, you'll suddenly notice remnants of the old trolley line beneath the cracks of the trail. And though it's sad the line no longer exists, at least the space was salvaged for folks looking for a manageable afternoon hike.

GARFIELD PARK

Like Cleveland's other large parks, Garfield Park was conceived as a romantically landscaped "public pleasure ground" where Clevelanders might spend a few hours enjoying rural conditions away from the noise and clamor of city life. Garfield Park was renowned for the grandeur of its groves and forests. Comprising high promontories and creek valleys, it featured a small lake and a mineral spring. A baseball diamond, football fields, tennis courts, and a swimming pool were added later. But beginning in the 1950s, lack of maintenance caused the park to deteriorate, prompting its lease in 1986 to Cleveland Metroparks.

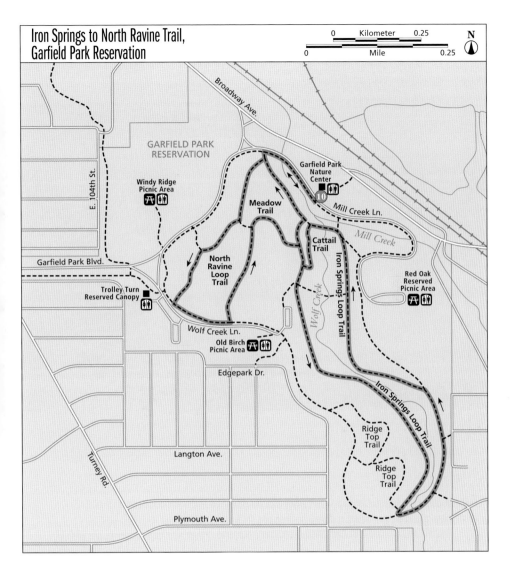

0   Kilometer   0.25

0   Mile   0.25

N

Broadway Ave.

GARFIELD PARK
RESERVATION

E. 104th St.

Windy Ridge
Picnic Area

Garfield Park
Nature
Center

10

Mill Creek Ln.

Meadow
Trail

Cattail
Trail

Mill Creek

Garfield Park Blvd.

North
Ravine
Loop
Trail

Iron Springs Loop Trail

Red Oak
Reserved
Picnic Area

Trolley Turn
Reserved Canopy

Wolf Creek Ln.

Old Birch
Picnic Area

Wolf Creek

Edgepark Dr.

Iron Springs Loop Trail

Turney Rd.

Langton Ave.

Ridge
Top
Trail

Ridge
Top
Trail

Plymouth Ave.

Perhaps best of all, you'll pass by Iron Springs, Green Springs, and the Old Boating
Pond along the way before hopping onto the North Ravine Loop Trail, a hilly hike
that highlights a mature, wooded ravine.

Runners and hikers alike will find a place here at Garfield Park Reservation. At
only about 2.7 miles of trails, you won't leave with a backbreaking workout under
your belt. But this reservation is about as good as it gets for hiking close to the city.
You won't have to worry about planning a day around conquering the trails here.

It's hard to believe you're in an inner-ring suburb and not rural Ohio. COURTESY OF THE CLEVELAND METROPOLITAN PARKS DISTRICT

Miles and Directions

0.0 You'll begin at the Garfield Park Nature Center parking lot. On the opposite side of the nature center, you'll find a paved all-purpose trail where you'll start the hike. Turn right (north) onto the trail. Shortly thereafter, you'll come to a sign with an orange maple leaf for the North Ravine Loop Trail. Turn left (southwest) onto the trail, continuing along as it turns south into the woods.

0.2 Turn right (west) to go down some stairs and you'll be immediately ushered to another set of stairs, this time to climb uphill.

0.4 You'll hike right into the all-purpose trail again. Turn left (east), hiking for a short period until the North Ravine Loop Trail turns back into the woods on the left, heading north.

0.7 Here you'll begin to see familiar territory as you hike closer to where you began the North Ravine Loop Trail. But on your right (east), you'll find a short connector trail—the Meadow Trail. Take this to the Iron Springs Loop Trail, a roughly paved trail that used to be a trolley route to Downtown Cleveland. Stay on this trail for just over a mile as it loops around an adjacent stream, heading back north toward the start of the trail on the eastern side of the stream.

2.1 The Iron Springs Loop Trail will come to a 19th-century stone bridge with your parking lot in sight. Hike across the stone bridge heading west toward the Cattail Trail. Turn left (south) onto the trail alongside a stream, hiking for a short distance before you reconnect with North Ravine Loop Trail from the beginning of your hike via a small section of the Iron Springs Loop Trail. Turn right (north) onto the North Ravine Loop Trail.

2.7 You'll return to the all-purpose trail you began on. Turn right (east) to return to the parking lot.

Hike Information

Local Information

Destination Cleveland; (216) 875-6680; www.thisiscleveland.com

Hike Tours

Cleveland Metroparks; (216) 635-3200; www.clevelandmetroparks.com
NEOHiking; www.meetup.com/NEOHiking
Cleveland Hiking Club; www.clevelandhikingclub.org

Other Resources

NEONaturalist; www.neonaturalist.com

GREEN TIP
Pass it down—the best way to instill good green habits in your children is to set a good example.

11 Hemlock to Deer Lick Cave Loop Trail, Brecksville Reservation

Chippewa Creek is the star of this section of Brecksville Reservation, flowing steadily throughout the year. Here, the reservation's extensive trail system, including the Bridle Trail and a portion of the famous Buckeye Trail, comes together, offering a winding hike with a constant back and forth between uphill climbs and downhill slopes. Oak-hickory forests rule the ridgetops, while cottonwoods, willows, and sycamores sit alongside the creek on the floodplain. The unusual sandstone formation of Deer Lick Cave makes this long rugged hike worth the trip.

Start: Across the street from Chippewa Picnic Area

Distance: 4.5-mile loop

Approximate hiking time: 2 hours

Difficulty: Easy with steep climbs and rough terrain

Trail surface: Forested natural surface and all-purpose trail

Best season: Year-round

Other trail users: Bicycles and motorized vehicles prohibited; horses on Bridle Trail portion only

Canine compatibility: Dogs permitted on 8-foot leash

Land status: Public

Fees and permits: None

Schedule: 6 a.m.–1 p.m. daily

Maps: www.clevelandmetroparks.com

Trail contacts: Brecksville Nature Center; (440) 526-1012; www.clevelandmetroparks .com

Finding the trailhead: Drive on I-77 heading south from Cleveland for about 14 miles. Take exit 149A to merge onto OH 82 driving east toward Brecksville. In 1.8 miles, turn right onto Chippewa Creek Drive. Chippewa Picnic Area will be on your right in less than 0.5 mile. GPS: N 41 18' 57.9456" / W 81 36' 3.492"

The Hike

Brecksville Reservation is an after-work favorite of many Clevelanders who enjoy a little sweat in the evening hours. Four and a half miles of winding, occasionally rough terrain await you. You'll climb steadily uphill before winding back down again, and repeat. Just as you think you've found a flat plain of sweet relief, it's time to march back up again. No, these climbs aren't anything that a Nepalese Sherpa would bat an eye at, but they're rigorous enough to make sure you'll feel it in your legs by the end.

Considering the number of trails around here, it's easy to take a wrong turn. If you do, it's hardly the end of the world. Anyone who loses himself or herself in this oak-hickory forest, outlined to the north by Chippewa Creek, is one lucky sod. Though the reservation is packed with an extensive trail system, it's surprisingly close to suburban Brecksville. So you'll easily find your way back on track should you get lost or decide to veer off trail because something caught your eye.

From the Chippewa Picnic Area parking lot, you'll want to cross the street you just drove in on (Chippewa Creek Drive) to catch the trailhead. Although most trails

*Deer Lick Cave is a popular sandstone rock overhang in the heart of Brecksville Reserva-
tion. Salt trapped in the sands deposited millions of years ago is picked up by water percolating
through the rock to the surface, which wildlife "lick."* ROBERT ANDRUKAT

around Cleveland are marked by a logo on a solid color backdrop, Brecksville Reservation uses a white hiker silhouette (a relative of the bathroom sign, perhaps?) on all
trails. To keep track of your trail, you'll simply need to coordinate the color of your
trail with the backdrop of the trail marker. To kick off the Hemlock Loop Trail, you'll
be looking for green.

    Heading northeast, you'll immediately start a gradual climb alongside a modest
creek—nothing torturous, though. In fact, you might even mistakenly think you're

in for a breeze. Sure, sure. Let us know how you feel by the end, especially on a hot summer afternoon when the sun seems to derive sick pleasure by pulling every last drop of hydration out of your body.

A little over a mile into your hike, you'll quickly realize you're standing directly over Chippewa Creek. Depending on the time of year, she might be flowing more like a river than a creek. Even in the heart of winter, when you expect every drop of water within a 60-mile radius of Lake Erie to be frozen, Chippewa Creek flows at a steady, relaxing rhythm.

Once you connect with the Bridle Trail heading south past Harriet Keeler Memorial Picnic Area—named after a late-19th-century, early-20th-century Cleveland educator and author of books for nature lovers—you'll be on your way to Deer Lick Cave Loop Trail, named after an unusual sandstone formation you'll pass along the way. But before you reach the caves, Deer Lick will merge with the Buckeye Trail, signified by a dab of light blue paint on surrounding trees generally referred to as "blue blazes."

Shortly after you begin the trek back north toward Chippewa Picnic Area where you started, you'll approach a set of stone steps that lead to Deer Lick Cave. Just follow the sound of flowing water.

Doing this hike in the winter promises an icy trail, an especially tricky adventure when hiking uphill. But if you're so inclined, you might be lucky enough to catch an intricate display of icicles hanging off the sandstone caves. If you didn't know any better, you'd think someone was putting on an ice show just for you. Otherwise, feel free to get your feet wet if you visit during the warmer months of the Cleveland year. As you leave, it'll be hard not to wonder who might have called those caves home, hundreds or even thousands of years ago.

DEER LICK CAVE

So how did Deer Lick Cave get its name, you might be wondering? It's rather self-explanatory, so long as you happen to be a geological nerd with a sense for sandstone and ancient ocean formations.

Ohio looked just a tad different millions of years ago, as did the rest of the world. For instance, an ancient ocean once covered the very region you're now hiking in—not just the region, but also the entire state. This formed sand deposits, leading to the slick-looking sandstone prevalent throughout Deer Lick Cave.

Now embedded in the stone is the salt once trapped within the very sands that formed the sandstone. So whenever water flows over the stone, it brings salt to the surface. Because you're an intelligent hiker using context clues and deductive reasoning, you've probably surmised that Ohio's plentiful deer population enjoys licking said salt, thus the name Deer Lick Cave.

Moving along, you'll start to get the feel you're in the backcountry. That means the Buckeye Trail (still merged with Deer Lick) is doing its job, sending your mind away from the troubles of everyday life. What else is nature for, right? Though it's admittedly disappointing when the trail creeps alongside Valley Parkway. Perhaps it's a metaphor for how it's nearly impossible for anyone to escape the realities of our everyday lives? Or maybe that's just hippie talk. Nevertheless, you'll soon be ushered away from civilization, lost once again on the trail. Your only sign of intelligent life (besides any companion you may be hiking with, let's hope) is a sign explaining the Buckeye Trail, accompanied with a map of the 1,444-mile trail that encompasses the state. But that's an adventure for another day (more like a summer). For now, it's time to part ways with the Buckeye Trail and finish today's journey along Deer Lick.

As the trail begins a winding downhill slope, it's your sign that the hike is regrettably coming to an end. You should even be able to catch a glimpse of your car in the Chippewa Picnic Area parking lot as you continue to descend.

At the end, you'll come out southwest of the parking lot on the opposite side of Cleveland Metro Parkway from where you began. Finish your hike, and bid farewell to Brecksville until another day.

Miles and Directions

0.0   Start north across Chippewa Creek Drive. You'll see a green sign with a picture of a hiker indicating the beginning of the Hemlock Loop Trail.

0.1   Turn right (northeast) over a wooden bridge and left (northwest) at the end of the bridge to begin a slightly uphill climb.

0.3   Continue straight over the bridge.

0.4   At the fork in the trail, take the bridge left (northwest).

1.2   On the right (north) you'll notice Chippewa Creek flowing much heavier than earlier. Continue straight.

1.3   You'll start to approach Chippewa Creek Drive again. Turn left (east) to briefly merge with the All Purpose Trail. Cross the street near the crosswalk and sign for Harriet Keeler Memorial Picnic Area. Continue the Hemlock Loop Trail across the street.

1.4   Stay right to join the Bridle Trail (yellow) toward the Deer Lick Cave Loop Trail (red).

1.6   Continue straight on the Bridle Trail.

1.8   Here you'll approach some wooden stairs. Take them up to the top and turn right (south) for the Deer Lick Cave Loop Trail.

2.0   Turn right (west) and then a sharp left (south) to head downhill.

2.6   At the bottom of the hill, turn right (south). You'll then cross a small bridge and begin another uphill climb.

2.8   Here you'll approach Valley Parkway. Join it briefly before reconnecting with the Bridle Trail / Deer Lick Cave Loop Trail on the right (south).

3.3   Stay left (north), merging with Deer Lick Cave Loop Trail and the Buckeye Trail, which is marked by blue paint on the surrounding trees.

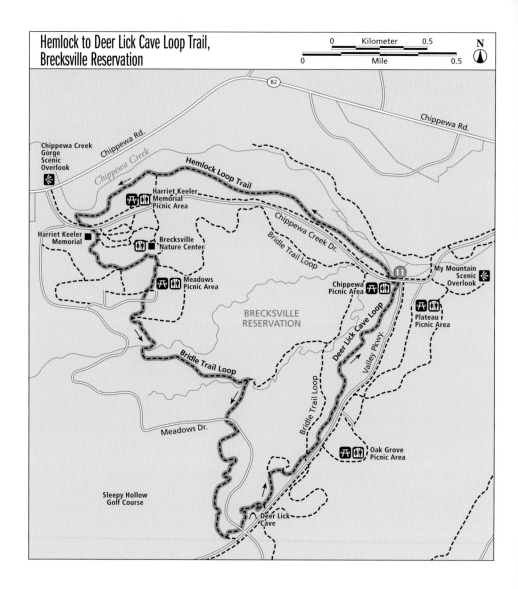

0   Kilometer   0.5

0   Mile   0.5

N

82

Chippewa Rd.

Chippewa Creek
Gorge
Scenic
Overlook

Chippewa Rd.

Chippewa Creek

Hemlock Loop Trail

Harriet Keeler
Memorial
Picnic Area

Chippewa Creek Dr.

Harriet Keeler
Memorial

Brecksville
Nature Center

Bridle Trail Loop

My Mountain
Scenic
Overlook

Meadows
Picnic Area

Chippewa
Picnic Area

Plateau
Picnic Area

BRECKSVILLE
RESERVATION

Deer Lick Cave Loop

Valley Pkwy.

Bridle Trail Loop

Bridle Trail Loop

Meadows Dr.

Oak Grove
Picnic Area

Sleepy Hollow
Golf Course

Deer Lick
Cave

3.4   Turn left (northwest) down stone steps to reach the Deer Lick cave, following the sound of lightly flowing water.

3.7   Stay right to continue on Deer Lick and Buckeye.

3.8   Turn left (north) onto the Bridle Trail very briefly, then back right (northeast) to continue along Deer Lick and Buckeye.

4.1   Continue straight on Deer Lick, leaving Buckeye. **Option:** Turn right (northeast) to continue on Buckeye and connect with the Salamander Loop Trail (1.5 miles).

4.5   Finish the Deer Lick Cave Loop Trail on the opposite side of Chippewa Creek Drive where you began.

Hike Information

Local Information
Destination Cleveland; (216) 875-6680; www.thisiscleveland.com

Hike Tours
Cleveland Hiking Club; www.clevelandhikingclub.org
Cleveland Metroparks; (216) 635-3200; www.clevelandmetroparks.com
NEOHiking; www.meetup.com/NEOHiking

Other Resources
NEONaturalist; www.neonaturalist.com

GREEN TIP
Borrow, rent, or share gear. It's wasteful to spend hundreds of dollars on new gear, unless you're a regular on the trails.

12 Sagamore Creek Loop Trail, Bedford Reservation

This hike has the diversity you'd expect in an overnight hike encompassing 20–plus miles. It has churning waterfalls, calming rivers, streams, and views of it all from ledges overlooking Sagamore Creek as you weave in and out of forested areas on 4.2 miles of moderate terrain. You'll feel like a true adventurer near the halfway mark as you're forced to cross the creek with only a handful of stones to guide the way.

Start: Trailhead is paved and marked as Bike and Hike Trail next to Cleveland Metroparks sign.
Distance: 4.2 miles
Approximate hiking time: 2 hours
Difficulty: Moderate due to creek crossings
Trail surface: Predominantly forested trail with portions of paved trail and road, partially on bridle trail
Best season: Year-round
Other trail users: Bicycles and motorized vehicles prohibited; horses on Bridle Trail portion only
Canine compatibility: Dogs permitted on 8-foot leash

Land status: Public
Fees and permits: None
Schedule: 6 a.m.–1 p.m. daily
Maps: www.clevelandmetroparks.com
Trail contacts: Cleveland Metroparks; (216) 635-3200; www.clevelandmetroparks.com
Finding the trailhead: Drive on I-77 heading south from Cleveland for about 10 miles. Take exit 153 toward Independence and merge onto East Pleasant Valley Road heading east. Continue for about 2.7 miles. Road will turn into Alexander Road for another 1.5 miles. Parking lot will be on right. GPS: N 41 21' 28.4142" / W 81 34' 7.4598"

The Hike

The parking lot comes and goes fairly quickly as you drive east along Alexander Road. Keep a sharp eye for what looks to be a glorified turnaround for cars. Once you pull in, you'll notice the Cleveland Metroparks trailhead kiosk that greets hikers at most official parking locations, letting you know you're where you're supposed to be.

After parking, head east toward a paved, relatively steep uphill climb. You'll notice a blue marker indicating you're on the Buckeye Trail as you continue south. This is part of the Metro Parks Bike and Hike Trail. As you hike, the trail begins to feel like a grand, elevated entrance to a palace. Trees line the path and immediately drop off to Sagamore Creek on your right and left, 100 feet or so below. The trail is clearly wide enough to welcome cyclists and hikers for a couple hundred feet until you approach a small sign on your right for the Buckeye and Sagamore Creek Trail next to another sign telling cyclists to keep moving. Head down this short slope into the forest where the trail becomes considerably rougher. It doesn't take long to understand why cyclists aren't welcome here.

Vic makes the second crossing of Sagamore Creek.

Enjoy the winding trip through the forest as you inch closer to the banks of Sagamore Creek. While still high above, you'll notice the occasional opening between trees, offering great views of the creek below. Notice again the trees marked in blue for the Buckeye Trail. You'll see that some hikers before you have carved faces into the paint.

Before long you'll be ushered out south toward Sagamore Road, hiking briefly alongside the road's guardrail. The field opens up briefly with the trail guiding you back toward the creek. It's easy to wander off trail here, especially in the winter or fall when snow or leaves are covering the trail. So long as you continue hiking west, parallel to the creek, you'll be fine. In fact, some off-trail adventure is encouraged here, especially if the water is warm enough to hop around in the creek. You might as well! You're going to get your feet wet when you have to cross later on anyway.

As you get closer to Valley View / Canal Road, you'll approach a small gravel turnaround for cars where another trail marker will greet you. At this point you can either follow the Bridle Trail back toward the creek for a crossing of about 50 feet, or hike on Sagamore Road to the intersection ahead. With the latter, you'll cross the creek using the road. Sagamore Creek Loop Trail will merge with the Bridle Trail on the northern side of the creek next to the Stephen Frazee House. The road will allow you to avoid getting your feet wet—for now. The return trip demands similarly wide

STEPHEN FRAZEE HOUSE

The Stephen Frazee House is a veritable piece of Ohio and American history. The brick home is one of the earliest settlements in the lower Cuyahoga Valley along the Ohio & Erie Canal. The early Ohio frontiersman purchased the property in 1806, only three years after the state joined the Union.

Thanks to the construction of the Ohio & Erie Canal, nearby farmers gained access to new markets using the water transportation route. However, Frazee gained his affluence by suing the state for flood damage to his corn and grasslands following construction of the canal.

Despite Ohio's birth coming from New England settlers, the Frazee House exhibits architectural characteristics more similar to mid-Atlantic culture. This is most likely because Frazee hailed from Pennsylvania before settling in the Connecticut Western Reserve portion of Ohio. The house's Federal style differs from typical New England fare by orienting the house's gable ends away from the street. This style can be found throughout central and southern Ohio, whereas northern areas are more likely to resemble their New England forefathers.

creek crossings you cannot avoid. A handful of stepping stones can help you along the way, but soaked shoes are inevitable if there's been any kind of recent rainfall or snow melting. Don't be a pansy!

The remainder of the trail is easy to navigate. Just as you knew you had to keep hiking west until the road intersection, now you know you have to continue east along the creek toward the parking lot, though there are some noticeable differences on the northern end of Sagamore Creek, namely a handful of towering ledges to the north, and your only set of switchbacks leading to steep climbs.

The end nears as you approach an open field filled with transmission towers that you would have passed driving in. Continue across the open field to the last batch of woods, leading directly back to the parking lot.

Miles and Directions

0.0 Start next to the sign for the Buckeye and All Purpose Trail on the eastern end of the parking lot. Turn right (south) to go uphill on the paved path. At the top of the hill, you'll see a sign indicating that you're on the Bike and Hike Trail.

0.2 Turn right (west) downhill, leaving the All Purpose Trail onto the Sagamore Creek Loop Trail also marked as the Buckeye Trail. Blue paint on the trees signifies the Buckeye Trail. After hiking downhill, you'll come to a small, unmarked overlook of Sagamore Creek.

0.6 Approach a small creek, cross it, and continue hiking uphill.

Keep an eye out for the trail markers so you don't miss turns like this one.

Sagamore Creek Loop Trail, Bedford Reservation

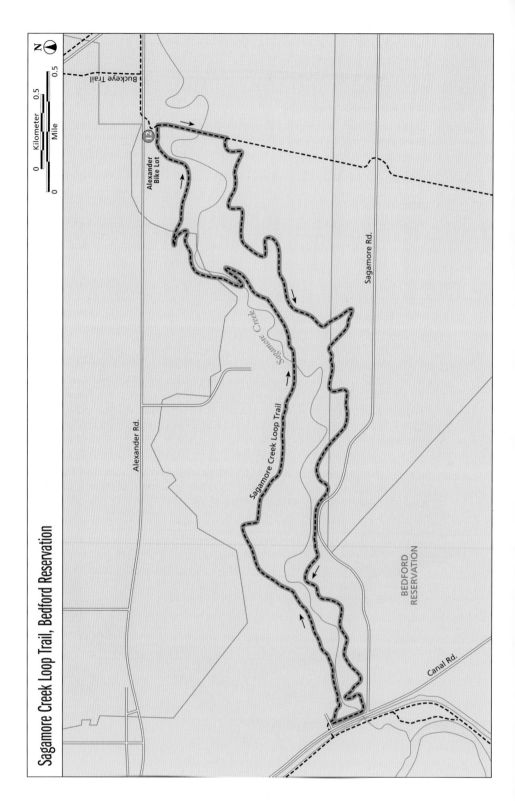

N

Kilometer
0   0.5

Mile
0   0.5

Alexander Rd.

Alexander
Bike Lot

12

Buckeye Trail

Sagamore Creek

Sagamore Creek Loop Trail

Sagamore Rd.

Canal Rd.

BEDFORD
RESERVATION

0.9 Cross another small creek and immediately turn back toward where you were coming from, but on the opposite side of the creek.

1.1 Another unmarked overlook opens up between trees with great views of Sagamore Creek a few hundred feet below. The opening comes next to a large tree with markings made by fellow hikers throughout the years.

1.4 Here you'll approach Sagamore Road. Walk alongside the road next to the guardrail. It may seem like you've lost the trail, but a tree up ahead marked blue lets you know you're not lost after all.

1.5 You'll come to a road sign with an arrow. Here you'll turn away from the road briefly before approaching a sign channeling you back toward Sagamore Road, away from the creek. **Option:** The trail is poorly marked as you approach an open field between the road and creek. For the sake of ease, you can stay on Sagamore Road until you reach Valley View Road / Canal Road. At this point, you'll turn right (north) to head over the creek, and soon approach a sign for the Sagamore Creek and Buckeye Trail next to the Stephen Frazee House.

1.8 Shortly after leaving Sagamore Road, you'll come to an open field between the creek and road. It's easy to lose your way here, especially in the winter and fall when snow or fallen leaves might cover the trail. But you can easily stay the course by continuing north toward Sagamore Creek. After approaching the creek, turn left (west) to follow the creek until you reach the yellow-marked Bridle Trail.

2.1 You'll approach a Sagamore Creek crossing along the Bridle Trail. It's easy to get across with the help of a few stones if you don't mind getting your feet wet. Otherwise, head back south toward Sagamore Road, and turn right (west) until you reach Valley View Road / Canal Road. Turn right (north) and cross the creek using the road, and pick up the Sagamore Creek Loop and Buckeye Trail again on the other side of the creek next to the Stephen Frazee House. Turn right (east) into the driveway for the house and another quick right (south) at the trail marker to resume the Sagamore Creek Trail, leaving Buckeye. This will shortly reconnect with the Bridle Trail on the opposite side of where you could have crossed earlier. This portion of the trail is marked much better, and you'll continue here heading northeast for the remainder of the hike.

3.1 The trail begins to move uphill, requiring a bit more energy than the first two-thirds of the hike.

3.3 You'll come to another water crossing even wider than before. Use the stones, and don't be afraid to get your feet wet. After you cross, go slightly uphill away from the creek and continue along the trail heading east.

3.8 Climb uphill for about 50 feet toward a switchback. Take the switchback left (north) for another climb. At the top of this climb, you'll want to turn right (east) to take another switchback.

3.9 Here you'll start to approach an open field filled with towering power lines. Continue across the field heading east, following the trail into the forest again toward the parking lot where you started.

4.2 Arrive back at the parking lot.

Hike Information

Local Information

Destination Cleveland; (216) 875-6680; www.thisiscleveland.com

Hike Tours

Cleveland Hiking Club; www.clevelandhikingclub.org
Cleveland Metroparks; (216) 635-3200; www.clevelandmetroparks.com
NEOHiking; www.meetup.com/NEOHiking

13 Hemlock to Bridle to Egbert to Buckeye Loop Trail, Bedford Reservation

Two creek crossings mean you'll want to pack dry towels and maybe even some dry clothes. This hike will take you alongside scenic Tinker's Creek via the occasionally rugged Bridle Trail, returning on some of the Buckeye Trail's best hiking as you pass the stunning Bridal Veil Falls and Tinker's Creek Gorge. It's an experience more than 10,000 years in the making since Ohio's last glacial period.

Start: Hemlock Creek Picnic Area Trailhead
Distance: 9.1 miles
Approximate hiking time: 4 hours
Difficulty: Difficult due to water crossings and varied terrain
Trail surface: Paved, crushed gravel, natural surface, and forested trail
Best season: Year-round
Other trail users: Bicycles; horses on Bridle Trail portion only; motorized vehicles prohibited
Canine compatibility: Dogs permitted on 8-foot leash
Land status: Public
Fees and permits: None
Schedule: 6 a.m.–11 p.m. daily

Maps: Cleveland Metroparks; (216) 635-3200; www.clevelandmetroparks.com
Trail contacts: Cleveland Metroparks; (216) 341-3152; www.clevelandmetroparks.com
Finding the trailhead: Drive south on I-77 from Cleveland for about 6 miles. Merge onto I-480 via exit 156 toward Youngstown. Keep right to take I-480 east toward Youngstown. In 4 miles, take exit 23 and turn right on Forbes Road. Take the first right onto Broadway Avenue. In about 1 mile take a slight left onto Union Street. Cleveland Metroparks entrance will be on the left. Turn left onto Egbert Road. At the end of the road turn right on Dunham Road, then another right on Button Road. GPS: N 41 22' 30.507" / W 81 34' 25.7592"

The Hike

Tinker's Creek is the star of this spectacular 9.1-mile hike. Flowing through the northern portion of Cleveland Metroparks' Bedford Reservation, the creek gets its name from Joseph Tinker, a member of Moses Cleaveland's surveying party. And unbeknownst to many—even Northeast Ohioans—the Tinker's Creek Gorge located on the latter portion of this hike is a certified National Natural Landmark.

You'll begin the hike on a combination of the Hemlock and Bridle Trails. As you might deduce from the trail name, this will take you east through deep hemlock forests as you hike alongside Tinker's Creek. The Hemlock Loop Trail itself is a short 0.8-mile jaunt along flat woodland trail with wildflowers in the spring. You have that option if 9 miles sounds a bit too daunting. Otherwise, you'll continue east on the Bridle Trail for a few miles before you come to a Tinker's Creek crossing.

Looking at the map, you can see the Bridle Trail has a couple of local connections. It's very easy to find yourself hiking uphill on one of these connections, not realizing you're off the planned route until you find yourself near someone's backyard. If this

Tinker's Creek flows powerfully at this point near the gorge through Bedford Reservation.
Courtesy of the Cleveland Metropolitan Parks District

happens, don't fret! Simply turn back around to your last junction and make sure you're continuing to hike east/northeast.

One of the bright spots of this hike is the tangible feeling that you're hiking someplace special. In fact, this area has been more than 10,000 years in the making since Ohio's last glacial period ended about 14,000 years ago. And it seems dear old Mother Nature used that time brilliantly to produce one of the region's most spectacular hikes.

Approaching the creek crossing, you'll no doubt need to roll your pant legs up. The creek here can rise as high as knee level or more depending on your height and whether or not there was a recent rain. Some might even wonder if this is indeed the correct route. But yellow Bridle Trail posts on opposite ends of the creek assure you that, yes, you will need to get your feet a little wet to proceed. Though if you're absolutely against crossing, you can take the local connector to Powers Road and work your way around the creek via Egbert Road where the Buckeye Trail you need intersects. But it's about a mile or more out of the way, so you'd serve your time best if you sucked it up and embraced the majesty that is Tinker's Creek.

OHIO HISTORY

Tinker's Creek is chock-full of Ohio history. First, Button Road that you drove in on has the distinction of being one of the Buckeye State's oldest roads, laid out in 1801. Before the United States was even sure Cleveland would remain American territory and not future Canadian land (if the results of the War of 1812 were different), Button Road was on the scene.

With a road, early settlers were able to access Tinker's Creek. Throughout the 19th century the creek provided water power for the region's earliest industries, including a gristmill, woolen mill, and a chair factory. Today, the park is appreciated for its natural diversity, including a dramatic 200-foot decline throughout the creek's 2-mile run in the reservation, a steep-walled gorge from soft blue shales, and twenty-nine different species of native trees. A botanist is simply giddy around these parts.

Continuing uphill on the other side, you'll soon connect briefly with the Egbert Loop Trail—a hike along the upper ridge through woodland forest above Tinker's Creek Valley. This will connect you to the Buckeye Trail for your western leg of the hike. As usual the blue blazes will signify your arrival to Ohio's trail of trails. Observe during your Buckeye hike a wealth of tree species, including basswood, beech, tulip, and more oaks and maples than your eye can take in.

Now south of Tinker's Creek, the Buckeye Trail (still combined with the Bridle Trail) will take you away from the flowing stream. But you'll realize it's worth it when you get to Bridal Veil Falls about three-quarters through the entire hike.

This waterfall flows over approximately 30 feet of shale with hemlocks lining the ridge above. A small parking lot sits nearby for those of us who prefer drive-by nature. But you're no slouch! Now about 6 miles into your hike, you've earned this sight.

Continuing west, the Buckeye Trail will soon break off from the Bridle Trail to turn south toward Sagamore Creek (Hike 12). You'll stay west on the Bridle Trail until the trail comes alongside Gorge Parkway where another, less arduous creek crossing awaits. Again, you can avoid the crossing by hiking further west up to Dunham Road to take the bridge and finish your hike the way you drove in. But in the spirit of the creek's namesake, the adventurous option is a more satisfying way to end your 9.1 miles.

Miles and Directions

0.0   Start hiking east alongside Tinker's Creek from the Hemlock/Bridle trailhead at the southern end of the parking lot.

0.3   Turn right (east) to stay on the Bridle Trail. **Option:** Turn left (west) to stay on the Hemlock Trail back toward the parking lot for a 0.8-mile hike.

0.6   You'll come to a junction. Stay to the right, closer to the creek. This portion of the trail is a short out-and-back leg that gives you some of the best views of the creek. In less than

Hemlock to Bridle to Egbert to Buckeye Loop Trail, Bedford Reservation

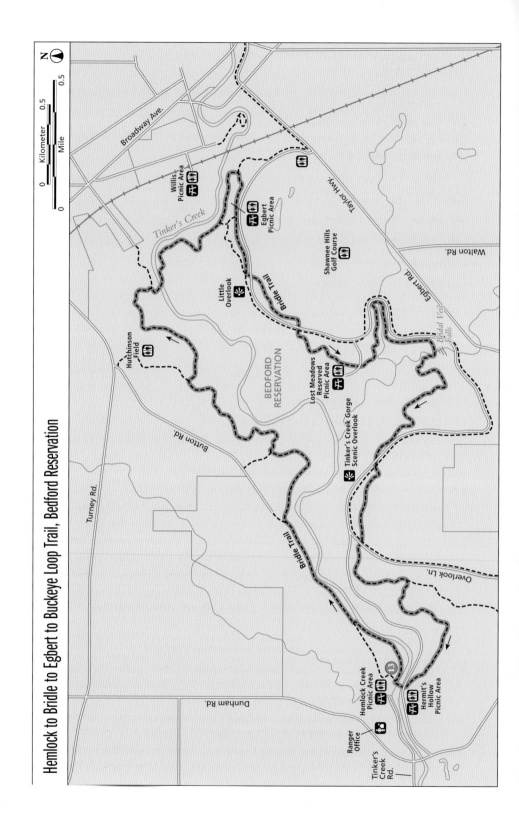

0.25 mile, you'll come to a dead end. Turn around back toward this junction, take a sharp right (northeast), and hike uphill.

1.1 Turn right (east) to stay on the Bridle Trail. Continuing straight will lead to Button Road, a residential street that connects to the park.

1.7 Here you'll turn right (southeast) to continue on the Bridle Trail.

2.4 Turn right (east) to stay on the Bridle Trail. Continuing straight (north) will lead to a softball field off of Grace Street.

3.0 On your right you will see a Bridle Trail crossing across Tinker's Creek. Depending on the height of the water, you may get your feet (or even pants) a little wet. Either way, you'll see a trail post on the southern end of Tinker's Creek where the Bridle Trail continues. Cross the creek toward that post heading south. **Option:** If you'd rather stay dry, you can either hike back to the parking lot from this point, or stay to the left and hike northeast up the hill. This will lead to a residential cul-de-sac. You'll run into Powers Road and will hike on the sidewalks of Bedford across some train tracks and onto Broadway Avenue. Turn right (southeast) onto Broadway Avenue. Continue hiking on the sidewalks along Broadway Avenue for 0.8 mile until Egbert Road just past the Northfield Road bridge. Here you'll turn right to head back east where you'll pick up the Bridle/Buckeye Trail alongside Egbert Road. Stay on this trail for a mile until you reach Cleveland Metroparks' Egbert Picnic Area and Trailhead parking lot along Gorge Parkway where you can pick up the Egbert Loop / Buckeye Trail. From here you'll continue west on the Buckeye Trail and will be back on track. You can pick up Miles and Directions below at the 4.2-mile marker. This may seem like a roundabout option to stay dry, but you'll at least get a glimpse of a town you otherwise might not have seen.

3.2 Stay to the left (southeast) closer to Tinker's Creek.

3.7 Turn left (east), hiking onto the Buckeye Trail. Continue following the blue blazes marked on surrounding trees.

4.0 Turn right (west) to stay on the Buckeye / Egbert Loop Trail.

4.2 You'll approach the Egbert Picnic Area and Trailhead parking lot. Continue hiking west across the parking lot and you'll find a trail marker for the Bridle Trail, leading you back into the woods.

4.4 Here you'll find a trail post for the Bridle/Egbert/Buckeye Trail. Continue past the marker heading west for about 50 feet where you'll approach another junction. Turn left (west) continuing on the Bridle/Buckeye Trail. **Option:** Turn right (east) to take the Egbert Loop Trail back to the parking lot.

4.5 You'll be heading southwest across the All Purpose Trail and Gorge Parkway. Pick the Bridle/Buckeye Trail back up across the street. You will crisscross the All Purpose Trail and Gorge Parkway a few more times throughout the rest of the hike. So long as you stay on the Buckeye Trail (until noted to leave), you'll be on the right track.

6.1 Take the wooden bridge over a small creek heading west. Shortly thereafter, you'll come to the Bridal Veil Falls overlook—a small waterfall flowing over 30 feet of shale with hemlocks lining the ridge above the falls.

7.8 Stay to the right at this junction to stay on the Bridle Trail, leaving the Buckeye Trail. **Option:** Turn left (south) to take the Buckeye Trail. Continuing south, this trail will cross Egbert Road in nearby Walton Hills, Ohio, the Metro Parks Hike and Bike Trail, and Dunham Road before running back into the bike trail. Here you can either turn back or continue even farther, turning right (west) onto the bike trail toward the Sagamore Creek Loop Trailhead, another hike listed separately in this book.

8.4 Cross Gorge Parkway yet again heading west, continuing on the Bridle Trail across the street. Here you'll find a post indicating another, final Bridle Trail creek crossing. Again, feel free to dive in (not literally, of course) if you don't mind getting a little wet. Otherwise, continue hiking west alongside Gorge Parkway and Tinker's Creek until Dunham Road. Here you'll turn right (north) onto paved road briefly, cross Tinker's Creek, turn right (east) onto Button Road, and finish hiking on the road toward the parking lot within sight.

9.1 Arrive at the parking lot, ending the hike.

Hike Information

Local Information

> **Destination Cleveland;** (216) 875-6680; www.thisiscleveland.com
> **Unmiserable Cleveland;** www.unmiserablecleveland.com

Hike Tours

> **Cleveland Hiking Club;** www.clevelandhikingclub.org
> **Cleveland Metroparks;** (216) 635-3200; www.clevelandmetroparks.com
> **NEOHiking;** www.meetup.com/NEOHiking

Other Resources

> **NEONaturalist;** www.neonaturalist.com

Looking back on the creek crossing

14 Sylvan to Castle Valley to Bridle Trail, North Chagrin Reservation

This is hardly the best-marked trail, but the diversity in vegetation and variety in trail composition make this hike an easy favorite of Northeast Ohioans. Start on the Sylvan Trail through the dense A. B. Williams Memorial Woods before connecting with the winding and occasionally rugged Castle Valley Trail that leads to the venerable Squire's Castle. Then enjoy a relatively easy stroll along Bridle Trail, composed of gravel and natural surface.

Start: At the North Chagrin Nature Center Trailhead
Distance: 5 miles
Approximate hiking time: 2 hours
Difficulty: Moderate due to steep climbs on the Castle Valley Trail
Trail surface: Paved, crushed gravel, natural surface, and forested trail
Best season: Year-round
Other trail users: Bicycles; horses on Bridle Trail portion only; motorized vehicles prohibited
Canine compatibility: Dogs permitted on 8-foot leash
Land status: Public
Fees and permits: None

Schedule: 6 a.m.–11 p.m. daily
Maps: www.clevelandmetroparks.com
Trail contacts: North Chagrin Nature Center; (440) 473-3370
Finding the trailhead: Drive on I-90 heading east toward Erie from Cleveland for about 13 miles. Keep right to take I-90 toward I-271. In 4 miles take the OH 91 exit 189 toward Willoughby Hills. Turn left onto SOM Center Road/OH 91. The entrance to North Chagrin Reservation will be on your left. Turn left onto Sunset Lane. At the end of the road, turn right onto Buttermilk Falls Parkway. North Chagrin Nature Center parking lot will be on your right. GPS: N 41 33' 40.0716" / W 81 26' 2.3814"

The Hike

From the North Chagrin Nature Center Trailhead, you'll hike east on a connector trail toward the orange-marked Sylvan Trail—a 1.25-mile loop on its own. The hike begins over nondescript crushed gravel as you hike east through the Forest Picnic Area. This leads directly into the A. B. Williams Memorial Woods where you'll find the beginning of the Sylvan Trail.

The A. B. Williams Memorial Woods become very dense with some of the most substantial root exposure in the book. Mind your step, so you can avoid falling flat on your face—always embarrassing regardless of the context.

This mixed forested area is home to beech, red maple, white ash, and shagbark hickory. Are you one of our bird-nerd friends? Then you'll want to keep your eyes peeled for black-capped chickadees and woodpeckers, though of course you can more easily hear the woodpeckers than spot them.

Continuing through the woods you'll soon come to the Castle Valley Trail junction. This will take you north a couple of miles toward Squire's Castle on mostly

Built in the 1890s by Feargus B. Squire, a founder of Standard Oil Company, the castle was to serve as the gatekeeper's house to his future country estate. The project was never completed, so Squire sold the property in 1922. Cleveland Metroparks purchased it three years later.
COURTESY OF THE CLEVELAND METROPOLITAN PARKS DISTRICT

SQUIRE'S CASTLE

Squire's Castle, with its massive stonewalls, arched doorways, and large tower, has tickled the imaginations of Metroparks visitors for decades. Built in the 1890s by Cleveland oil pioneer Feargus B. Squire, it was only intended to serve as a gatekeeper's lodge. The original plans called for a large country home to be built behind the lodge.

Although the larger home was never constructed, Squire used the gatekeeper's lodge as a weekend retreat in the early 1900s. The "castle" was constructed from siltstone quarried in what is now Cleveland Metroparks' Euclid Creek Reservation. The castle had several bedrooms, living areas, a large kitchen, and a breakfast porch. All of the castle rooms had white plaster walls, elegant woodwork, and leaded glass windows. The castle's majestic beauty remains, but gone are the door, fixtures, woodwork, and glass windows.

natural trail. And it's on this trail where the trail markers—or lack thereof—might throw you off. Luckily, it's easy to correct yourself should you happen to take a wrong turn. Ultimately you want to go north, so having a compass (let's be honest: a compass app) would be a good idea.

Another potentially confusing junction comes at the River Grove Reserved Picnic Area. You'll know you're here when you come out of the woods to a wide-open field with a parking lot just ahead. Continue hiking through this area and you'll find the Castle Valley Trail continues on the other end. To your right is the Bridle Trail you'll be taking on your return trek.

Now as you get closer to Squire's Castle, you'll likely hear families with kids running around. This is easily one of the most popular hiking areas in the region, probably because of the rough, sometimes very steep terrain that makes for a fun challenge. And coming from this direction, your reward is the quasi-historic Squire's Castle (quasi-historic, because it's obviously not a real medieval castle) at the northern terminus of the Castle Valley Trail. You'll then backtrack slightly until you return to the picnic area where you'll take the Bridle Trail back to the Sylvan Trail.

Keeping track of the Bridle Trail can also be a bit of a tricky feat. But as you can tell, easy navigating is not a highlight of this hike.

If you continue on the Bridle Trail west for too long, you may find yourself at the Buttermilk Falls Trailhead. This isn't necessarily a bad thing if you have the time to add the 1.6-mile Hickory Loop Trail to your itinerary. But to finish your hike, you'll need to keep an eye out for a left turn that will take you south back to the beginning of the Sylvan Loop Trail. You'll then simply turn right to exit the woods and backtrack on the connector trail you used to start your hike.

Though the trail markers leave something to be desired, this truly is a personal favorite. What North Chagrin Reservation lacks in trail markers is more than made up for in trail possibilities. Meaning, there are many more routes and connections to be explored than what is written here. Truth be told, North Chagrin Reservation will make you want to don your Indiana Jones fedora and start exploring.

Miles and Directions

0.0 Start from the North Chagrin Nature Center parking lot, hiking east on crushed gravel connector trail from the southeastern end of the parking lot. You'll cross Buttermilk Falls Parkway and another parking lot next to a picnic area where the Sylvan Loop Trail begins.

0.2 Begin the Sylvan Loop Trail, staying to the right to continue hiking due east.

0.4 You'll come to another junction, this time for the Bridle and Buckeye Trail. For now, continue hiking east on Sylvan Loop Trail. Soon you'll come to another marker where you'll turn right (south) to stay on Sylvan Loop Trail.

0.9 Continue straight (north) for the Castle Valley Trail. Shortly after that, you'll come to another marker for the Buckeye and Bridle Trails, but we still want to stay north on the Castle Valley Trail. You'll hike on this trail for a significant amount of time until you reach Squire's Castle.

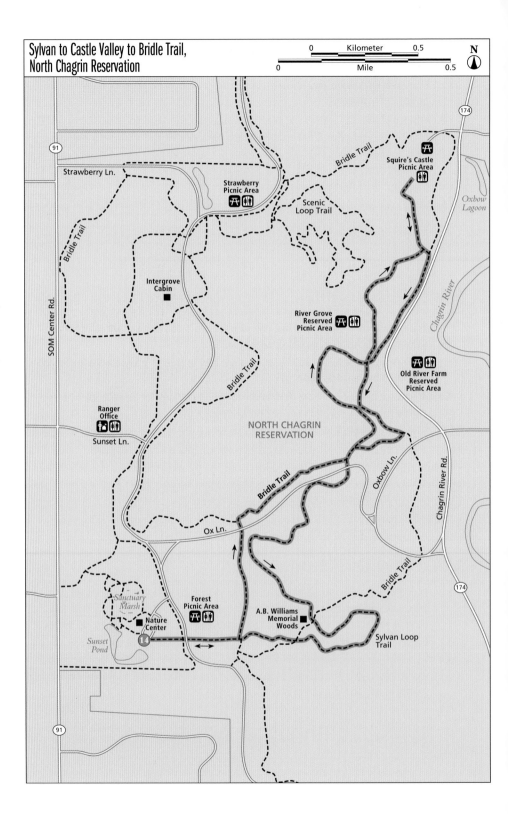

Kilometer
0   0.5

Mile
0   0.5

N

91

Strawberry Ln.

Strawberry
Picnic Area

Bridle Trail

Scenic
Loop Trail

Bridle Trail

Squire's Castle
Picnic Area

174

Oxbow
Lagoon

Bridle Trail

Intergrove
Cabin

SOM Center Rd.

River Grove
Reserved
Picnic Area

Chagrin River

Old River Farm
Reserved
Picnic Area

Ranger
Office

Sunset Ln.

NORTH CHAGRIN
RESERVATION

Bridle Trail

Oxbow Ln.

Chagrin River Rd.

Ox Ln.

Bridle Trail

174

Sanctuary
Marsh

Nature
Center

Forest
Picnic Area

A.B. Williams
Memorial
Woods

Sylvan Loop
Trail

Sunset
Pond

14

91

1.7 Continue hiking north to cross Oxbow Lane. Stay straight, away from the Bridle Trail to continue on the Castle Valley Trail.

1.8 Hike down some stairs and turn left (north) at the bottom to hike over a small wooden bridge over a ravine.

2.1 Hiking east, you'll go down more steps heading toward a picnic area. You'll pass this area with a basketball court as the trail winds north, still on the Castle Valley Trail.

2.2 Turn left (north) to hike through a large grassy field and parking lot. This may seem unorthodox, but you'll notice markers for the Castle Valley Trail that note the trail continues in the woods on the other side of the field past the Chestnut Shelter.

2.7 Turn left (north) for a steep, uphill climb. You'll notice the Bridle Trail adjacent to you at this junction. The area is poorly marked. But if you somehow end up on the Bridle Trail, simply continue hiking north and you will arrive at Squire's Castle shortly.

2.9 Arrive at Squire's Castle. When you're done visiting the castle, return where you came from at 2.7. You should arrive around the 3-mile mark. This time, take the Bridle Trail hiking south.

3.4 Cross the driveway for the grassy field you hiked past earlier. You'll see a sign for the Bridle Trail as you continue hiking south. After you hike this short leg next to the field, you'll come to a junction you visited earlier. You don't want to repeat the Castle Valley Trail, so you'll turn left (south) to continue on the Bridle Trail.

4.3 Turn left (south) at this Bridle junction to cross Oxbow Lane. You'll take this trail for a vast majority of the remaining hike.

4.6 Arrive back at the Sylvan Loop Trail junction you hiked past at the beginning of the hike. Turn right (west) and take this connector back to your car.

5.0 Return to the parking lot to end your hike.

15 Look About Lodge to Bridle/Buckeye to Sulphur Springs to Squaw Rock Trails, South Chagrin Reservation

The scenic Chagrin River flows through the eastern edge of South Chagrin Reservation alongside hemlocks, beeches, oaks, and hickories that make for brilliant fall colors. Become better acquainted with the powerful river as you hike along Squaw Rock Loop Trail on the banks of the Chagrin River, home of an intricate sculpture that leaves much to interpretation.

Start: Look About Lodge, 37374 Miles Road, Bentleyville
Distance: 4.5 miles
Approximate hiking time: 2 hours
Difficulty: Moderate due to steep climbs
Trail surface: Paved, crushed gravel, natural surface, and forested trail
Best season: Spectacular fall colors
Other trail users: Bicycles; horses on Bridle Trail portion only; motorized vehicles prohibited
Canine compatibility: Dogs permitted on 8-foot leash
Land status: Public
Fees and permits: None
Schedule: 6 a.m.–11 p.m. daily

Maps: www.clevelandmetroparks.com
Trail contacts: Cleveland Metroparks; (440) 247-7075
Finding the trailhead: Drive south on I-77 from Cleveland for approximately 6 miles. Take exit 156 merging onto I-480 toward Youngstown for about 7 miles. Keep left and take exit 26 for I-480 toward I-271/Erie PA/US 422/Warren. In 1.5 miles keep right to take US 422 E toward Warren. Take the OH 91 exit toward Moreland Hills/Solon. Turn left onto SOM Center Road/OH 91. In about 2 miles turn right onto Miles Road. Look About Lodge is 1.2 miles ahead on your right. GPS: N 41 25' 23.8506" / W 81 25' 17.1264"

The Hike

South Chagrin Reservation faces similar marking challenges as its relative to the north (Hike 14). But like North Chagrin, the fun you'll have on the trails themselves makes up for any difficulty you may have in tracking your hike. Spread across Bentleyville, Solon, and Moreland Hills, South Chagrin Reservation features a wide range of trails, rich spring wildflowers, and of course the crown jewel, the Chagrin River—designated a Scenic River in July 1979.

You'll begin behind Look About Lodge—a landmark on the National Register of Historic Places—where you'll find the increasingly familiar blue blazes of the Buckeye Trail. Hiking into the woods, you'll immediately become enveloped by dense forest with fairly rough terrain. This will lead to the red-marked Look About Lodge Trail, which you'll use to connect to a series of trails. Look About Lodge features a series of hemlock ravines and occasional views of the surrounding creeks.

Sulphur Springs Courtesy of the Cleveland Metropolitan Parks District

Hiking west, you'll soon link up with the Bridle Trail—a flat, wide, and easy trail that connects to most of the reservation's trails. You'll use it to connect with the purple-marked Persing Trail to hike north along a narrow, dense path filled with mature beech, hickory, and large oak trees. Persing will guide you back east after hiking north to reconnect with the combined Look About Lodge and Bridle Trails, which you'll take back south. You won't be with Look About Lodge for long, as the Bridle Trail breaks off to wind its way south along with the blue blazes of the Buckeye Trail. Continue hiking this south through the previous Persing junction to find your orange-marked Sulphur Springs connection that leads through the Sulphur Springs Picnic Area where you'll hike next to a small stream. Continue south through the picnic area until you return to the dense woodland you've grown accustomed to. Maintain your southern hike on the combined Sulphur Springs and Buckeye Trail, still east of the Chagrin River tributary.

Before long the Bridle Trail will merge with your hike as you continue southwest. But Sulphur Springs will soon turn away to the west. You could stay on the loop for a shorter hike, but you can get more miles by continuing on the Bridle Trail south toward Hawthorn Parkway after crossing the tributary.

SQUAW ROCK

The intricate carvings of Squaw Rock date back to 1885 when artist and blacksmith Henry Church created the sculpture. According to Cleveland Metroparks, Church walked through the Chagrin River at night to sculpt the large sandstone boulder that rests on the banks of the river.

See if you can spot the various designs within the sculpture. One that immediately sticks out is a quiver of arrows along with the four phases of the moon. You might also notice the giant serpent (how can you not?), an eagle, a dog, a skeleton, and a baby in a papoose—a type of bag used to carry a small child on one's back. Most notable, however, is the carving of a woman with a shell behind her that brings to mind Botticelli's *The Birth of Venus* painting from the late 15th century.

Much like the aforementioned Italian classic, much of Church's work has been left to interpretation. Over a century later, it remains unclear exactly what Mr. Church was trying to convey with his sculpture. But if his intention was to draw Clevelanders and visiting hikers to the banks of the Chagrin River, then it was a masterful success.

After a brief jaunt on this leg of the Bridle, you'll come to a junction where the Buckeye and part of the Bridle break off to the west. Instead, you'll want to turn left to continue south across the All Purpose Trail and Hawthorn Parkway. You should still be seeing the blue blazes here too. Follow this trail as it loops around to Arbor Lane, which you'll also cross. This will take you through the Bentley Village Service Department. You may feel a bit off track, but blue blazes painted on surrounding markers will let you know you're still on the right track.

Now only on the Buckeye Trail, you'll use this leg as a connector to the Hatchet Ridge Trail. You're only on this brown-marked trail briefly to connect to Squaw Rock. But if you were to turn south, you would find yourself in a former Boy Scout winter camp with great views of the Chagrin River. But you'll also get plenty of great views off the Squaw Rock Loop.

When you reach the white-marked Squaw Rock Loop, you'll turn right to hike south toward a long series of wooden steps that take you down to the Chagrin River. The trail turns back north as you hike alongside the river where you'll find spectacular views of the surprisingly powerful river, not to mention the crown jewel of South Chagrin—Squaw Rock itself. Just past the Squaw Rock carvings, you'll continue your hike toward a small waterfall where families will take a dip on a hot afternoon, though park officials will tell you this isn't permitted.

Continuing north, you'll leave the Squaw Rock Loop thanks to a northern connector trail that goes around the Squaw Rock Picnic Area and runs right into the Shelterhouse Loop Trail. You'll take this yellow trail west as it loops through a

Squaw Rock

woodland ravine and back northeast to the All Purpose Trail, which you'll use briefly to return to the crushed gravel of the Bridle Trail. The Bridle Trail will then return you to the Look About Lodge Loop Trail after hiking alongside Chagrin River Road and across a small creek crossing to end your hike.

Most will find this hike moderate due to the occasional steep climbs. Whatever your level of fitness, the Chagrin River is not to be missed. The trails west of the river are bonuses to one of Cleveland Metroparks' most popular reservations.

Miles and Directions

0.0 Start south behind Look About Lodge where you'll find blue blazes marking the Buckeye Trail near the trailhead for the hike. As you enter the woods here, the trail will immediately bend to the right (southeast), and you'll see a red trail marker for the Look About Lodge Loop Trail. Continue hiking west along various ridges and rocky terrain on Look About Lodge.

0.1 Turn right (west) up some natural stone steps and take the bridge over a stream crossing. Continue on Look About Lodge briefly before turning left (south) to join the purple-marked Persing Trail. Follow the narrow trail as it bends west and shortly thereafter north.

0.3 Continue west on Persing as it cuts through Bridle Trail.

0.6 Turn right (west) to stay on Persing for another 0.1 mile.

0.7 The Persing Trail will end and you'll rejoin the Look About Lodge Trail. First the trail will take you north before winding back down south. Next you'll come to the Bridle Trail. Take this south toward the Sulphur Springs Loop Trail. **Bailout:** Stay on Look About Lodge Trail to return to your parking lot if you need to stop.

1.3 On your left you will see two blue blazes for the Buckeye Trail, which combines with Sulphur Springs Loop Trail. Take this to go downhill at a slight grade away from the Bridle Trail, hiking northeast. Soon you'll hike through the Sulphur Springs Picnic Area and Trailhead where you'll hike alongside a small stream with just as small a waterfall running over shale. Continue hiking south through this picnic area with the stream on your right.

1.4 You'll reach the southern end of the parking lot and find blue blazes marking trees as you reenter the woods for the Sulphur Springs Loop Trail.

1.6 At this Buckeye Trail junction, turn right (southwest) to continue on Sulphur Springs Loop Trail. **Option:** Turn left (east) for the Bridle Trail, which winds north back toward the parking lot for a shorter hike.

1.7 Stay to the left (south) to hike onto the Bridle Trail. **Option:** Turn right (west) to stay on the combined Bridle/Sulphur Springs Trail that loops back north toward your trailhead.

1.8 Turn left (south) to hike on the combined Buckeye and Bridle Trails toward Hawthorn Parkway. Continuing straight (west) toward SOM Center Road will take you far away from the reservation.

1.9 Cross the All Purpose Trail and Hawthorn Parkway, continuing the Buckeye/Bridle Trail right across the street, hiking south.

2.3 Continue following the blue blazes to hike east toward Arbor Lane.

2.5 Cross Arbor Lane hiking east and stay to the right to hike through the Bentley Village Service Department. You'll occasionally see blue blazes marked on surrounding markers to let you know you're still on the Buckeye Trail.

2.6 After you pass the department, you'll see a blue blaze directing you back east into the woods.

2.9 Turn left (north) as the Buckeye Trail merges with the Hatchet Ridge Trail. In less than 0.1 mile, the Buckeye Trail will break off to the left (north). You'll want to stay right (east) on Hatchet Ridge toward the Squaw Rock Loop Trail and Chagrin River.

3.0 Arrive at the Squaw Rock Trail and turn right (south). This will take you to a series of wooden stairs you'll want to take down to the Chagrin River. At the riverbank, the trail will guide you north to continue alongside the Chagrin River on Squaw Rock Loop Trail.

3.3 You'll come to another set of stairs that lead down to Squaw Rock. Take these and the Squaw Rock Trail will continue on the ground level, hiking north.

3.5 Here you'll see a small Chagrin River waterfall with a gentle pool of water within the river. Come in the summer and you might find families taking pictures of the waterfall.

3.8 At the northernmost point of the Squaw Rock Loop Trail, you'll take a connector trail north past the Squaw Rock Picnic Area and toward the All Purpose and Shelterhouse Trails.

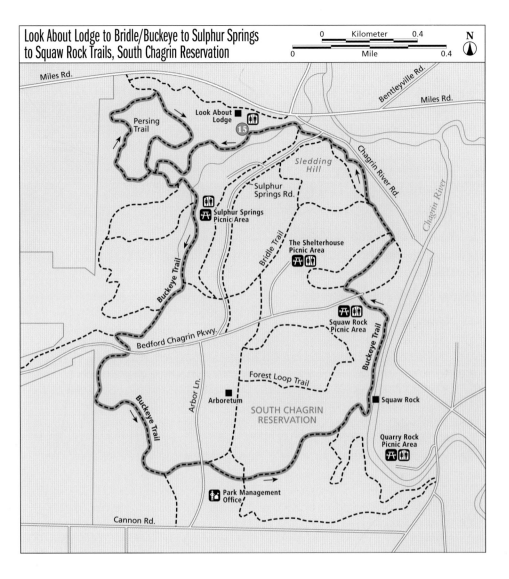

Kilometer
0   0.4
Mile
0   0.4

N

Miles Rd.

Bentleyville Rd.

Miles Rd.

Persing Trail

Look About Lodge

15

Chagrin River Rd.

Sledding Hill

Chagrin River

Sulphur Springs Rd.

Sulphur Springs Picnic Area

Bridle Trail

The Shelterhouse Picnic Area

Buckeye Trail

Squaw Rock Picnic Area

Buckeye Trail

Bedford Chagrin Pkwy.

Forest Loop Trail

Buckeye Trail

Arbor Ln.

Arboretum

SOUTH CHAGRIN RESERVATION

Squaw Rock

Quarry Rock Picnic Area

Park Management Office

Cannon Rd.

Soon you'll cross Bedford Chagrin Parkway, where you'll join the Shelterhouse Trail, hiking northeast.

3.9 You'll run into the All Purpose Trail. Turn left (north) for a brief all-purpose hike onto a bridge crossing. This will serve as a brief connection to the Bridle Trail, which you'll turn right on to hike north back toward the parking lot. Continue hiking on the Bridle Trail, parallel to Chagrin River Road.

4.0 Cross Sulphur Springs Drive and hike through a small creek crossing, keeping west. It's easy to miss this turn and it might be tempting to turn left along Sulphur Springs Road, so keep an eye out for that creek crossing underneath a bridge. After crossing the creek, you'll climb uphill and turn left to keep hiking west back toward the parking lot.

4.3 Turn left (southwest) to rejoin the red-marked Look About Lodge Trail from the beginning of your hike. **Option:** You can also stay straight on the combined Look About Lodge/Bridle Trail alongside Miles Road to return to the parking lot. Turning left will give you a more interesting hike in the woods.

4.5 Take the first right (north) to end your hike where you started behind Look About Lodge.

Hike Information

Local Information

Destination Cleveland; (216) 875-6680; www.thisiscleveland.com

Hike Tours

Cleveland Hiking Club; www.clevelandhikingclub.org
Cleveland Metroparks; (216) 635-3200; www.clevelandmetroparks.com
NEOHiking; www.meetup.com/NEOHiking

Other Resources

NEONaturalist; www.neonaturalist.com

16 Sugar Bush Trail to Royalview Loop, Mill Stream Run Reservation

There's a calming sensation throughout this 4-mile hike as you wind through forest mixed with pine and oak trees. Climbs are gentle and gradual, so you'll be surprised when you're suddenly hiking alongside a ledge several hundred feet high during the final stretch of the loop. The panoramic view alone is a tremendous sight, worthy of the trip to Strongsville.

Start: Royalview trailhead is adjacent to the parking lot.
Distance: 4-mile loop
Approximate hiking time: 1.5 hours
Difficulty: Moderate due to length
Trail surface: Natural surface, forested trail
Best season: Year-round
Other trail users: Motorized vehicles and horses prohibited; bicycles on Royalview Loop Trail portion only
Canine compatibility: Dogs permitted on 8-foot leash
Land status: Public

Fees and permits: None
Schedule: 6 a.m.–11 p.m. daily
Maps: www.clevelandmetroparks.com
Trail contacts: Brecksville Nature Center; (440) 526-1012; www.clevelandmetroparks .com
Finding the trailhead: Drive on I-71 heading south from Cleveland for about 17 miles. Take exit 231A to merge onto OH 82 E/Royalton Road. Continue for 1 mile. Take the first right onto Royalview Lane and use the first parking lot on your left after about 400 feet. GPS: N 41 18' 57.7008" / W 81 36' 2.4438"

The Hike

Mill Stream Run cuts through several Northeast Ohio communities, including Berea, Middleburg Heights, North Royalton, and Strongsville. Nineteenth-century communities were born around here to take advantage of the nearby Rocky River and its tributaries, though they were hardly the first to settle here. Native American artifacts dating back more than 8,000 years have been found here. As time marched on, Mill Stream Run Reservation continued to be a favorite of surrounding residents, hosting hikers, mountain bikers, and the Cleveland West Road Runners' annual Fall and Spring Classic.

Upon arrival, you might find yourself slightly confused. The trail map posted onsite is slightly different than what you'll find online. On the Cleveland Metroparks website, the Sugar Bush Loop Trail is clearly marked in orange, connecting with the Royalview Loop Trail marked in brown. Onsite, you'll see a yellow and red Royalview trail that might throw you off at first glance. These are mountain biking trails also reserved for hikers. But any confusion or uneasiness that you might feel washes away about 5 minutes into the hike when you realize there's nothing else around you. So unless you purposely wander off-trail like an overexcited puppy—a genuine concern for hikers such as myself—finding your way around this 4-mile loop

MILL STREAM RUN RESERVATION OVER TIME

Mill Stream Run Reservation cuts through several Northeast Ohio communities, including Berea, Middleburg Heights, North Royalton, and Strongsville. But in a different era, it was the 19th-century towns of Albion, Sanderson's Corners, and Slab Hollow that blossomed along the eastern branch of the Rocky River and its tributaries. First the sawmills and gristmills came, then a basket factory, taverns, blacksmith shops, and tailors soon followed. Stepping even further back in time, Native Americans called this area home more than 8,000 years ago, living off the diverse plant and animal life that remain vibrant to this day.

Today, of course, you won't find tribes of Native Americans, or operating mills of any kind. You can, however, scream yourself silly as you slide down the Chalet toboggan chute in the heart of winter. What more can you ask for?

Royalview Loop, Mill Stream Run Reservation Courtesy of the Cleveland Metropolitan Parks District

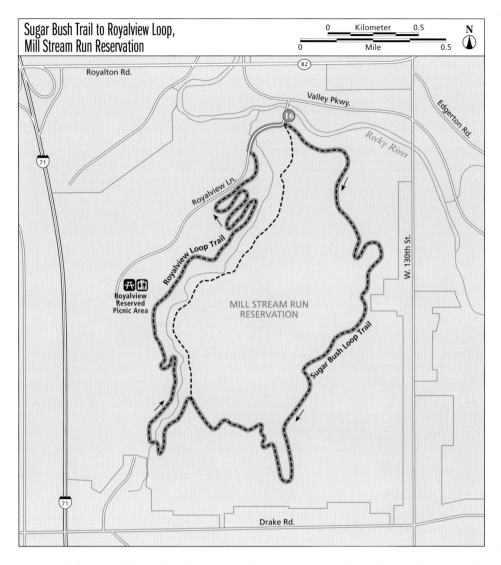

0   Kilometer   0.5

0   Mile   0.5

N

Royalton Rd.

82

Valley Pkwy.

Edgerton Rd.

16

Rocky River

71

Royalview Ln.

Royalview Loop Trail

W. 130th St.

Royalview
Reserved
Picnic Area

MILL STREAM RUN
RESERVATION

Sugar Bush Loop Trail

71

Drake Rd.

won't be a problem. Plus there are markers every 0.5 mile to let you know you're making progress.

Now that your worries have vanished, take this opportunity to relax. Moderate only because of length, the trail is a calming hike through a variety of switchbacks that only gradually increase in elevation. But it's nothing you'll notice in your legs or breath unless you've had one too many Twinkies in your time.

Short, wooden bridges are scattered throughout the trail to guide you over small pockets of ravines. As the oak and pine trees grow in number, surrounding you from all angles, you'll realize just how remote this place actually *feels*. The crunch of your shoe on forested trail is louder than anything else you'll hear. Yet in reality (and sadly depending on your general outlook), civilization beckons nearby. You'll be reminded

Mill Stream Run Reservation covered in winter snow

you're not quite off the grid as you reach the southern tip of the hike where large country-style homes sit along Drake Road, peeking into Mill Stream Run Reservation. A bit of envy might even set in. How lucky to have this as your backyard? Or more critically, one might wonder if suburban sprawl is threatening these very reservations. (Hint: They are.)

After turning away from the quiet homes, you'll start inching closer to the ridges overlooking Mill Stream, a tributary of the Rocky River. At this point you'll realize there was a purpose to all those gradual switchbacks during the first half or so of the hike, as you notice you're now about 500 feet above the stream. It's fair to say this might be the most scenic portion of the hike, so long as you're careful to mind your step and not send yourself tumbling down below. Like all of the hikes, this is one you can repeat in every season for an almost completely different view. Come in the heart of winter to see the typically steady stream freeze completely over. Depending on the amount of snow, you might not even realize there's a stream down below.

Before hiking too long along the ledges, you'll be guided back into the heart of the forest and returned to the Royalview Trailhead via the Sugar Bush Trail.

Miles and Directions

0.0 Start at the northern trailhead on your left as you drive into the parking lot, marked in yellow. In about 50 feet, stay left (northeast) at the split to continue along the yellow trail.

0.8 Houses along Drake Road begin to appear over the horizon as you reach the southern tip of the trail.

1.1 Take the bridge south and turn left (east) after crossing.

1.6 Cross the creek heading northeast. This will be one of your best photo opportunities.

2.1 Take a sharp right (north) to continue on Sugar Bush Loop Trail.

2.8 Turn right (east) following signs for Sugar Bush, signified by an orange maple leaf. You'll come to a small set of large logs with conveniently carved steps.

3.9 Bear left (northeast) to stay away from Royalview Loop Trail and finish on Sugar Bush.

4.0 Arrive back at the parking lot.

Hike Information

Local Information
Destination Cleveland; (216) 875-6680; www.thisiscleveland.com

Restaurants
The Brew Kettle; (440) 239-8788; www.thebrewkettle.com

Hike Tours
Cleveland Hiking Club; www.clevelandhikingclub.org
Cleveland Metroparks; (216) 635-3200; www.clevelandmetroparks.com
NEOHiking; www.meetup.com/NEOHiking

17 Hinckley Lake to Buckeye Trail to Whipp's Ledges Loop Trail, Hinckley Reservation

This is, perhaps, one of the most diverse hikes in the Cleveland area, boasting an array of all-purpose, moderate lakeside and rough trail—the latter courtesy of the Buckeye Trail. Relax and enjoy the serenity of 90-acre Hinckley Lake, or put on your Spidey tights to climb on the giant boulders of Whipp's Ledges.

Start: East Drive parking lot south of Bellus Road
Distance: 4.8-mile loop
Approximate hiking time: 2 hours
Difficulty: Ultimately easy with occasional bouts of moderate terrain on the Buckeye Trail
Trail surface: Paved, gravel, grassy, natural surface, and forested trail
Best season: Fall for spectacular colors
Other trail users: Bicycles and motorized vehicles prohibited; horses on Bridle Trail portion only
Canine compatibility: Dogs permitted on 8-foot leash
Land status: Public

Fees and permits: None
Schedule: 6 a.m.–11 p.m. daily
Maps: www.clevelandmetroparks.com
Trail contacts: Brecksville Nature Center; (440) 526-1012; www.clevelandmetroparks .com
Finding the trailhead: Drive south on I-71 from Cleveland for approximately 23 miles. Take exit 226 for OH 303 toward Hinckley/S Carpenter Road for 3.7 miles. Turn right on Hinckley Hills Road/OH 606, then in 0.8 mile take the first left onto Bellus Road. In 0.8 mile take the first right onto East Drive. The parking lot is on the right. GPS: N 41 13' 38.2614" / W 81 43' 2.7834"

The Hike

This hike is easily a personal favorite. It seems trite to describe any aspect of nature as "breathtaking," "beautiful," or "relaxing." But the visually dominating 90-acre Hinckley Lake is worthy of all these descriptors, yet there's absolutely nothing trite or boring about this portion of Hinckley Reservation's mixture of crushed gravel, grassy, all-purpose, and forested trail.

Heading south you'll begin hiking briefly along a small leg of the All Purpose Trail with walkers and joggers passing you by. Before long, you'll come to the East Drive Scenic Overlook on your right, offering your first panoramic view of Hinckley Lake. It's a sight to see in any season. You'll then continue alongside the lake, dropping into a brief portion of forested trail on your way to gravel trail that follows alongside the lake. Trail runners are particular fans of this loop.

As you continue along the trail, you'll notice the park has highlighted a variety of trees with small plaques. Tulip, red maple, American beech, and northern red oak are just a few you'll hike past.

Whipp's Ledges honors the bizarre story of former property owner and cattle emperor Robert Whipp (see sidebar). Courtesy of the Cleveland Metropolitan Parks District

Just after a mile, you'll come to State Road. Hinckley Lake Loop continues south, which you can, of course, take for a shorter hike. But to experience more of the reservation, it's worth continuing across the street toward the Buckeye Trail. As usual you'll see trees painted with the famous blue blazes.

The Buckeye Trail begins as a grassy trail alongside small creeks, quickly turning into forested trail. The rough trail with occasional climbs and slopes is a stark contrast to the easy and serene Hinckley Lake Loop Trail. This leads to a parking lot for Whipp's Ledges, but you'll take a sharp right uphill to stay on the Buckeye Trail for a hair longer. At the top of the hill, you'll see a set of wooden stairs about 100 feet on your left with a sign indicating the beginning of the Whipp's Ledges Trail (brown oak leaf trail marker). You'll follow the stairs, climbing eastward toward the famous ledges, a common rock climbing area for Northeast Ohioans. The trail will then take you in between large boulders where hikers have carved messages for nearly 150 years, but, of course, you'll follow the Leave No Trace rule of hiking and refrain from carving your own message. You'll then loop back toward the Whipp's Ledges parking lot, repeating a small portion of the Buckeye Trail back toward Hinckley Lake Loop to continue alongside the lake.

THE NAME BEHIND THE LEDGES

Whipp's Ledges rise 350 feet above Hinckley Lake and were formed more than 250 million years ago. But geological nerdiness aside, the real intrigue lies in the story of the ledges' namesake—Robert Whipp, recounted best by local writer Allan Lewicki.

Born in England in 1824, Robert Whipp began his life in the family business as a butcher. Following the sheep blight of 1845, Whipp ended up in Brunswick, Ohio, by way of New York City and Cleveland. By 1877, Whipp amassed a personal wealth of $100,000 and 2,000 acres—Trump standards in this era, but obviously without the TV deal and roadkill toupee.

Now at this point, Whipp was a widower. So naturally his housekeeper and neighbor, Hanna Spensley, suggested he take up with her daughter Rachel, who was thirty years younger when they eventually married in 1877. Foreshadowing the marital bliss of (pick your current Hollywood disaster couple), Whipp allegedly was contemplating divorce three weeks into marriage. The rumor that Rachel, who had a boyfriend behind Whipp's back named Taylor, was bearing the fruit of another man's loins probably didn't make matters better.

Next, Rachel approached her brother Lon and Taylor with a plot to murder Whipp and make it look like a suicide. The story unfolded like an episode of 19th-century *Law and Order: SVU.*

On September 15, 1877, Lon and Taylor attempted to chloroform Whipp before hanging him. Unfortunately for our criminal *masterminds,* they didn't account for Mr. Whipp's size—over 6 feet tall and 250 pounds. He fought them off, leading to the arrest of Lon, Taylor, and even his *lovely* wife, Rachel, though at the trial, Whipp could not positively identify Taylor, so only Lon and Rachel served any time—just one year of a seven-year sentence. Rachel then disappeared with Taylor in southern Ohio for the rest of their days.

Whipp, meanwhile, faded as well. His cattle empire but a whimper of its former glory, he lived out his final twelve or so years at Kline Farm on Hinckley Ridge. But hey, at least he got some really cool ledges named after him!

Returning to Hinckley Lake Loop Trail is much more gentle compared to what you just experienced on the Buckeye and Whipp's Ledges trails. The remaining mile or so winds alongside the lake, taking you to the Hinckley Lake Boathouse and through a spillway beach near a pedestrian bridge that leads back to your parking lot. Overall, this moderate hike is one of the more picturesque hikes you'll find in the Greater Cleveland area. Make sure you bring a camera, so you can make like Ansel Adams and capture nature at its finest.

The Hinckley Lake Dam powers through all of Ohio's vastly different seasons.

Miles and Directions

0.0 After parking, go back out toward the Cleveland Metroparks entrance sign, and cross the road you just drove in on, East Drive, heading north onto the All Purpose Trail. Continue hiking southeast along the paved path.

0.3 You'll come to the East Drive Scenic Overlook for a beautiful panoramic view of Hinckley Lake.

0.4 Here you'll approach a driveway. Turn right (west) downhill toward Hinckley Lake and cross East Drive where you'll see a sign for the Hinckley Lake Loop Trail (blue heron trail marker). Take the trail and start descending down toward the lake, winding through the woods.

0.6 You'll approach a sign for the Hinckley Lake Loop Trail. Continue south. You'll soon come to a small slope that takes you right alongside Hinckley Lake.

1.3 Here Hinckley Lake Loop Trail meets with the Buckeye Trail. Continue straight (east) onto the Buckeye Trail, crossing State Road and past the Whipp's Ledges Picnic Area. You'll then hike uphill briefly and follow the Buckeye Trail into the woods, heading southeast. Continue on the Buckeye Trail until you reach the Whipp's Ledges Loop Trail.

1.9 You'll come to a parking lot for the Whipp's Ledges Loop Trail. Take a sharp right (southeast) to stay on the Buckeye Trail. Hike up the hill for about 50 feet and turn left (north). You should see a marker for the Whipp's Ledges Loop Trail (brown oak leaf trail marker) in front of a large collection of stairs. Turn right (east) up the stairs.

Hinckley Lake to Buckeye Trail to Whipp's Ledges Loop Trail, Hinckley Reservation

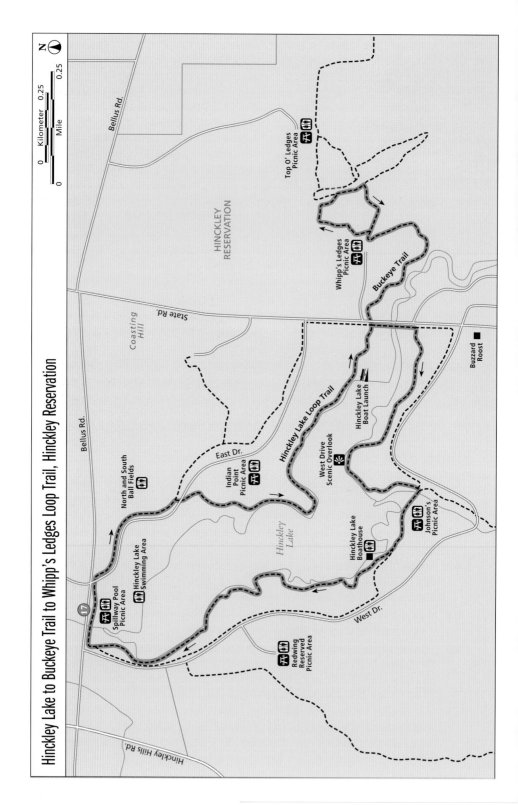

2.1   You're now at Whipp's Ledges. Hike to the top of the hill toward the highest boulders. Turn left (west) for about 10 to 20 feet, and take a quick right (north) uphill. At the top of the climb, take another right (south). As you continue hiking, you should notice the blue blazes of the Buckeye Trail behind the ledges. After walking behind the ledges, you'll approach stones made into steps. Take the stones downhill in between two large boulders that will be towering over you shortly. Markings on the boulders show people have been hiking here since the late 19th century, but don't take it as a pass to leave your own mark!

2.5   You'll come to a tree with several blue blazes on it. Turn right (south) downhill on some stones. Continue downhill, following trees marked with the blue blazes. At the bottom of the hill, turn right (northwest) again to continue on the Buckeye Trail. Continuing along the trail, it will turn into gravel as you return to the Whipp's Ledges parking lot. Take a sharp left (southeast) at the parking lot to repeat the previous portion of the Buckeye Trail back to the Hinckley Lake Loop Trail you left.

3.0   Arrive back at the Hinckley Lake Loop Trail, and turn left (south) to hike parallel to State Road. Take this and the upcoming pedestrian bridge over the East Branch Rocky River. After crossing the river, you'll come to a post for the Hinckley Lake Loop Trail. Turn right (west) to continue hiking the trail.

3.8   Turn right (northwest) onto the All Purpose Trail along the western edge of Hinckley Lake.

4.0   You'll arrive at the boathouse, and the All Purpose Trail splits from Hinckley Lake Loop. Stay to the right and head downhill closer to the lake.

4.8   Next to a dam, you'll come to a junction where you'll want to head downstairs into the Spillway. Hike across the Spillway to a pedestrian bridge 50 to 100 feet ahead of you. Take the bridge over the stream to a set of stone stairs that lead back toward the parking lot where you started. At the top of the stairs, stay left to continue on the All Purpose Trail heading north. Hike this small portion toward Bellus Road. Turn right (east) at the intersection back to where you started the hike.

Hike Information

Local Information
Visit Medina County; (330) 722-5502; www.visitmedinacounty.com

Local Events/Attractions
Every March 15 the buzzards return to the **Buzzard Roost** near the corner of State Road and West Drive. Join the Annual Return of the Buzzard festivities starting at 7:30 a.m. until the first buzzard is spotted.

Hike Tours
Cleveland Hiking Club; www.clevelandhikingclub.org
Cleveland Metroparks; (216) 635-3200; www.clevelandmetroparks.com
NEOHiking; www.meetup.com/NEOHiking

Lake County

ere you'll find three Lake Metroparks hikes, one on the coast of Lake Erie in the City of Mentor, and one of the largest botanical gardens in the country with Holden Arboretum—a botanist and hiker's dream.

18 Chapin Forest Reservation Trails

More than 5 miles of mature woodland trails traverse Chapin Forest's 390 acres in rural Kirtland, Ohio. Hikers can tackle the trails one-by-one or easily connect them all to experience the reservation's diversity. Wide travels give way to rocky terrain with a variety of oaks, maples, tulips, hemlocks, and beeches lining the trails. If nothing else, come for the scenic overlook off Lucky Stone Loop where on a clear day you can catch a glimpse of the Cleveland skyline 18 miles away.

Start: At the Hobart Road parking lot
Distance: 4.5 miles
Approximate hiking time: 1.5–2 hours
Difficulty: Mostly easy with moderate climbs and terrain on Lucky Stone Loop Trail
Trail surface: Crushed limestone and natural surface
Best season: Year-round
Other trail users: This trail is groomed for skiing in the winter, along with ski and snowshoe rentals. Hikers are still welcome all year.
Canine compatibility: Yes, on a leash
Land status: Public
Fees and permits: None
Schedule: Open 6 a.m.–11 p.m.

Maps: www.lakemetroparks.com/parks/documents/Chapin-Forest-Reservation-trail-map042312.pdf
Trail contacts: Lake Metroparks; (440) 639-7275; www.lakemetroparks.com
Finding the trailhead: Drive east from Cleveland on I-90 for 16.3 miles. Take exit 189 for OH 91. Turn left onto SOM Center Road for just under a mile and turn left again onto Chardon Road for 2.6 miles. Continue onto Euclid Chardon Road for 1.2 miles. Turn left onto Hobart Road and the destination will be on the right in 0.4 miles. GPS: N 41 35' 23.2224" / W 81 22' 10.9092"

The Hike

Chapin Forest might not seem like the place to be for a lengthy hike. True, its longest trail—Lucky Stone Loop—clocks in at just around 1.5 miles. But it's surprisingly easy to combine multiple trails to hike the entire reservation from the southwest corner to the northeast.

You'll find the Whispering Pines and Beech Woods trailhead at the northwestern end of the parking lot. Compacted gravel covers the trail before you turn into the evergreens of the Whispering Pines trail, home to barred owls, woodpeckers, and itself a one-time state forest. Interestingly the state forest still owns this land that Lake Metroparks leases. The whole lowland area off Hobart Road is used as a place to study growth rates on trees. Nearly all the woods down there were planted by the state, and if you look carefully you'll notice all the trees growing in rows—both evergreen and deciduous trees. And in just 0.25 mile, you'll be back out to the gravel of Beech Woods, hiking toward Arbor Lane.

The beeches of Beech Wood Trail continue onto Arbor Lane, joining maples, oaks, and wild cherry trees for an interesting mix. Still on compacted gravel, the trail

You can see the Cleveland skyline 18 miles away on a clear day from this overlook.

FREDERIC H. CHAPIN TO THE RESCUE!

Concerned with encroaching development, Frederic H. Chapin purchased today's Chapin Forest property in 1949 and donated it to the Ohio Division of Forestry. Though he knew some of the forest might be logged, he also knew the state would replant, maintain, and manage the forests—better than leaving the pristine woodland in the hands of potentially overzealous developers of the mid-20th century. And thanks to his efforts, the 390 acres of Chapin Forest survive today for Clevelanders to enjoy. So the least the powers that be at Lake Metroparks could do was name the reservation after him.

runs wide. That's because this was once a logging road, perhaps robbing Whispering Pines of its former state forest status.

Arbor Lane will connect to Lucky Stone Loop. A brief connector trail links the two loops and is marked by the blue blazes of the Buckeye Trail. To make matters simple, you'll continue following the blue blazes north on Lucky Stone Loop toward the Historic Sperry Quarry overlook. From here on a clear day, you can see the Cleveland skyline 18 miles away. Spot it with a friend and you'll inevitably shriek, "There it is!"

Lucky Stone then winds downhill where you'll connect with the 0.8-mile Turkey Trail. This out-and-back leg leads to the 1-mile Quarry Loop Trail, still marked in blue blazes, with the 0.1-mile Stonecutters Loop just off the eastern end. The blue blazes will lead you to it easily enough.

Back at the Quarry Loop, you'll backtrack through Turkey to reconnect with Lucky Stone and hike the southern leg of its loop. This portion is far rockier than the

Here's your trailhead for the Chapin Forest Reservation with Whispering Pines on the left.

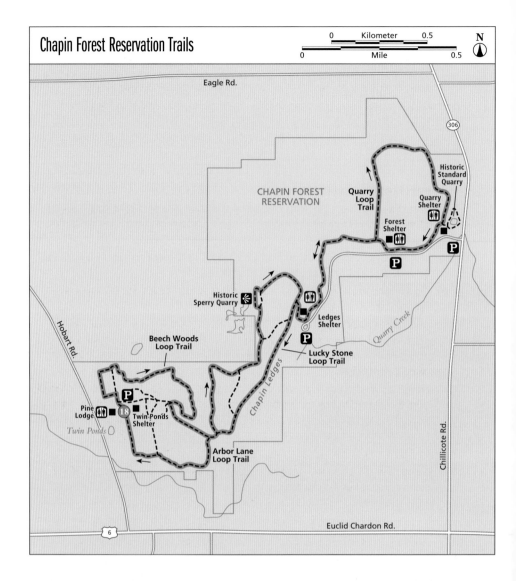

northern portion, living up to its name thanks to the plethora of Sharon Conglomerate stone formed over 300 million years ago. These stones are sometimes referred to as "lucky stones," hence the trail's name.

Following your rocky hike, you'll return to Arbor Lane. This time you'll follow the blue blazes to hike new terrain of the Arbor Lane Loop. The blazes will lead you back to the southern end of the parking lot, finishing your Chapin Forest hike.

Miles and Directions

0.0 Start on the gravel trailhead for the Whispering Pines and Beech Woods trailhead at the northwestern corner of the parking lot. Hike north briefly before turning left (west) into the pines for a brief loop on grassy trail that will wind back out onto Beech Woods.

0.1 Turn right (north) to continue hiking Whispering Pines. You'll pass a short connector en route to the northern end of this yellow-marked trail.

0.2 Emerge from the woods and turn left (north) to hike Beech Woods. Continue hiking Beech Woods as the trail quickly winds east.

0.6 Turn left onto the Arbor Lane Loop Trail, hiking southeast. **Option:** Continue southwest on Beech Woods to complete the mile loop.

0.8 Stay to the left at the Lucky Stone Loop junction with blue blazes lining the trail. Less than 0.1 mile later you'll turn left again (north) to hike the loop clockwise. You'll return by this junction on your end hike.

1.1 Pass a bypass on your right, keeping to the left to continue hiking northeast. **Bailout:** Turn right onto the bypass to shorten your hike significantly.

1.2 Ignore another bypass, keeping left to hike north. **Bailout:** Another option if you need to end early.

1.3 Arrive at the Historic Sperry Quarry overlook, a mini-loop within the trail. Follow the loop west to north. If it's clear, you might be able to see the Cleveland skyline 18 miles away. Continuing on Lucky Stone, the trail will trek northeast before bending south downhill toward the Turkey Trail.

1.6 Turn left (southeast) downhill onto asphalt trail toward the Ledges Shelter parking lot. You'll return to this junction later to hike the southern leg of Lucky Stone Loop. At the bottom of the downhill, turn left (northeast) onto the flat, gravel-covered Turkey Trail, also covered in the blue blazes. Follow this 0.8-mile trail northeast to the Quarry Loop Trail.

2.1 Turn left (north) onto the 1-mile Quarry Loop Trail.

2.7 Take the junction for the tiny Stonecutters Loop Trail. Backtrack to where you left Quarry after completing this 0.1-mile loop.

2.8 Ignore the Buckeye Trail junction. Though tempting, this will take you out of Chapin Forest.

2.9 Return to the Quarry Loop Trail and continue hiking south as the trail bends west.

3.1 Stay along the perimeter of the Forest Shelter to return to the Turkey Trail junction.

3.2 Continue onto the Turkey Trail, backtracking to where you left Lucky Stone Loop.

3.6 Return to Lucky Stone Loop. Hike north back up the asphalt trail and stay to the left onto gravel trail lined by wooden posts. At the top of the hill, turn left to hike the southern leg of Lucky Stone, west.

3.7 Stay to the left to hike up a series of large stones, heading southwest. Continue hiking in this direction, ignoring two bypasses you've already passed on the northern side, until you return to Arbor Lane Loop.

4.1 Emerge to a rather large gravel junction. Keep left (west) toward yet another junction where you'll turn left (south) to hike a new leg of Arbor Lane. The blue blazes will follow you for the remainder of your hike.

4.3 Ignore an Arbor Lane bypass on your right (north). Continue west as you near the end of your hike.

4.5 Arbor Lane turns north back to the parking lot where you'll end your hike next to Twin Ponds Shelter.

Hike Information

Local Information

Lake County Visitors Bureau; (440) 975-1234; www.lakevisit.com

Hike Tours

Cleveland Hiking Club; www.clevelandhikingclub.org
Lake Metroparks; (440) 639-7275; www.lakemetroparks.com
NEOHiking; www.meetup.com/NEOHiking

GREEN TIP

Hiking and snowshoeing are great carbon-free activities during the cold holidays. Cleveland's a winter city— embrace it!

19 Girdled Road Reservation Loop Trails

Wooden stairs and steep climbs greet you early on along the 0.68-mile Chickadee Trail with hemlocks lining the trail to the approximately 4-mile Oak Leaf Loop Trail—a relatively flat hike alongside Big Creek until the Green Darner Trail. The latter is a short 0.3-mile loop around a man-made wetland leading back to the second half of Oak Leaf. You'll backtrack the Chickadee Trail in the end where you can either finish early or add on the Valley View Overlook or 1.2-mile Surveyor's Woods Loop Trail near where the first surveyors of Girdled Road set up camp in 1798. This is the largest park in the Lake Metroparks system, protecting 935 acres of pristine habitat.

Start: At the Chickadee Trailhead
Distance: 5.2 miles
Approximate hiking time: 2 hours
Difficulty: Moderate due to the distance
Trail surface: Crushed limestone
Best season: Year-round
Other trail users: This trail is groomed for skiing in the winter.
Canine compatibility: Yes, on a leash
Land status: Public
Fees and permits: None
Schedule: Open 6 a.m.–11 p.m.
Maps: Lake Metroparks; (440) 639-7275; www.lakemetroparks.com

Trail contacts: Lake Metroparks; (440) 639-7275; www.lakemetroparks.com
Finding the trailhead: Drive east from Cleveland on OH 2 for approximately 11 miles as it merges with I-90. Follow signs for I-271 toward Erie, PA, to stay on I-90 E for 15.5 miles. Take exit 200 for OH 44 toward Chardon/Painesville and turn left onto OH 44 S. In 0.2 mile, turn left onto Auburn Road and then the second right onto Concord Hambden Road. Turn left onto Williams Road in 2 miles and right onto Cascade Road in 0.9 mile. Destination will be on the right. GPS: N 41 40' 2.082" / W 81 10' 40.0542"

The Hike

Lake Metroparks' Girdled Road Reservation is perhaps one of the most underappreciated hikes in the region. West Siders and city dwellers alike remain largely unfamiliar with the park. Maybe it goes back to the *deep-rooted* (but ultimately laughable) East Side / West Side rivalry Clevelanders like to pretend is a real thing. Whatever the poor reasoning for overlooking this 932-acre gem nestled within leafy Concord Township, now is the time to remedy the indifference it has received by hitting all but two of the reservation's trails in this 5.2-mile hike.

You'll begin by hiking south out of the parking lot where trailheads for the Chickadee and Surveyor's Woods Loop Trails will greet you. For now, you'll want to take the 0.68-mile Chickadee Trail south through a long series of wooden stairs that can make for steep climbing. Like many of the trails in Northeast Ohio, you'll find hemlocks, hemlocks, and *even more* hemlocks lining the trail along your initial hike to the Oak Leaf Loop junction.

Melanie notices the snowshoe trail off of Oak Leaf.

When you arrive at the gravel-covered Oak Leaf, you can obviously take the trail either clockwise or counter-clockwise. Looking at a map, it's clear connecting the trails yourself is hardly a difficult feat, not to mention the trails are very well marked by the folks at Lake Metroparks. For our purposes, hike the loop counter-clockwise so you can get straight to some of the best views of the Big Creek on your right. This will lead to the 0.4-mile Big Creek Valley Trail, which is actually just the Buckeye Trail, but Lake Metroparks officials decided to give the trail their own name as it cuts through Girdled Road Reservation. Anyway, you'll want to continue on the Oak Leaf Loop.

Soon after the Big Creek junction you'll come to a bypass that will shorten the Oak Leaf Loop Trail in half. If you're looking for a shorter hike and have little interest in seeing the ducks hanging around Green Darner (season-pending of course), then that's an option. But who doesn't love ducks or wetlands?

Farther south you'll come to a junction for the Green Darner Loop Trail and a continuation of Oak Leaf. Take the Darner connection and hike around the 0.3-mile man-made wetland counter-clockwise until you hook back up with Oak Leaf, which at this point is an out-and-back leg off the main loop. You'll hike this back north to the previous junction, staying to the right to continue hiking north along the eastern

GIRDLED ROAD RESERVATION

"Girdled Road" might strike some as an odd name for a park reservation. What do roads have to do with nature? Naturally, there's a historic connection behind the naming.

Purchased by Lake Metroparks in 1965, the reservation takes its name from the first road created by the area's early European settlers that connected the young City of Cleveland to the Pennsylvania state line in the early 1800s. Now you might wonder what "girdled" means. Girdling a tree is a rather harsh-sounding process of removing the bark around a tree to stop nutrients from keeping said tree alive. This makes it easier to later remove the dead tree and widen a road.

There you have it! The beautifully lush Girdled Road Reservation gets its name from a slow and painful method of killing trees.

Summer skies at the Valley View Overlook

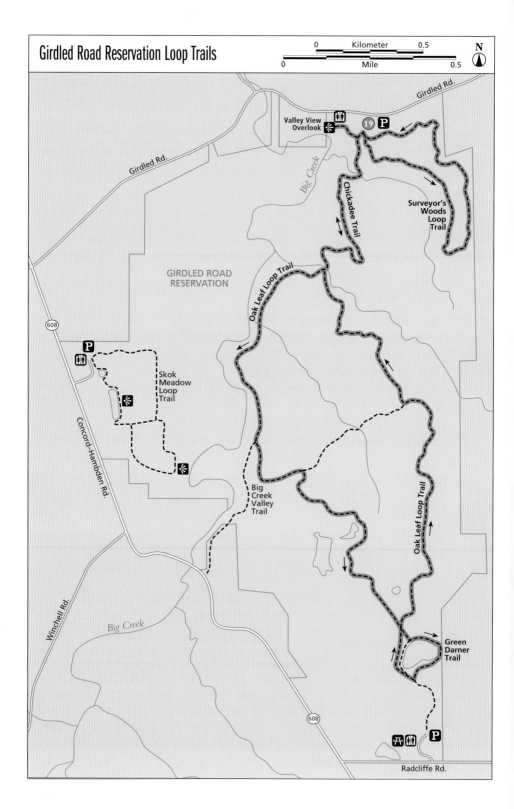

Girdled Road Reservation Loop Trails

Kilometer
0   0.5

Mile
0   0.5

N

Girdled Rd.

Valley View
Overlook

19   P

Girdled Rd.

Big Creek

Chickadee Trail

Surveyor's
Woods
Loop
Trail

GIRDLED ROAD
RESERVATION

Oak Leaf Loop Trail

608

P

Skok
Meadow
Loop
Trail

Big
Creek
Valley
Trail

Oak Leaf Loop Trail

Concord-Hambden Rd.

Winchell Rd.

Big Creek

Green
Darner
Trail

608

P

Radcliffe Rd.

leg of the Oak Leaf Loop. Take this all the way back to the Chickadee Trail to back-track the out-and-back toward the trailhead.

At the trailhead, you now have the option to end early or grab a couple more sights. To the west you have the Valley View Overlook less than 0.1 mile away with panoramic views of Big Creek and the surrounding forest. East you have the 1.2-mile Surveyor's Woods Loop Trail, an easy jaunt along the ridges above Big Creek. Chances are you'll want to add as much to your itinerary as possible with your new-found appreciation for Girdled Road Reservation.

Miles and Directions

0.0 Start the Chickadee Trail out-and-back trail from the southwestern end of the parking lot hiking due south. Stay to the left, ignoring signs for the Valley View Overlook Trail.

0.7 Arrive at the junction for the Oak Leaf Loop Trail. Continue straight, hiking southwest. You'll return on your left once you finish the loop.

1.2 You'll come to a junction for the Big Creek Valley Trail, a 0.43-mile out-and-back hike heading south, slightly to the west. But we're going to stay to the left (southeast) to continue on the Oak Leaf Loop Trail.

1.4 If you need to bail out or prefer a shorter hike, now is your opportunity to take the Oak Leaf Loop connector trail by staying straight and hiking northeast. Otherwise, turn right (south) to continue on the full Oak Leaf Loop Trail.

2.0 Take the Green Darner Trail connector by turning left (east) for a brisk 0.33-mile loop around a small pond. Take another left (east) once you arrive at the pond to hike around it clockwise until you run back into the Oak Leaf Loop Trail.

2.2 Turn right (north) at the southern tip of the pond to rejoin the Oak Leaf Loop Trail, hiking alongside the western end of the pond. Shortly thereafter, you'll come to another Green Darner junction, but we're going to stay straight hiking due north on Oak Leaf back toward the junction where you originally left Oak Leaf for the Green Darner. When you arrive, stay to the right on the Oak Leaf trail to hike north along the eastern portion of the loop back toward your first Chickadee Trail junction.

3.1 Ignore the connector trail by turning right (north) to continue hiking back to the Girdled Road parking lot where you started.

3.5 Return to the Chickadee Trail junction. Turn right (north) to repeat this portion of the hike back toward the parking lot.

4.0 Now you're back at one of your first junctions with the parking lot in plain sight to the north. You can either turn right (north) to finish your hike or you can do a quick 0.07-mile detour to an overlook by staying straight and hiking west. Once you arrive at the overlook, you'll hike back to this junction.

4.1 Arrive back at the junction where you started hiking toward the overlook. Turn left (north) to get back on Chickadee toward the parking lot. Shortly after you'll come back to the trail junction where you started your hike. You can end here or turn right (south) for a 1.22-mile hike along the Surveyor's Woods Loop Trail. If you decide on the loop, turn right (south) to hike this loop counter-clockwise.

4.3 You'll come to a connector on your left that you can take if you need or want to shorten the hike. Otherwise, continue east to finish the entirety of the loop.

Small pond in Girdled Road Reservation

4.9 Now you're at the opposite end of the aforementioned connector. Ignore it and continue straight hiking north toward the Girdled Road parking lot.

5.2 Return to the Surveyor's Woods Loop Trailhead. Turn right (north) to hike not even 0.1 mile back to the parking lot and end your hike.

Hike Information

Local Information

Lake County Visitors Bureau; (440) 975–1234; www.lakevisit.com

Camping

By reservation only

Hike Tours

Cleveland Hiking Club; www.clevelandhikingclub.org
Lake Metroparks; (440) 639-7275; www.lakemetroparks.com
NEOHiking; www.meetup.com/NEOHiking

20 Gorge to Bridle/Buckeye Trail, Penitentiary Glen Reservation

Hike over a variety of paved, gravel, and natural trails that run over 424 acres of grassy fields, open meadows, forest, and wetlands that northern cardinals and cottontail rabbits call home. More than 7 miles of trails fill the reservation named after the deep gorge that splits it. Take the 141-step staircase down for a look at Stoney Brook Falls in the middle of the gorge.

Start: At the Penitentiary Glen Nature Center
Distance: 2.7 miles
Approximate hiking time: 1 hour
Difficulty: Easy
Trail surface: Crushed limestone
Best season: Year-round
Other trail users: None
Canine compatibility: Yes, on a leash
Land status: Public
Fees and permits: None
Schedule: Open 6 a.m.–11 p.m.

Maps: www.lakemetroparks.com/select-park/documents/Penitentiary-Glen-Reservation-trail-map041013.pdf
Trail contacts: Lake Metroparks; (440) 639-7275; www.lakemetroparks.com
Finding the trailhead: Drive east from Cleveland on I-90 for a little over 20 miles. Take exit 193 for OH 306 South. Turn right onto OH 306 South. In a mile, turn left onto Chillicothe Road and take the second right onto Kirtland Chardon Road. The destination will be on the right in 2 miles. GPS: N 41 36' 43.6788" / W 81 19' 56.4306"

The Hike

You might think you're in for a snoozer of a hike when you first take notice of all the paved trails surrounding the parking lot. But within the first 0.3 mile, you'll feel lost in the woods as you hike high up on a ridge with steep falls surrounding you. Needless to say, watch your step. Nobody lands that fall comfortably.

You'll find a paved path at the northwestern end of the parking lot that'll take you (briefly) alongside the Glen Meadow & Orchard train tracks before dumping you onto the gravel-covered Gorge Rim Loop Trail. This 1-mile trail travels smoothly downhill toward the hemlock ravine of Penitentiary Gorge. As the trail bends northwest, you'll find 141 steps that lead down to relaxing Stoney Brook Falls.

Finishing your Gorge Rim hike, you'll come out of the woodland to an open expanse of greenery to connect with the Bridle Trail. Hike this gravel trail west, and near here you'll find a sign warning that the next 3 miles are rugged. Of course, this is your welcoming to the usually challenging Buckeye Trail. As usual blue blazes will guide your way along the trail, though contrary to other hikes, the blue blazes are painted on trail markers as opposed to trees. Nevertheless, they're impossible to miss. Overall, this is a very well-marked hike.

Jarret hikes down the Buckeye Trail. Unlike most Buckeye Trail markings, the blue blazes in Penitentiary Glen are on posts instead of trees.

Staying on the Buckeye Trail, you'll get the rugged terrain the sign promised as you escape into dense woods and narrow trail with roots sticking out of the ground. The surrounding habitat provides a nice cover from the summer sun.

About 0.5 mile into the Buckeye Trail, you'll come to a surprisingly steep climb. You might second-guess it, but you are indeed supposed to take this on. Don't be afraid to get your hands and knees dirty. After all, it's part of the fun.

The remainder provides a much easier hike compared to earlier portions of the Buckeye Trail. Emerging from the woods, you'll hike alongside a serene pond that might have a fisherman or two casting a line. Shortly after the pond, the Buckeye Trail splits west, leaving you hiking east on a mostly grassy Bridle Trail. You'll cross the Stoney Brook as you hike alongside Booth Road. Shortly after you'll come to

Gorge to Bridle/Buckeye Trail, Penitentiary Glen Reservation

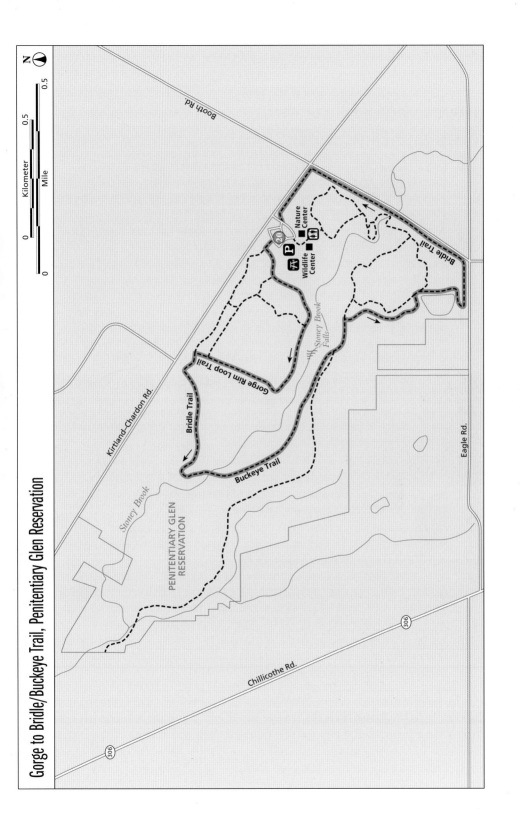

Kilometer

Mile

N

Booth Rd.

Nature Center

Wildlife Center

Bridle Trail

Gorge Rim Loop Trail

Stoney Brook Falls

Bridle Trail

Buckeye Trail

Kirtland-Chardon Rd.

Stoney Brook

PENITENTIARY GLEN RESERVATION

Chillicothe Rd.

Eagle Rd.

306

306

20

Glen Meadow where you can simply cut through the field to the parking lot now in sight to end the day.

Not the most challenging hike in the book, but the Buckeye Trail makes the visit to Penitentiary Glen plenty worthwhile.

Miles and Directions

0.0 Start at the northwest corner of the parking lot near the Glen Meadow & Orchard train tracks. Take the paved path that goes alongside the tracks to the right, hiking north. This leads to the trailhead for the Gorge Rim Loop Trail in about 200 feet. Turn left (southwest) onto Gorge Rim.

0.1 Here you'll come to the junction for Gorge Rim and the Rabbit Run Loop. Stay straight to continue on Gorge Rim, hiking west alongside the railroad tracks.

0.2 Ahead looks like a continuation of the trail, but it's just a service route that goes over the tracks. Turn right (southwest) onto a series of boardwalks that will guide you through the woods. This will last less than 0.1 mile, at which point you'll hike onto wide, natural trail.

0.3 Ignore the Gorge Rim Shortcut and continue hiking north across a wooden bridge. In less than 0.1 mile you'll come to a series of wooden stairs (steps) that take you down to Stoney Brook Falls, a brief out-and-back excursion off Gorge Rim. **Bailout:** Turn right (east) to cut through the longer Gorge Rim Loop toward Rabbit Run.

0.4 Arrive at Stoney Brook Falls. Return up the stairs to where you left the Gorge Rim Loop and turn left to continue hiking north.

0.8 Ignore the Rabbit Run junction and continue straight (east) where you'll see another junction just ahead for the Bridle Trail. Turn left (north) here. **Option:** Turn right (south) on either Rabbit Run or the Bridle Trail for a shorter loop back to the parking lot.

0.9 Turn left (south) to continue on the combined Buckeye/Bridle Trail. A sign will greet you here that reads RUGGED TERRAIN NEXT 3 MILES. Continue following the blue blazes.

1.3 Here you'll arrive at a surprisingly steep hill, almost like a trench running uphill. Trees line the path, however, offering assistance if you need it.

1.6 Arrive at the wide and flat Kirtland Connector Trail that runs on gravel surface. Turn left (south) to continue on the Buckeye/Bridle Trail. Continue following this trail as it wraps the east side of a nearby pond and fisherman's dock.

2.1 Now south of the pond, turn left (east) to hike onto the Bridle Trail, parallel to Eagle Road. As you can see on the map, you'll continue hiking on this leg of the Bridle Trail as it follows the adjacent roads. Soon the trail will turn northeast to run alongside Booth Road where you'll cross the Penitentiary Gorge—a small stream that won't provide any trouble.

2.6 Turn left (northwest) to hike across the Glen Meadow field that sits in front of the Nature Center parking lot.

2.7 End your hike at the Nature Center parking lot.

A gravel stone trail cutting into the woods

Hike Information

Local Information
Lake County Visitors Bureau; (440) 975-1234; www.lakevisit.com

Local Events/Attractions
Nature Center and Wildlife Center open 9–5 every day but Thanksgiving and Christmas

Hike Tours
Cleveland Hiking Club; www.clevelandhikingclub.org
Lake Metroparks; (440) 639-7275; www.lakemetroparks.com
NEOHiking; www.meetup.com/NEOHiking

GREEN TIP
Carpool, bike, or take public transportation to the trailhead.
The planet will thank you.

21 Holden Arboretum

Cleveland's East Side has bragging rights for Holden Arboretum, with its wonderful cultivated gardens and rugged forest trails that offer hikers a little bit of everything. And with 15,800 accessioned plants and plant groupings, wildlife, and 3,600 acres—one of the largest arboreta in the United States—there's plenty for a wandering adventurer to explore on a variety of easy man-made and rugged natural trails.

Start: Warren H. Corning Visitor Center

Distance: 6.7 miles

Approximate hiking time: 4 hours

Difficulty: Moderate due to occasionally rugged terrain on Old Valley

Trail surface: Crushed limestone and forested trail

Best season: Year-round

Other trail users: Public

Canine compatibility: Dogs on leashes are welcome on the trails.

Land status: Open to the public with admission

Fees and permits: Cost is $6 for nonmembers ages 13 and older; $3 for children ages 6 to 12. Children under 5 are admitted free. College students $1 off admission with a student ID.

Active duty military and family are free with ID. Holden members are free.

Schedule: Trails are open year-round.

Maps: Holden Arboretum; (440) 946-4400; www.holdenarb.org

Trail contacts: Holden Arboretum; (440) 946-4400; www.holdenarb.org

Finding the trailhead: From Cleveland, drive east on OH 2 for approximately 11 miles as it merges with I-90. In 10 more miles, take exit 195 for OH 615/Center Street. Turn right for 0.5 mile before turning left onto Chillicothe Road. Take the first right onto Baldwin Road and another right onto Booth Road in 1.3 miles. Take the first left onto Sperry Road and the destination will be on your right in 2 miles. GPS: N 41 36' 40.3416" / W 81 18' 4.3668"

The Hike

Find the Old Valley Trail at the trailhead, located on the south end of the Corning Visitor Center lawn, west of the parking lot. The trail begins near the entrance to the Display Garden with its hedge, lilac, and viburnum collections. Follow the gravel surface west as it converges with the Highlights Trail. You'll use this as a simple connector to the Pierson Creek Loop Trail. Signs are plenty to guide you along the way.

The trail becomes far less manicured and smooth when you start hiking the combined Pierson Creek, Woodland, and Old Valley Trails. You'll hike northwest past Foster Pond, continuing on the windy trail as it bends in all directions. The Woodland Trail will leave you as you hike west just before Pierson and Old Valley split north. Following this trail will take you to the rugged loop of Pierson Creek. You can always skip it and simply continue on Old Valley, but hiking beside the creek channel is a sight to see, especially as the wildflowers bloom. In total the loop is about 0.5 mile long, covering the northern portion of Holden Arboretum.

You'll return to Old Valley for your longest continuous stretch on the arboretum's lengthiest, most rugged hike. This particular leg of Old Valley offers seclusion and a

Heath Pond at the Holden Arboretum
COURTESY OF THE HOLDEN ARBORETUM

respite from the sweltering sun (if you're hiking in the summer, of course). The narrow, natural trail remains true to its rugged core as it meanders south to the Strong Acres Loop Trail.

Hanging west off Old Valley, Strong Acres Loop is a 0.75-mile hike along grassy trail with terrific views of the surrounding meadow. Bluebirds, bobolinks, meadowlarks, and tree swallows surround the loop. Again, you can just as easily skip this loop and continue on Old Valley. But it's a nice change of pace from the dense woodland you're accustomed to thus far. Besides, you'll return to Old Valley shortly.

Returning from Strong Acres, your last leg of the Old Valley will wind east to connect you to the Highlights Extension Trail, which in turn will quickly link to the Helen S. Layer Rhododendron Garden Trail—winner for longest trail name in the book.

The aforementioned trail will greet you at a tall gate used to prevent deer and other animals from ruining the gardens beyond. Be sure to close the gate behind you as you pass by and continue hiking south.

This southern loop includes 1.8 miles of trail with nearly 1,000 rhododendrons in bloom at its peak in late May and early June. First you'll hike north along Heath Pond to the similarly named Eliot and Linda Paine Rhododendron Discovery Garden. You'll see trails here, but they aren't marked on the official map. Feel free to browse at your own pace before hiking back south past Heath Pond to explore the trails around the Hourglass Pond. When you're done, you'll backtrack to where you left the Highlights Extension Trail.

From here you'll hike back north to the Display Garden Trail briefly to connect with the Bole Woods Trail. Hike east along the northern shore of Corning Lake and across Sperry Road to begin your eastern loop through the Bole Woods—a National Natural Landmark of mature beech-maple forest. On your return you'll link with the 1.5-mile Corning Lake Trail, hiking south and west alongside the lily pad–covered lake.

A pergola at the Holden Forest and Garden COURTESY OF THE HOLDEN ARBORETUM

HOW TO WIN FATHER OF THE YEAR

Albert Fairchild Holden should receive posthumous Father of the Year recognition.

Holden's daughter Elizabeth Davis Holden tragically succumbed to scarlet fever in 1908 at the age of 12. Following the tragedy, Albert Holden struggled with how best to memorialize his lost child. First he thought to bequeath his trust to Harvard University's Arnold Arboretum before his sister, Roberta Holden Bole, convinced Mr. Holden to create an arboretum in Cleveland as a sanctuary for adults and students interested in learning the basics of horticulture.

Following his own passing in 1913, Holden left a trust agreement that an arboretum be created after a life interest was secured for his surviving daughters, Emery May and Katharine Davis. The family realized such an undertaking needed to start as soon as possible and begun searching for a location.

Finally, in 1931, the Holden Arboretum was established. More than 80 years later, the arboretum continues to serve the Northeast Ohio community admirably. Mr. Holden can rest in peace knowing the entirety of Greater Cleveland will remain forever grateful for his daughter's memorial.

Stream crossing at the Holden Arboretum Courtesy of the Holden Arboretum

Near the southwest corner of the lake, you'll find gravel trail that you'll hike northeast back to an earlier junction where you began your Bole Woods hike. Hiking north, you'll simply follow the converged trails north back to start with your car now in sight.

Miles and Directions

0.0 Start hiking west on a paved connector that attaches the western end of the parking lot to the trails. Stay right to take the well-manicured Display Garden gravel trail, following signs northwest toward Pierson Creek Loop, Woodland, and Old Valley Trails.

0.1 Stay straight at the Blueberry Pond Trail junction to continue hiking northwest. You'll then hike down some stairs toward narrow gravel trail. Continue hiking toward Pierson Creek, taking a small bridge over a ravine. After the bridge, you'll be hiking north on less-manicured gravel trail. **Option:** Turn left (south) to hike the 0.5-mile Blueberry Pond Trail for a much shorter hike.

0.2 Foster Pond is on your right (northeast) off the Pierson Creek Loop Trail.

0.3 Turn right (northwest) to continue hiking on Pierson.

0.5 Here you'll follow a trail marker to turn left to continue hiking north on Pierson and Old Valley.

0.6 Arrive at the Pierson Creek Loop. Turn right (north) to hike the loop counter-clockwise. You'll return here at the end of the loop via the wooden stairs you can see in front of you.

0.9 Hike west down a 174-step wooden staircase. At the bottom, turn left (south) onto natural dirt trail. This will wind down a few more steps toward a bridge to cross Pierson Creek. You'll then take a handful more stairs after the creek to continue the trail, west.

The Holden Gardens

1.3 Take a sharp right (north) away from the creek to hike onto the Old Valley Trail.

1.8 Bear right (west) toward the 0.75-mile Strong Acres Loop Trail. **Option:** Continue on Old Valley to skip Strong Acres for a shorter hike.

1.9 A sign will push you out to the wide-open meadow of Strong Acres. Stay to the right (west) of the V-cut grass to hike the short loop counter-clockwise.

2.3 You'll approach grassy connector trails, but you'll want to stay left to continue hiking east on Strong Acres.

2.7 Finish Strong Acres Loop and backtrack to where you left Old Valley. You'll then turn right (southeast) when you return to Old Valley.

2.9 Turn left (east) away from a rifle range on private property. You'll hike downhill and suddenly come across a lot of stones on the trail.

Holden Arboretum

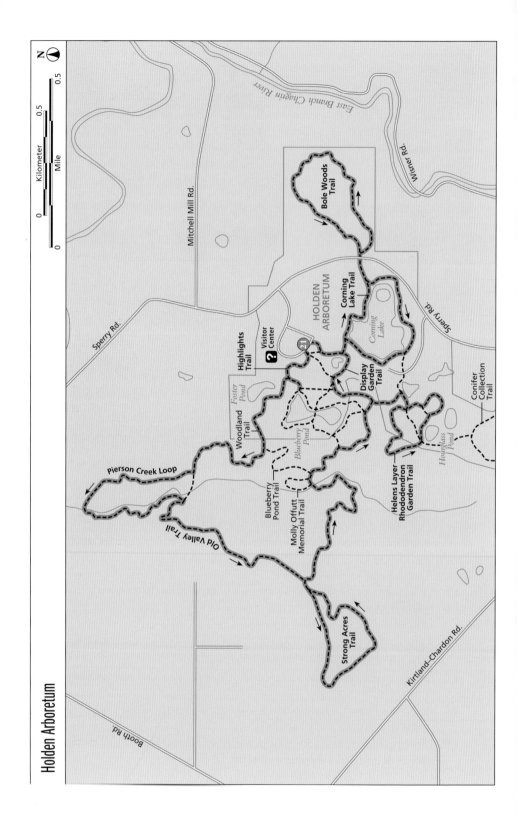

3.1 Continue hiking across a small stream on Old Valley that will lead to a boardwalk. On your right you'll find ninety-six uphill stairs you'll need to take, hiking east. At the top of the stairs, turn right (southeast) onto a man-made, smooth gravel trail section of Old Valley. Stay on this trail until it connects with the purple-marked Highlights Extension Trail.

3.3 You'll come to a junction for the Woodland and Old Valley Trails. Turn right (south) toward the Dawes Memorial Overlook. On your right will be a brief out-and-back leg for the Dawes Memorial Overlook. Ultimately you'll need to continue hiking east on the Old Valley Trail.

3.4 Stay right (east) to hike on to the Highlights Extension Trail off Old Valley. This will lead to the gated Helen S. Layer Rhododendron Garden Trail. Hike past the gate south.

The Stebbins Gulch Waterfall in the Holden Arboretum
Courtesy of the Holden Arboretum

3.5 Continue hiking south over a bridge toward a sign marking the Helen S. Layer Rhododendron Garden. You'll soon arrive at Heath Pond where you'll want to turn right (east) to hike to the Eliot and Linda Paine Rhododendron Discovery Garden.

3.6 Arrive at the garden. You'll see trails populate the area for leisure exploring. Ultimately you'll want to return to the entrance to eventually hike back to Heath Pond. One option is to simply hike the small, northern loop around the garden counter-clockwise.

3.7 Backtrack to Heath Pond and continue hiking west, past the junction that leads back to the Helen S. Layer Rhododendron Garden Trailhead.

3.8 Turn right (north) to hike alongside Sherwin Pond. After the pond, the trail will loop west to south toward the Hourglass Pond.

4.1 Go straight through a four-way intersection, hiking east next to Hourglass Pond. Soon you'll pass a small trail that bisects this southern loop. Continue southeast, following the trail as it quickly loops back northwest and toward a previous junction near Heath Pond.

4.3 Turn right (east) to backtrack through the Helen S. Layer Rhododendron Garden Trail gate to return to where you left the Highlights Extension Trail.

4.5 Hiking north on Highlights Extension will eventually turn into the yellow-marked Garden Trail. This will lead to the Myrtle S. Holden Wildflower Garden where you'll turn right (east) to hike around the southern end of Lotus Pond. Soon this will turn back into the Highlights Extension Trail as it runs into the orange Bole Woods Trail. At the Bole Woods Trail junction near Lotus Pond, continue straight (east) to hike the 1.5-mile National Natural Landmark Trail.

4.7 As you're hiking east, you'll see where you'll take the Corning Lake Trail later on. For now, continue hiking onto grassy trail toward Bole Woods.

5.0 Cross Sperry Road and stay right (southeast) to hike the loop of Bole Woods counter-clockwise. You'll hike this trail until you return to Sperry Road.

5.8 Back at Sperry Road, follow signs across the street toward Corning Lake, hiking west.

6.0 Turn left (south) toward the Sugarbush Observation Blind, leading to the Corning Lake Trail. Continue hiking this trail west to north as the trail wraps around the lake. Along the way you'll pass the Sugarbush Overlook. Visit quickly if you like, but you'll need to return via Corning Lake.

6.2 Turn right (northwest) at the southwestern corner of Corning Lake. The trail will soon merge onto gravel surface.

6.4 End your Corning Lake hike and turn left (west) onto a portion of gravel trail you covered while hiking toward Bole Woods.

6.5 Stay to the right (north) onto the Highlights Trail, hiking back toward the parking lot. Follow this windy trail back to the beginning of your hike, now easily in sight.

6.7 End your hike at the Holden Arboretum parking lot.

22 Mentor Lagoons Nature Preserve Loop Trails

Billed as the newest nature preserve in the state of Ohio, the Mentor Lagoons Nature Preserve offers 450 acres of dense woodland hiking and easy strolls along the coast of Lake Erie, where you'll get some of the best views of our beloved Great Lake in the book, rivaling the Cleveland Lakefront Nature Preserve (Hike 2).

Start: Trailhead, just past the Marina Office building
Distance: 3.0 miles
Approximate hiking time: 1.5 hours
Difficulty: Easy
Trail surface: Gravel, packed and natural surface
Best season: Year-round
Other trail users: Bicycles and electric carts (for handicapped accessibility) are permitted, except on the Marsh Rim and Shoreline Loop Trails.
Canine compatibility: Dogs permitted on leash, except on Lakefront Loop and Marsh Rim Trail
Land status: Public

Fees and permits: None
Schedule: Daily, dawn to dusk
Maps: www.cityofmentor.com
Trail contacts: City of Mentor Parks & Recreation; (440) 974-5720; parks@cityofmentor.com
Finding the trailhead: From I-90, take exit 195 (OH 615/Center Street). Head north for approximately 4.3 miles. Continue north onto Hopkins Road for 0.7 mile. Turn right onto Lake Shore Boulevard (161 feet), then take an immediate left onto Harbor Drive. Turn right at the stop sign and continue on Harbor Drive into the park entrance. GPS: N 41 43' 35.6046" / W 81 20' 17.1234"

The Hike

Mentor Lagoons Nature Preserve might not seem to have many trails to offer at face value. But natural, easy connections between the six trails make for a nice trek along the shores of Lake Erie.

You'll begin hiking north on gravel-covered Lakefront Trail with forest and cattails lining the way. Within just 0.2 mile you'll be at a junction for the Marsh Rim Trail, which will take you into dense woodland trail similar to what you will experience in other Cleveland-area hikes. Here the trail is made up of very soft dirt with fallen leaves mixed in. Roots sprouting out of the ground will force you to watch your step even more so than usual.

Unsurprisingly, Marsh Rim lives up to its name. With the exception of an unseasonal drought, expect to get the hiking boots a tad muddy here as you make your way east and north again to connect with the northeastern terminus of the Lakefront Trail. Once here you'll coast over relatively wide gravel-covered trail along the coast of Lake Erie. Though your view is obstructed most of the way by various trees and small brush, you'll soon reach an opening with a park bench where you can enjoy

Enjoying the view of Lake Erie off the Lakefront Trail

the lake in all its glory. But keep in mind this won't be your only Lake Erie encounter on the hike.

Continuing west on the Lakefront Trail, you'll start to wind back south toward where you started your hike. In fact, you could continue south to finish a shorter loop. Others will want to turn right onto the short, 0.6-mile Woods Trail to connect to the Shoreline Loop for an even closer encounter with Lake Erie.

Though just 0.3 mile, the Shoreline Loop will actually take you onto the beach, which is one of the last remnants of natural, wild beach in Ohio. Here you'll encounter Ohio endangered plant species like the coastal little bluestem, purple sandgrass, beach pea, and sea rocket. Some hikers might wonder whether or not they've lost the trail. Not so. To be fair, trail markers are few and far between at this point, but trust you are on the right track by continuing west along the shore. This will take you to a small graveled parking lot that you'll take south away from the lake to the Marina Overlook Trail.

UNTOUCHED BEACH

The Mentor Lagoons Nature Preserve contains the largest untouched beach between Cleveland and the Pennsylvania border. In the mid-1920s the property was slated to become a Venice of the North, but this plan failed due to the stock market crash. A conservation effort began in the early 1960s with the formation of the Mentor Marsh State Nature Preserve. This continued through 1996 and 1997 with the City of Mentor's purchase of 450 acres to create a nature preserve. The area is a popular hiking spot and also serves as an Important Birding Area, attracting over 150 neo-tropical birds and butterflies as they migrate in the fall and spring.

The Marina Overlook Trail starts as a simple road along the marina with cars parked on either side. Again, you might begin to wonder whether or not you're actually on a trail, but keep an eye out on the left for an opening into the woods and a trail marker where the Marina Overlook Trail continues. This brief jaunt through the woods will link you back to the Lakefront Trail where you started, backtracking slightly south to return to the trailhead.

Miles and Directions

0.0   Start off from the parking lot at the trailhead on the northeastern corner adjacent to the MENTOR LAGOONS sign, hiking north on the Lakefront Trail with forest lining the trail on your left. Before long, you'll approach a junction on the left for the Marina Overlook Trail, but we're going to continue straight toward the Marsh Rim Trail.

0.2   Turn right (east) onto the Marsh Rim Trail and into the woods.

0.8   At the end of the Marsh Rim Trail, you'll take a sharp left onto the Lakefront Loop Trail to hike north toward Lake Erie.

1.2   Now you're back on a gravel trail as you turn left (southwest) onto the Lakefront Trail, hiking alongside Lake Erie.

1.8   Leave the Lakefront Trail turning right (west) onto the Woods Trail. **Option:** Stay straight, hiking south to finish the Lakefront Trail and end your hike early.

2.1   Turn right (north) for a brief out-and-back hike onto gravel trail toward Lake Erie. You'll hike down some man-made stairs that will put you right up against the lake for some beautiful scenery. Afterward, backtrack to where you just were and continue straight (south).

2.3   You'll come right to the shoreline, but don't mistake this for a dead-end. You'll want to turn left (southwest) onto the Shoreline Loop, hiking uphill briefly as it starts to move away from the shoreline. Eventually you'll be pushed onto the beach where you'll want to continue hiking west onto a dirt parking lot. From here you're going to want to hike south, and soon the path will begin to turn east onto the Marina Overlook Trail.

2.6   On your left (north) you'll see a marker for the Marina Overlook Trail that will take you back into the woods, hiking uphill and continuing east back toward the parking lot.

3.0   Here you'll run back into the Lakefront Trail. Turn right (south), and you'll take this back into the parking lot at the trailhead where you started your hike.

Top: *A couple rests on a bench at the edge of Lake Erie.*
Bottom: *Modest waves crash against the coast in Mentor.*

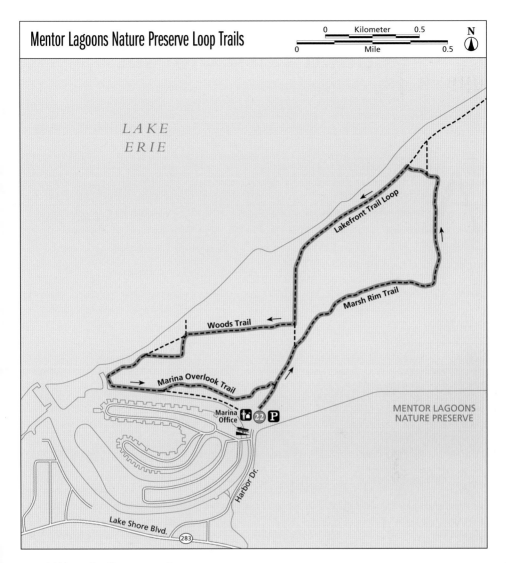

LAKE ERIE

Lakefront Trail Loop

Marsh Rim Trail

Woods Trail

Marina Overlook Trail

Marina Office

MENTOR LAGOONS NATURE PRESERVE

Harbor Dr.

Lake Shore Blvd.

283

Hike Information

Local Events/Attractions

The **National Park Service** maintains the home and library of the 20th president, the James A. Garfield National Historic Site on Mentor Avenue (www.nps.gov/jaga/index.htm).

Hike Tours

Guided hikes are arranged through the **Mentor Marsh Nature Center:** www.cmnh.org/site/Conservation/NaturalAreas/MentorMarshPrograms.aspx; (440) 257-0777; or rdonalds@cmnh.org.

Geauga Park District

As you experience the hikes in this section, you'll find some of the most pronounced greenery in the entire Greater Cleveland region when hiking in the spring and summer. Come fall and it's a tapestry of oranges and browns as the season turns to winter when Geauga County, the heart of Cleveland's snow belt, is blanketed in the kind of picturesque snow typically reserved for Hallmark Christmas movies.

Geauga parks offer some of the most remote hikes in the book, rivaling Ohio's only national park with trails that put you in the middle of nowhere—in a good way.

23 Bridle to Ansel's Cave to Trout Lily Trails, The West Woods

Seven miles of trails traverse through West Woods' 902 acres of woodlands and streams. Ansel's Cave is the highlight of this hike, though it's more than just an interesting rock formation. Local legend suggests the cave might have served a far greater purpose during the mid–1800s.

Start: Horse Trailer Parking Lot
Distance: 5.4 miles
Approximate hiking time: 2 to 2.5 hours
Difficulty: Moderate due to hills
Trail surface: Hard-packed dirt, gravel
Best season: Year-round
Other trail users: Horses on Pioneer Bridle Trail and portions of Ansel's Cave Trail
Canine compatibility: Dogs welcome (must be on leash)
Land status: Park land
Fees and permits: None
Schedule: Trails open dawn to dusk daily
Maps: Geauga Park District; www.geaugapark district.org; (440) 286-9516

Trail contacts: Geauga Park District; www .geaugaparkdistrict.org; (440) 286-9516
Finding the trailhead: Drive south from Cleveland on I-77 toward Akron for about 7 miles. Take exit 156 to merge onto I-480 East toward Youngstown for just over 8 miles. Take the exit on the left for I-271 North for approximately 2.5 miles. Take exit 29 for US 422 and turn right onto OH 87 East/Chagrin Boulevard in another 1.5 miles. At the traffic circle, continue straight onto Pinetree Road and take a slight right onto South Woodland Road in a mile. In 2.3 miles, turn left onto OH 87 East for 5.2 miles. Destination will be on right at 9465 Kinsman Road, Russell, OH. GPS: N 41 27' 44.0712" / W 81 18' 18.5394"

The Hike

The Pioneer Bridle Trail, where you'll start your hike, is a mix of your typical forested, dirt trail. Open to horseback riders and (obviously) hikers, the trail makes a large loop west before coming back around toward Silver Creek. Along the way you'll pass junctions for both the Affelder Link and Music Street Trails. Both are out-and-back trails that you're welcome to take for added mileage, but it would include a decent amount of backtracking that we're going to avoid.

Shortly after the second Silver Creek crossing, you'll hike north to a four-way junction. To your left is the 0.3-mile Discovery Trail and straight ahead continues the Pioneer. Ignore both, as you'll be covering them later, and turn right onto a short connector trail. This will take you to a parking lot with the Turkey Ridge and Deer Run shelters. Follow the asphalt trail in front of the Turkey Ridge shelter to the south toward the Ansel's Cave Trail. Follow the Ansel's Cave Trail and head east to continue to hike around the trail counter-clockwise. At this point you'll return to forested trail.

The legendary Ansel's Cave sits at the northern end of the loop. Unfortunately the cave faces a similar fate as the Ice Box Cave in Cuyahoga Valley National Park's

Plenty of rumors surround the fabled Ansel's Cave. Runaway slaves in the Civil War, bootleggers; Ansel's Cave has maybe seen it all.

Virginia Kendall Unit (Hike 38). That is, the cave is closed off to hikers due to the spreading of white-nosed syndrome—a spreading killer of the area's bat population.

Some might feel daring and want to cross the barricade. This wouldn't be a wise choice, as signs warning you that you will be prosecuted if caught populate the area. Admire from afar (which really isn't that far) and continue hiking the loop west.

Not far past the end of the loop, you'll return to a previous junction with the Ansel's Cave Link Trail. Now you can take the junction west through the Ansel's Cave Link Trail into the West Woods Nature Center's parking lot. In front of the center you'll see a sign for 0.1-mile-long Trout Lily Trail—worth taking for the scenic overlook of Pebble Brook. After the overlook, you'll simply backtrack on Trout Lily, keeping an eye out for the Discovery Trail. The aptly named Discovery Trail is entirely paved, so not a very rigorous hike, but worth the 0.3 mile for the educational signs about the area that line the trail. You'll no doubt *discover* something new. Get it? Discover?

The Discovery Trail will lead southeast back to an earlier junction for the Pioneer where you first followed the connector trail to the Ansel's Cave Trail. Now you'll turn left to head back north on the Pioneer Bridle Trail for the remainder of the hike, weaving in and out of the woods parallel to the park driveway.

THE LEGEND OF ANSEL'S CAVE

According to local legend, Ansel's Cave has had its fair share of residents over the years, most notably in the mid-1800s. Many of you are (hopefully) familiar with a piece of American history called the Civil War. Local legend says that the large rock outcroppings once provided shelter to Civil War soldiers and runaway slaves on the Underground Railroad.

Later on the cave (again, allegedly) even welcomed Prohibition-era bootleggers. But before the soldiers, runaway slaves, and bootleggers came through, some believe a man by the name of Ansel Savage claimed the cave for himself. Apparently setting up unverified residency in a cave is worthy of receiving naming rights.

Hiking the West Woods will leave you with the feeling that the entirety of Cleveland's eastern suburbs would have made for an incredible national park had sprawl not axed its grind to the forest. But it did, so no point causing oneself a headache over what could have been. Enjoy the hike as it is and the smiling faces that seem to routinely populate the park's trails.

Miles and Directions

0.0 Start at the Pioneer Bridle Trail from the southwestern end of the parking lot, hiking southeast into the woods. In about 200 feet you'll come to a junction for the Pioneer Bridle Trail. This is where you'll return at the end of the hike. For now, turn right (south) to continue hiking the loop counter-clockwise.

1.0 You'll hike to the Pioneer Bridle and Affelder Trail junction. Continue hiking south on the bridle trail. **Option:** Turn right (west) for the 1.1-mile Affelder Link Trail. This is an out-and-back trail, not a loop. (Round trip would be 2.2 miles.)

1.7 Now you'll approach the Music Street Link Trail junction. Once again, you're going to ignore the post and continue hiking northeast on the Pioneer Bridle Trail. **Option:** Turn right (south) for the 0.7-mile Music Street Link Trail. This, again, is an out-and-back trail that ends at Music Street. (Round trip would be 1.4 miles.)

2.1 On your left is the Discovery Trail junction. You're going to turn right (east) onto a short connector trail to hike toward nearby Turkey Ridge Shelter within a small parking lot. You're going to hike alongside the parking lot to the eastern end past some restrooms. Next to the restroom you'll find the trailhead for Ansel's Cave on driveway-esque gravel. Hike back into the woods, still heading east. **Option:** Continue hiking north on the Pioneer Bridle Trail if you wish to end your hike early.

2.4 Turn right (east) to continue on the Ansel's Cave Trail toward the caves. **Option:** Turn left (southwest) to take the Ansel's Cave Link Trail back toward the Pioneer Bridle Trail.

2.5 Now you're at the junction for the loop around Ansel's Cave. Follow the yellow arrow pointing you to the east as the trail bends south to complete the loop around Ansel's Cave counter-clockwise. You'll return to this junction after completing the loop.

2.7 Continue straight (north) to follow signs for the Ansel's Cave Long Loop.

Bridle to Ansel's Cave to Trout Lily Trails, The West Woods

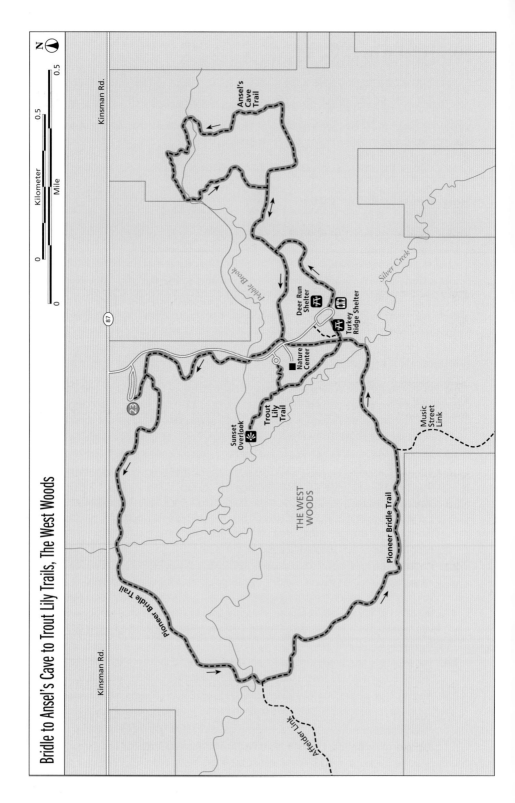

A narrow dirt trail splits the forest.

2.9 Signs will force you to turn left (north) onto a narrow boardwalk. Soon you'll return to trail, but this portion is much more narrow than earlier with a plentiful amount of roots sticking out of the ground.

3.3 Arrive at a boardwalk that will usher you around Ansel's Cave.

3.7 Return to the junction where you began the loop around Ansel's Cave. Turn right (west) to hike familiar territory back toward the Ansel's Cave Link Trail junction.

3.8 Now you're back at the junction where you left the gravel portion of the Ansel's Cave Trail. This time, continue straight (west) toward the West Woods Nature Center and Trout Lily Discovery Trail. **Option:** Turn right (north) to take the Pioneer Bridle Trail back to the parking lot, skipping the Trout Lily Trail and Sunset Overlook.

4.1 Cross the street heading northwest to the parking lot for the West Woods Nature Center. Keep left alongside the nature center and you'll find the Trout Lily trailhead, leading to the Sunset Overlook.

4.3 Arrive at a junction alongside a small pond. Turn right (northwest) to follow signs for the Sunset Overlook.

4.4 Stay to the right (northwest) to continue toward the Sunset Overlook. You'll then find stairs and a platform where you can enjoy the overlook.

4.5 Arrive at the Sunset Overlook. When you're done, backtrack to the previous junction next to the pond.

4.6 Return to the junction and keep right (southeast) for the Discovery Trail.

4.8 Arrive back at the previous Pioneer Bridle Trail junction where you skipped the Discovery Trail. Now you'll turn left (north) back onto Bridle Trail, continuing this trail until you return to your parking lot.

5.0 Cross the street heading east to continue on the Pioneer Bridle Trail. Soon you'll cross the street again heading west just past the West Woods Nature Center, and wind in and out of the woods until you return to the first junction you encountered in the hike.

5.4 Return to your first trail junction, and continue straight (west) back to the parking lot where you'll end your hike.

Hike Information

Camping

Camping at nearby **Punderson State Park**

Hike Tours

Check newsletter or website: www.geaugaparkdistrict.org

24 McIntosh to Harvest Loop Trail, Orchard Hills Park

Orchard Hills Park's 237 acres served as a golf course in a former life. The property has since been reborn as a Geauga Park District reforested landscape behind Patterson Fruit Farm's Farm Market thanks in part to a partnership with the Western Reserve Land Conservancy, funded in part by the Water Resources Restoration Sponsorship Program of the Ohio Environmental Protection Agency, the Clean Ohio Conservation Fund, and other public funds. Habitat restoration is the primary focus of the natural resource management plan for Orchard Hills Park.

Start: On the paved Cricket Trail right along the western edge of the parking lot and in front of Orchard Hills Lodge
Distance: 2 miles
Approximate hiking time: 40 minutes
Difficulty: Easy
Trail surface: Crushed limestone
Best season: Year-round
Other trail users: Bicycles, joggers, dog walkers, winter skiers
Canine compatibility: Dogs on leash
Land status: Public
Fees and permits: None
Schedule: Open 6:00 a.m–11:00 p.m.
Maps: Available at nature centers or online

Trail contacts: Geauga Park District; www .geaugaparkdistrict.org; (440) 286-9516
Finding the trailhead: Drive east from Cleveland for approximately 11 miles on OH 2 East as it merges with I-90 East. Keep right to stay on I-90 E for 10.5 miles, following signs for I-271 South. Take exit 189 for OH 91 in 4.2 miles and turn left onto SOM Center Road for just under a mile before turning left onto Chardon Road. In 2.6 miles, continue onto Euclid Chardon Road for 1.4 miles, and turn right onto Tibbets Road for 1 mile. Continue onto Caves Road for 0.4 mile, and the destination will be on the right. GPS: N 41 33' 41.778" / W 81 22' 2.3736"

The Hike

Driving into Geauga Park District's Orchard Hills Park, you'll immediately sense openness unlike any other hike in the book. And after hiking to the McIntosh/Harvest Trail junction just 0.1 mile into your hike, you'll get a clue of the property's former life as a golf course from the layout of the landscape.

Hiking northwest on the crushed gravel of the McIntosh Trail, you'll quickly be lost in an expanse of greenery and apple orchards. (Note the apples are the property of Patterson Farm. As the Soup Nazi would say, *No apple for you!*) Considering restoration plans only kicked off in 2010, you'll be impressed with the park's immense vegetation. But you'll never come into dense woodland like in a majority of this book's hikes. Instead you'll be in for a leisurely stroll, hardly dropping a bead of sweat along the way.

Just under 1.5 miles into the hike, right after passing a fishermen's pond, McIntosh will turn into the paved Harvest Trail to loop around the southern and eastern

Jarret marches on alongside the impressive natural growth that has taken hold since Orchard Hills ceased operating as a golf course.

ends of Orchard Hills. You can stay on flat land by keeping left on Harvest as the trail bends north, but hiking uphill to Patterson Fruit Farm offers an interesting, quick glimpse at their operation. The hike through headquarters is brief before you pick the trail back up again to hike downhill toward the Cricket Trail once again. As you hike downhill you'll notice you can see the Orchard Hills Lodge and parking lot, meaning you can easily get back to the car regardless of which of the two remaining trail options you take.

For today, take the first left off your downhill hike to take the Cricket Trail northwest and connect with the Sedge Trail. This will quickly take you over a small bridge that spans across a Chagrin River tributary before dumping you back at the parking lot.

Thanks for this relaxing jaunt goes to—as you might have guessed—the Patterson family, who has managed the property for five generations and built the original golf course in 1962. After the course closed in January 2007, the Pattersons altruistically

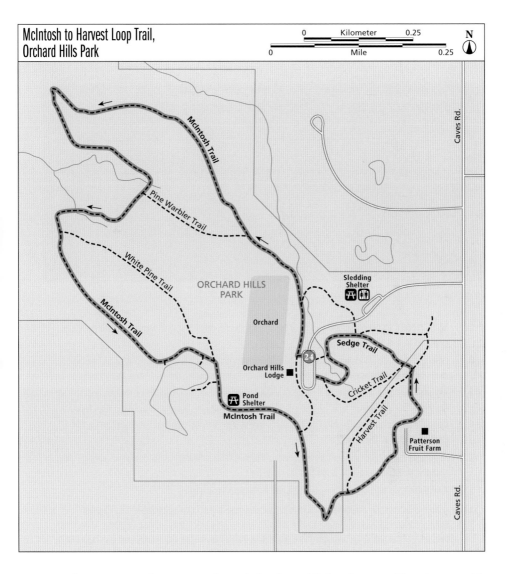

0   Kilometer   0.25

0   Mile   0.25

N

McIntosh Trail

Pine Warbler Trail

White Pine Trail

McIntosh Trail

ORCHARD HILLS
PARK

Orchard

Sledding
Shelter

Caves Rd.

Sedge Trail

Orchard Hills
Lodge

Cricket Trail

Pond
Shelter

McIntosh Trail

Harvest Trail

Patterson
Fruit Farm

Caves Rd.

agreed to permanently preserve the park for the public's enjoyment. Teaming up with the Western Reserve Land Conservancy and, of course, Geauga Park District, the Pattersons did just that. Now you may have an apple.

Miles and Directions

0.0 Start on the paved Cricket Trail right along the western edge of the parking lot and in front of Orchard Hills Lodge. Hike north toward the McIntosh Trail junction next to a small pond.

0.1 Keep left to hike north onto the paved, 1.6-mile McIntosh Trail. You'll quickly be lost in an expanse of greenery and apple orchards.

Wide view of Orchard Hills Park

0.7 Stay straight to continue on the McIntosh Trail, hiking southwest. **Bailout:** Turn left (southeast) onto the Pine Warbler Trail.

0.9 Ignore the White Pine Trail junction and continue hiking south on McIntosh. The trail will soon bend southeast.

1.2 After hiking past a couple of fishing platforms on a small pond, you'll turn right (south) to continue on McIntosh. Just under 1.5 mile into the hike, right after passing a fishermen's pond, McIntosh will turn into the paved Harvest Trail to loop around the southern and eastern ends of Orchard Hills.

1.4 McIntosh turns into paved trail as it loops back to the parking lot. To continue hiking, stay straight (south) to merge onto the Harvest Trail.

1.5 Turn right to hike northeast uphill toward Patterson Fruit Farm.

1.6 Arrive at Patterson Fruit Farm. Hike along the western end of the property north past Orchard Hills Café. Here you'll find a sign directing you back toward the Orchard Hills main entrance. This will take you onto downhill trail, hiking north. At the bottom of the downhill, bear left to take the Cricket Trail to the parking lot. You should see it easily now on your left (west).

1.8 Take another left (west) onto the Sedge Trail, following the trail south over a small bridge that will dump you on the eastern end of the parking lot.

2.0 End your hike at the Orchard Hills parking lot.

Hike Information

Hike Tours

Cleveland Hiking Club; www.clevelandhikingclub.org
Geauga Park District; www.geaugaparkdistrict.org; (440) 286-9516
NEOHiking; www.meetup.com/NEOHiking

25 Big Creek Circuit Trails

Scenic Big Creek Park comprises 642 wooded acres in Chardon Township. A 6.4-mile network of trail loops surround picnic and parking areas with designated cross-country skiing trails that make Big Creek a year-round destination. Keep an eye out for the Buckeye Trail, which cuts through the entire park north-to-south.

Start: Deep Woods parking lot
Distance: 3.3 miles
Approximate hiking time: 1 hour
Difficulty: Moderate with some hills
Trail surface: Packed gravel
Best season: Year-round
Other trail users: Birders
Canine compatibility: Yes, but please pick up after your dog, and must be leashed
Land status: Public
Fees and permits: None
Schedule: N/A
Maps: www.geaugaparkdistrict.org/documents/bigcreek.pdf

Trail contacts: Geauga Park District; www.geaugaparkdistrict.org; (440) 286-9516
Finding the trailhead: Drive east from Cleveland for approximately 11 miles on OH 2 East as it merges with I-90 East. Keep right to stay on I-90 E for 15.5 miles, following signs for I-271 South. Take exit 200 for OH 44 toward Chardon/Painesville. Turn left onto OH 44 South for 3 miles, then left onto Clark Road for 1.8 miles. Turn right onto Robinson Road, and the destination will be on your right in 0.8 mile. GPS: N 41 37' 8.4252" / W 81 12' 23.1804"

The Hike

Big Creek includes several short trails, but it's possible (not to mention easy) to combine them all for a satisfying hike filled with dense forest, winding trails, and ravines. You'll begin from the southernmost parking lot to pick up the 0.3-mile Deep Woods Trail—one of Big Creek's cross-country-friendly trails. This trailhead sits behind a playground adjacent to the Deep Woods Shelter next to the Wildflower Trail. Completing the brief Deep Woods Trail will take you back behind the adjacent shelter, and you'll simply return to the playground to start the Wildflower Trail.

The Wildflower Trail, as its name implies, is one of the best spring wildflower trails in the park. It is essentially a connector to the mile-long Hemlock Trail, which forms a loop around the southern end of the park. As the trail starts to turn north, you'll find the trail combines with the Buckeye Trail as blue blazes cover trees lining the trail. Ignore the trail continuing straight. This is where you'll return from at the end of your hike. Instead you'll turn right to take the Beechwoods Trail toward the Ruth Kennan Trail east. (If you need to bail out, you can always simply finish the Hemlock Trail.)

After wrapping around the handicapped-accessible Ruth Kennan Trail, you'll follow the 0.1-mile-long Cascade Trail north through the Aspen Grove parking lot to reach the Trillium Trail. Stay straight to hike alongside Aspen Grove, one of the park's

Tall grass and wildflowers surround the Lincoln Cascade.

two fishermen-friendly ponds. This will take you along a ridge above one of Big Creek's tributaries as you hike your way north toward Maple Grove. At the northernmost point of the Trillium Trail, you'll find a connector trail that leads north to the Maple Grove picnic area parking lot. Take it to head toward the White Oak Trail, which is another cross-country skiing trail in the winter. As you finish the loop north, you'll find a junction for the Buckeye Trail that leads you through the camping area. While it may be tempting, it's best to finish the White Oak Trail unless you want to find yourself miles away from your trailhead. Leave that for another day's adventure or reserve a lean-to or tent pad and stay overnight.

Once you finish the White Oak Trail loop, you'll backtrack south to reconnect with the Trillium Trail and hike the western leg of this loop. Continue hiking your way west (including the 0.1-mile Boreal Trail that loops off and back to Trillium), and you'll return to the parking lot where you left the Beechwoods/Buckeye Trail. Follow this trail due south until you return to the aforementioned Beechwoods and Hemlock junction. Now you'll simply turn right to finish the Hemlock Trail and reemerge to your parking lot from the southwest.

THANK YOU, MR. MATHER

Samuel Livingston Mather is the man we get to thank for today's Big Creek Park. In 1926, Mr. Mather purchased nearly 1,000 acres of Chardon Township land in hopes of creating an affluent resort—not entirely unlike Mr. Rockefeller's original ambitions with Forest Hill (Hike 6).

Unfortunately for Mather (not to mention the entirety of the United States), the Great Depression put a halt to his plans. Instead, Mather donated 505 acres of the land to the State of Ohio in 1955, which was later leased to the Geauga Park District in 1965. Later additions brought the total acreage to 624, and in 1990 the State of Ohio officially transferred ownership of Big Creek Park to the Geauga Park District.

In reality, we have the Great Depression to thank for crushing Mather's dreams and instead giving us Big Creek Park. But because it's rather odd to be thankful for the worst economic catastrophe in our nation's history, we instead give full credit to Samuel Livingston Mather.

Connecting all of these trails may seem like a task in and of itself. If that's ever the case, feel free to wander around and enjoy these trails as you see fit. You won't want to miss this area rich with beech and maple woods, spring flowers, and songbirds that migrate here from the tropics.

Miles and Directions

0.0 Start hiking north from the northern end of the parking lot. Bear left at the Deep Woods Shelter, hiking northeast past a small playground with two different trail entrances side-by-side. For now, you'll take the one on the right to hike north into the woods on the Deep Woods Trail.

0.1 Stay straight to hike north on a short out-and-back leg of the Deep Woods Trail. You'll return here shortly to finish the short loop.

0.2 Arrive at a picnic table under a shelter and at an overlook bench at the end of the out-and-back. Backtrack to 0.1 where you'll turn left (east) to finish the small loop back at the playground.

0.3 You'll emerge from the woods next to the Deep Woods shelter. Hike through the picnic area very briefly to find the playground and Deep Woods Trailhead once again. This time you'll hike west on the Wildflower Trail to the immediate left of the Deep Woods Trail.

0.6 Turn right (west) down a light slope onto the Hemlock Trail. A short side trail after crossing the bridge will take you down to Big Creek, the park's namesake.

1.0 Pass a service road that might look like a trail to some. Continue hiking north on the Hemlock Trail until you reach the Beechwoods Trail. After the service road, you'll start to notice the blue blazes of the Buckeye Trail.

1.1 Turn right (east) onto Beechwoods. You'll return to this junction at the end of your hike.

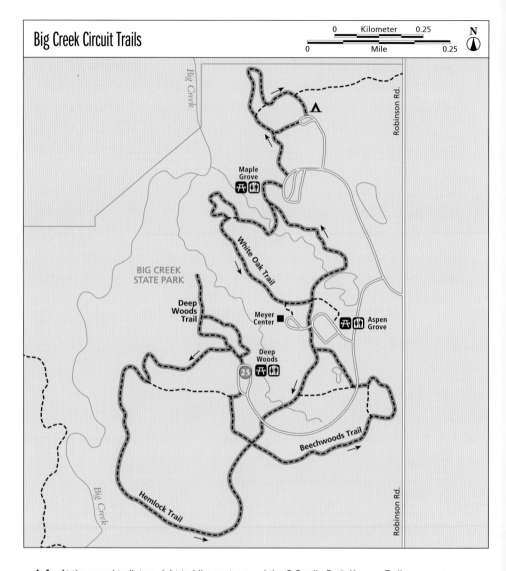

0   Kilometer   0.25

0   Mile   0.25

N

1.4 At the paved trail, turn right to hike east around the 0.2-mile Ruth Kennan Trail.

1.5 Take the first exit off Ruth Kennan by turning right (west). Hike across the driveway you drove in on and you'll find a trail marker for the paved Cascade Trail. This will lead to a bridge over Linton Cascade pond, a small body of water covered in lily pads with the sound of frogs croaking. Within this 0.1 mile you'll come to the Aspen Grove parking lot. Turn left (west) to stay on the Cascade Trail. You'll notice the Beechwoods/Buckeye Trail south of you. For now, continue hiking on Cascade as it wraps north around the parking lot to the Donald W. Meyer Center on the northwest corner of the parking lot.

1.7 After passing the paved walkway to the Meyer Center, you'll take a dirt trail north around the amphitheater toward the Trillium Trail. Continue hiking straight (north) when you reach the 0.7-mile Trillium loop.

Short bridge crossing over a dry creek

1.9 Turn right (north) onto a connector trail for the Maple Grove parking lot. Hike through the parking lot due north for the White Oak Trail.

2.1 Keep left on White Oak to continue hiking north, ignoring the campground connector on your right. You'll come to another junction in less than 0.1 mile that you'll ignore for now. Continue hiking north.

2.2 Turn left (northeast) toward some shelters. You've now technically left White Oak for the Buckeye Trail, but only briefly until you turn right (south) onto grassy trail to reconnect with White Oak.

2.3 At the gravel parking lot, turn right (west) onto a leg of the White Oak Trail you previously passed. Follow this trail briefly until you can turn left (south) and backtrack to where you left the Trillium Trail.

2.5 Back at the Trillium Trail, turn right (northwest). Soon you'll come to stairs that guide you down a switchback and across a bridge on your left (south).

2.7 Turn right (north) onto the 0.1-mile Boreal Trail. This will loop north-to-south and reconnect with the Trillium Trail.

2.8 Again at the Trillium Trail, turn right to continue hiking the trail as it winds southeast.

3.0 Turn right (south) to hike through the Donald Meyer Center parking lot to backtrack the Cascade Trail to the Beechwoods/Buckeye Trail.

3.1 Leave the paved Cascade Trail to turn right (south) onto the gravel-covered Beechwoods/ Buckeye Trail. You'll hike downhill briefly before crossing a Big Creek tributary and your parking lot's driveway. Continue hiking south on this trail until you return to an earlier junction with the Hemlock Trail.

3.3 Turn right (west) onto the Hemlock Trail. In less than 0.1 mile, the trail will bend north to guide you to the southern end of the Deep Woods parking lot to end your hike.

26 Whitetail to Lake to Beechnut Trails, Beartown Lakes Reservation

East Side runners and hikers love Beartown Lakes for the reservation's fast trails that glide throughout its 149 acres and around 22 acres of open water. Nestled between Auburn and Bainbridge Townships with beech-maple woods offering a respite from the antagonizing sun, Beartown Lakes is a perfect summer retreat. Come back when the snow falls for sledding near Lower Bear Lake.

Start: At the Whitetail trailhead
Distance: 2 miles
Approximate hiking time: 45 minutes
Difficulty: Easy
Trail surface: Crushed limestone
Best season: Year-round
Other trail users: None
Canine compatibility: Yes, but please pick up after your dog, and must be leashed
Land status: Public
Fees and permits: None
Schedule: N/A
Maps: www.geaugaparkdistrict.org/parks/beartown.shtml

Trail contacts: Geauga Park District; www.geaugaparkdistrict.org; (440) 286-9516
Finding the trailhead: Drive south from Cleveland on I-77 just over 7 miles. Take exit 156 for I-480 East toward Youngstown for 8.6 miles. Continue onto US 422 East for 9.1 miles. Take the OH 306 exit toward Bainbridge Road/Chagrin Road and turn right onto OH 306 South/Chillicothe Road for 1.2 miles. Turn left onto Taylor May Road. In 2.7 miles, turn right onto Quinn Road, and the destination will be on the right in 1.5 miles. GPS: N 41 21' 18.1398" / W 81 17' 45.9594"

The Hike

Beartown Lakes Reservation's park map and trails are incredibly easy to navigate. You'll find a trailhead at the northern end of the parking lot, hiking north into the woods on gravel trail. Soon you'll split to the left for a windy hike on the Whitetail Trail, Beartown Lakes Reservation's longest trail at 1.5 miles.

Your initial woodsy hike will quickly be interrupted by a brief jaunt past a sledding hill before submerging once again into the woods, the trail now natural and dirt covered. Whitetail will then take you over a tributary of the adjacent Spring Creek as you wind south on flat, easy trail. Nothing takes long at Beartown, so suffice it to say you'll be at the southwestern corner of Lower Bear Lake just as you were starting to reach a Zen state of mind on Whitetail.

Whitetail ends as it pushes you out onto the paved Lake Trail that runs around Lower Bear Lake. This will be your first chance to truly admire one of the reservation's three lakes, teeming with amphibian and reptile favorites like frogs, water snakes, and turtles. Birds such as the great blue heron and green heron use Lower Bear Lake as a feeding area because of the tasty bass and bluegills that swim below. Lower Bear Lake is also a migratory stop-over for hungry ducks and geese.

The Whitetail Trail merges onto the Lake Trail at the southwestern corner of Lower Bear Lake— one of three lakes at the property that indeed used to harbor bears.

ARE BEARS AFOOT?

A name like "Beartown Lakes" lends itself to an obvious question. Are there bears? Once upon a time, the answer was yes.

David McConughey and his family were the first to settle Bainbridge Township in 1811. A man by the name of Robert Smith soon followed with his family. Together, they cleared tracts of land and built log cabins in the spot we now call Beartown Lakes Reservation. Wolves, deer, and elk were plentiful in the region. And of course, bears.

The story goes that one of McConughey's sons harvested five bears in one day. The impressive abundance of bears in the region naturally led to naming the area Beartown.

But more important, one has to wonder why there is no monumental statue to a man who harvested *five* bears in one day. Can you imagine being that guy's brother, and following that story when Mom asks how your day was? Now we know who should star opposite Sylvester Stallone if Rocky Balboa ever takes to time travel.

Whitetail to Lake to Beechnut Trails, Beartown Lakes Reservation

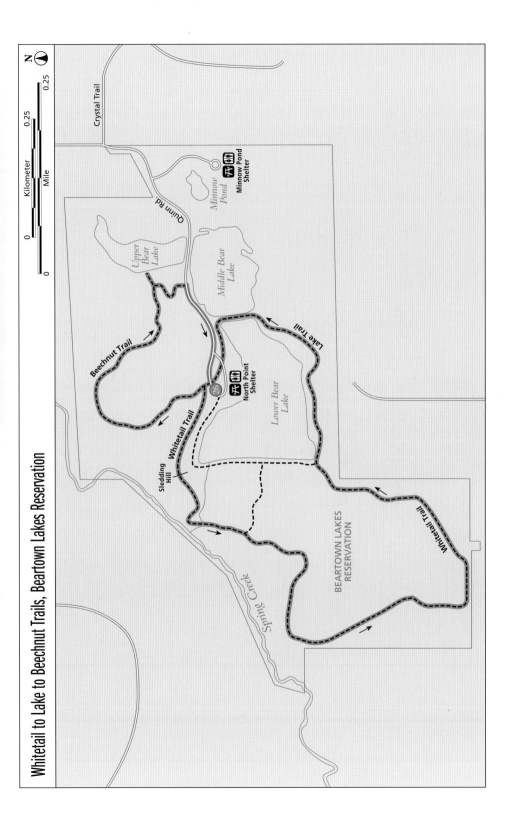

Melanie gets ahead of the hike.

You'll then continue east over a nearby wooden bridge that takes you back into the woods, albeit very briefly before you reemerge between Lower Bear and Middle Bear Lakes. One of the reservation's three fishing platforms sits just north of you.

Following the Lake Trail will take you back to the start, where you could very well end your hike. But you can also head back to your trailhead and stay north to hike the 0.6-mile Beechnut Trail for a taste of the reservation's wildflowers, large trees, and wetlands. This brief northern loop also connects you to some secluded views of Upper Bear Lake with a park bench calling out to you for relaxation.

Beechnut ends at the park road, so simply hike west along the road back to the parking lot. Looking for more? You can hike the entirety of the 0.7-mile Lake Trail loop around Lower Bear Lake if you're itching to take in every last foot of trail the park has to offer.

Miles and Directions

0.0 Start by hiking north into the woods off the parking lot. The trail will quickly split between Whitetail Trail and Beechnut Trail. To begin, keep left (west) to hike Whitetail. You'll return here later to hike Beechnut.

0.2 Cross a tributary of nearby Spring Creek and continue your hike south.

0.3 Ignore the connector trail on your left that leads due east to the Lake Trail. Continue hiking for the southern loop of the Whitetail Trail. Follow this loop for the next 0.7 mile when you'll be guided out of the woods to the southwestern corner of Lower Bear Lake next to a wooden bridge.

1.0 Arrive at the southwestern corner of Lower Bear Lake. Turn right (east) over the bridge to hike back into the woods onto the paved Lake Trail.

1.2 The Lake Trail winds north, still paved, splitting in between Lower Bear Lake and Middle Bear Lake.

1.3 Turn left (west) back toward the parking lot and the trailhead where you started. **Option:** You can end your hike once you arrive back at the parking lot.

1.4 Back at the first junction, continue hiking north this time to take the Beechnut Trail.

1.7 A short out-and-back leads to a view of Upper Bear Lake with a park bench for rest. When you're done, continue hiking south on Beechnut.

1.8 Arrive at the park driveway and turn right (west) for a 0.2-mile hike back to the parking lot.

2.0 End your hike. **Option:** For another 0.7 miles, you can hike just the Lake Trail around Lower Bear Lake. But this will cover some previously explored terrain.

Hike Information

Hike Tours

Cleveland Hiking Club; www.clevelandhikingclub.org
NEOHiking; www.meetup.com/NEOHiking

Summit County

Many of the hikes in northern Summit County include hills, rocky outcroppings, waterfalls, and ravines. Metro Parks, Serving Summit County manages three of these hikes with the City of Stow looking after the jaunt around Adell Durbin Park & Arboretum and the City of Hudson taking care of the serene trail around Hudson Springs Lake.

Sand Run Stream will grab your attention as you cross along the Mingo Trail in the appropriately named Sand Run Metro Park. ROBERT ANDRUKAT

27 Adam Run Loop Trail, Hampton Hills Metro Park

Adam Run makes for an easy, scenic loop on a well-marked trail through ravines and a number of other streams that were created more than 10,000 years ago when glaciers retreated from Northern Ohio. Black walnut, elm, oak, and sycamore trees offer a habitat for the area's bird and wildlife population. But your senses will most enjoy the scent of white pine, planted nearly 50 years ago by the Girl Scouts.

Start: Main entrance on Akron-Peninsula Road
Distance: 3.2 miles
Approximate hiking time: 1.5 hours
Difficulty: Easy
Trail surface: Rough forested trail
Best season: Any heavy spring rains may close the trail due to washouts.
Other trail users: Hikers and runners only
Canine compatibility: On a leash (8-foot max)
Land status: Public
Fees and permits: None for individuals and families; a Special-Use Permit may be required for large/organized hiking groups
Schedule: Daily 6 a.m.–11 p.m.

Maps: www.summitmetroparks.org or the free Metro Parks mobile app
Trail contacts: (330) 867-5511 or www.summitmetroparks.org
Finding the trailhead: Drive south on I-77 for almost 20 miles before taking exit 143 for OH 176. Turn left onto Wheatley Road for approximately 3 miles and then a slight left onto Everett Road for 0.6 mile. Take a right onto Riverview Road for 1.7 miles and another left onto Ira Road for just 0.3 mile. Finally, turn right onto Akron Peninsula Road, and the destination will be on the left in 1.2 miles. GPS: N 41 10' 0.9948" / W 81 34' 0.9048"

The Hike

Adam Run is a great introduction to the fine work of Metro Parks, Serving Summit County. What you'll notice early on is how well marked the trails are. You would have to make a special effort to get lost here.

Hampton Hills Metro Park is simple. There are just two trails—Adam Run and Spring Hollow. Together the trails form a figure eight. Both are loops with Spring Hollow cutting the longer Adam Run loop in half for a 1.6-mile hike. Being the face of fitness and adventure that you surely are, you are of course going to take on the 3.2-mile Adam Run for a more substantial hike and to see more of the beauty that is Hampton Hills.

From the parking lot you'll be greeted by a large Metro Parks sign at the trailhead directing you east onto the forested trail. The trail itself is flat and manageable for most hikers with the occasional bridge showing up to help you over one of the many streams in the park. Metro Parks notes that an unusual plant called rush lines the banks of the streams that run alongside Adam Run Valley.

The trails inside the Hampton Hills Metro Park COURTESY OF SUMMIT METROPARKS

Adam Run Loop Trail, Hampton Hills Metro Park

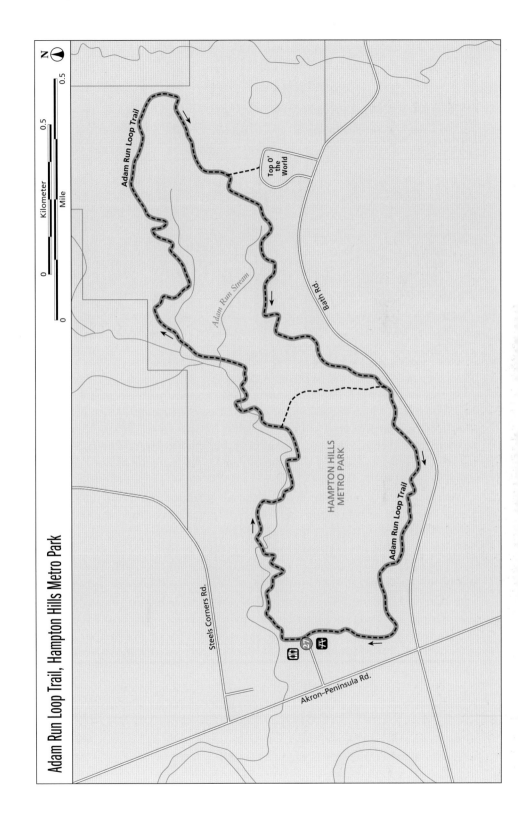

Adam Loop Trail in the thick of the fall season COURTESY OF SUMMIT METROPARKS

Black walnut, elm, oak, and sycamore trees largely make up the tree life in the area, offering homes to birds and other wildlife. But a personal favorite is the smell of white pines that were planted by Girl Scouts in the late 1960s. Who doesn't love the smell of pine? Indeed, the Girl Scouts deserve the gratitude of our happy and satisfied nostrils.

Also deserving of our gratitude are Rhea and Reginald Adam, who donated 162 acres of farmland to help create the 278-acre Hampton Hills Park, also in the late 1960s. Hampton Hills has since stretched its grasp to 655 acres after signing a lease in 2010 for the adjacent Hardy Road landfill.

Remember as you're hiking to ignore the junction for Spring Hollow. This will shorten your hike in half, and you're going to want to soak in every last second of your time in Hampton Hills. And thanks to the aforementioned simplicity of the park's layout, you won't encounter but two more junctions—one for the Top O' the World overlook and the other being the opposite end of Spring Hollow as it reconnects with Adam Run. When you're done, the trail will conveniently dump you right back to your parking lot.

If you're like most hikers, chances are you'll be itching to do this trail again. Another fun way to experience Adam Run would be to strap on a pair of trail running shoes and go for a run. Chances are you will see Akron-area runners of all ages using the smooth trail for their workout. As the name of the trail implies, Adam Run does indeed make for a fun trail run in addition to a hike.

Miles and Directions

0.0 Start from the trailhead at a Metro Parks sign at northeastern edge of the parking lot. Hike into the woods and you'll immediately come to a sign directing you to stay left for the Adam Run Loop and Spring Hollow Trails heading east.

0.8 You'll come to the Spring Hollow divide junction. Continue straight on Adam's Run heading northeast for the longer loop. **Option:** Turn right (southeast) to complete the shorter Spring Hollow Trail.

0.6 Turn right (west) away from the Top O' The World sign to continue hiking on Adam Run back toward the parking lot. You'll follow this trail hiking southwest for the remainder of the hike.

3.2 Return to the trailhead and parking lot where you started your hike.

Hike Information

Local Information

Top O' the World entrance on Bath Road is closed during winter and the rainy season in spring.

28 Dogwood to Mingo Trail Loop, Sand Run Metro Park

Ravines are plentiful in this scenic gem nestled in the heart of Summit County's Sand Run Metro Park. Moderate, occasionally rough, terrain encompasses a majority of this hike's trail, surrounded by a laundry list of plant and animal life. And despite the trail's proximity to suburban and urban life, much of the hike feels as if you've traveled a wormhole to a prehistoric time. But don't worry, this isn't Jurassic Park and a Tyrannosaurus rex will not pluck you out of a restroom.

Start: Trail begins on western end of the Shadow Field Area
Distance: 4.4-mile loop
Approximate hiking time: 2 hours
Difficulty: Moderate with steep and rough terrain
Trail surface: Rough forested trail
Best season: Year-round
Other trail users: Hikers and runners only
Canine compatibility: On a leash (8-foot max)
Land status: Public
Fees and permits: None for individuals and families; a Special-Use Permit may be required for large/organized hiking groups
Schedule: Open daily 6 a.m.–11 p.m.

Maps: www.summitmetroparks.org
Trail contacts: Metro Parks, Serving Summit County; (330) 867-5511; www.summitmetro parks.org
Finding the trailhead: Drive south on I-77 for 25 miles. Take exit 138 for Ghent Road, keeping right at the fork in the road. In 1.5 miles, turn left onto Smith Road for another 1.5 miles before turning right onto Sand Run Road. Take this for just 0.5 mile before taking the second left onto Sand Run Parkway, continuing east until the parking lot on the right in approximately 1.7 miles. GPS: N 41 8' 2.3784" / W 81 33' 34.9272"

The Hike

You'll kick things off hiking west across the Shadow Field Area into the woods, where you'll come up to restrooms and signage identifying the trails. You'll want to start on Dogwood Trail, heading west to hike the southern portion of the loop. The trails here are forested and manageable for most hikers. More than anything, it's a scenic hike through relatively dense forest covered in wildflowers throughout the spring and summer. If you're looking for a challenge, Metro Parks encourages hikers to keep an eye out for the numerous plants and animals that call Sand Run home. You name it—oaks, tuliptrees, American beeches, hemlocks, ferns, woodpeckers, and owls and squirrels of nearly every stripe. Best of all, you're unlikely to hike far before seeing ravine after ravine after ravine. It's a photographer's nirvana.

As you continue through Sand Run Metro Park, hiking southeast, you'll eventually come out of the woods onto the Hawkins Area soccer field with a parking lot on your left, due south. Here's where it's easy to get a little confused, because it's not readily apparent that you're supposed to hike across the soccer field due west. Rest

Crossing the scenic ford on Sand Run Stream, a tributary of the Cuyahoga River.
ROBERT ANDRUKAT

assured, you'll find posts on the opposite side of the field if you remain steadfast. Worst-case scenario is you'll run into one of the very friendly members of the park staff, ready and willing to point you in the right direction.

By the way, it's worth repeating that the helping hands of Metro Parks at Sand Run are some of the kindest park staffers you're bound to hike past. Nearly everyone is ready to offer a wave and a smile, adding an additional element of positivity that nature—as lovely and awe-inspiring as she is—simply cannot provide, unless, of course, you're with Bambi and his singing animal friends.

After hiking back into the forest, you'll continue hiking northwest toward Sand Run Parkway until you see Shady Hollow Pavilion, a beautifully constructed, maroon-colored cabin. Work your way down around the cabin, taking a set of wooden stairs to continue hiking west alongside Sand Run Parkway until you cross the road heading north on Mingo Trail about a mile away. Crossing the ravine here will offer perhaps your best opportunity at a scenic photograph if you're feeling artsy. Otherwise,

GENERAL WADSWORTH

During the Revolutionary War Ohio was still considered the Wild West, but the Buckeye State did play an integral role in the largely underappreciated War of 1812. Ohio's role in the Battle of Lake Erie—a United States Navy victory that ensured control of the lake—is well remembered, despite being a blip in the radar of American history. The glory (and artistic renderings, naturally) went to Commodore Oliver Hazard Perry.

Meanwhile, Brigadier General William Wadsworth—a sixth generation descendant of one of the founders of Hartford, Connecticut—was doing his part to protect Western New York and the Niagara River from the British. During the war, Wadsworth had camped in what is now Sand Run Metro Park, and his former campsite is now known as the Wadsworth Area and Shelter just off Dogwood Trail.

Wadsworth's most famous battle was the Battle of Queenston Heights near Niagara Falls. Though he faced his enemy bravely, refusing to show his back to the enemy in the event he was shot and would appear cowardly, Wadsworth perhaps could have used a little more rest and relaxation alongside the ravines of Sand Run. The battle was lost on October 13, 1812, and the British took Wadsworth prisoner.

continue along Mingo until you're reconnected with the northern portion of Dogwood, just past the crushed limestone Jogging Trail. This final stretch, about a mile or a little less, will take you right back to the parking lot where you started, ending the loop.

Miles and Directions

0.0 Hike south toward a Metro Parks sign and Wadsworth Shelter. Continue west across Shadow Field toward a sign indicating trailheads for the Dogwood and Mingo Trails. You'll come to restrooms and a post with trail indicators. Turn left (south) to begin the Dogwood Trail. Now stay right to go uphill and continue on Dogwood.

0.8 Trail opens to a soccer field heading west with a parking lot to the south. Continue across the middle of the field or follow signs around the northern edge to the other side where the Dogwood Trail continues downhill.

1.5 After hiking east along a downhill, you'll come to Shady Hollow Pavilion where you'll begin the Mingo Trail. Continue over the wooden bridge and climb the adjacent stairs heading north.

1.8 Cross a wooden bridge after a small stream and bear left, heading west. You'll come to a steep climb in about 50 feet that lasts about another 50 feet, if not slightly more.

2.5 Continue across another wooden bridge over a stream, and hike north past Sand Run Parkway back into the woods where a steep climb awaits. After hiking uphill, you'll be

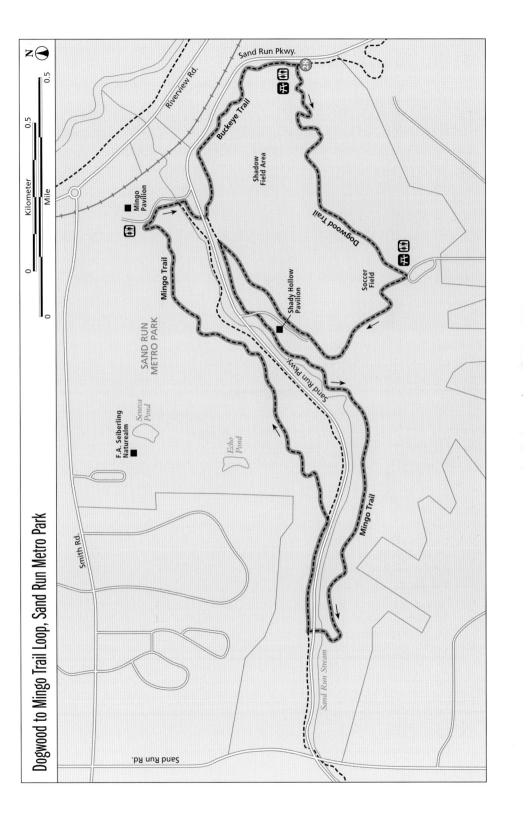

Dogwood to Mingo Trail Loop, Sand Run Metro Park

Smith Rd.

Sand Run Rd.

Riverview Rd.

Sand Run Pkwy.

SAND RUN METRO PARK

F.A. Seiberling Naturealm

Seneca Pond

Echo Pond

Mingo Pavilion

Mingo Trail

Buckeye Trail

Shadow Field Area

Dogwood Trail

Shady Hollow Pavilion

Soccer Field

Sand Run Pkwy

Mingo Trail

Sand Run Stream

28

N

Kilometer

Mile

0.5

0.5

0

about 100 feet above Sand Run Parkway, hiking parallel to the road and heading east back toward the start of the hike.

3.7 You'll approach a park driveway. Take this briefly, hiking southeast toward the Sand Run Metro Parks entrance.

3.9 The driveway will turn into a bridge, crossing a stream toward a small waterfall. On the other side of the stream, you'll find a sign for the Mingo Trail. Continue following the sign.

4.0 Continue across the street. Turn left (east) for a 200-foot or so climb uphill.

4.4 Turn away from Sand Run Parkway to the right (south), and you'll find the parking lot you started from due south.

Hike Information

Local Information

The vehicle ford on **Sand Run Parkway** may be closed after heavy rainfall.

Local Events/Attractions

The **F. A. Seiberling Nature Realm** visitor center is located nearby at 1828 Smith Road, Akron.

GREEN TIP
**Pack out what you pack in; even food scraps
can attract wild animals.**

29 Hudson Springs Park Loop Trail

This is an easy, pleasant hike on smooth gravel and dirt trail around a 50-acre lake, winding in and out of woods along soft, rolling hills. Scenic views and wildlife sighting opportunities await you on this fast, 2.1-mile hike in Hudson.

Start: Trailhead is in the southern end of the parking lot.
Distance: 2.2 miles
Approximate hiking time: 45 minutes
Difficulty: Easy
Trail surface: Crushed limestone
Best season: Year-round
Other trail users: Bicycles
Canine compatibility: Allowed on leash; pick up waste—waste bags provided at trailhead
Land status: Public
Fees and permits: Non-residents pay to fish
Schedule: Dawn to dusk, 365 days
Maps: www.hudson.oh.us

Trail contacts: Hudson Park Office; (330) 653-5201
Finding the trailhead: Drive on I-77 heading south from Cleveland for about 6.4 miles. Take exit 156 to merge onto I-480 driving east toward Youngstown for a little over 21 miles. Then, take exit 41 toward Frost Road for a short drive. Turn right onto Aurora Hudson Road. In less than a mile, the road will turn into Hudson Aurora Road. One mile later, turn left onto Stow Road. The park entrance will be on your left in less than a mile. GPS: N 41 15' 5.0898" / W 81 24' 27.8424"

The Hike

Hudson Springs Park is in a world of its own as far as the best hikes near Cleveland go. Seriously. It's not part of any metro, state, or national park system like the other thirty-nine in this book. Hudson Springs is a quaint City of Hudson park that is best known for its eighteen-basket disc golf course and wildlife sighting opportunities, including ducks, geese, fox, deer, heron, owls, and hawks. But that doesn't mean there aren't worthy trails to explore with scenic lake views. There most definitely are.

Arrive at Hudson Springs Park right off Stow Road, parking on the northwestern corner of the Hudson Springs Lake. More than 250 acres of parkland await you with a 50-acre lake at the center of it all. You'll see three picnic pavilions near the trailhead next to a kid's playground to the north. Kayaks and canoes rest near a small dock south of the parking lot near where you'll end your hike.

Start your hike on the smooth gravel trail heading north as the trail wraps around the northern end of the lake. Some of the best views will grab you early on.

Two trails make up Hudson Springs Park—red and yellow. The only difference between the two is that the yellow skips a half-loop into some northern woods early on in the hike. But because this hike is just a hair over 2 miles, you won't be burning too much extra gas for the brief excursion.

When you arrive at the red trail junction, you'll head north into the woods where you might catch some Frisbee golfers in action. Following the red trail, you'll wind

Peaceful Hudson Springs Lake is a popular fishing spot with blue gill, perch, trout, bass, carp, and catfish.

northeast to southeast where you'll reconnect with the yellow trail to continue hiking in the woods as you make your way around the eastern edge of Hudson Springs Lake. The terrain here can be a tad more rigorous with a few small hills thrown in, but nothing that will warrant a call to the paramedic. Before you know it, the trail will usher you back into the parking lot where you started your short journey, passing those small docks mentioned earlier on the right.

Though hardly a strenuous hike, this is by far one of the most community-oriented hikes in the Cleveland region. Meaning, you'll find many runners, frolfers (Frisbee golfers), and kayakers populating the area as soon as the temperature reaches a reasonable level. You'll also notice during your hike numerous, unmarked footpaths that connect the loop to the surrounding Hudson community. On the whole, this is what any city park should aspire to be.

Miles and Directions

0.0 Begin the yellow trail from the western point of the northernmost parking lot alongside Lake Erie. Hike west on the smooth gravel trail alongside the lake.

0.4 Turn left heading north to stay on the red trail, taking you away from the lake and into the woods.

0.5 You'll approach a junction. If you keep going straight, you'll be guided to an open field near the parking lot to the west. Instead, bear to the right (northeast). You'll hike past Frisbee golf equipment as you continue through the woods.

Hudson Springs Park Loop Trail

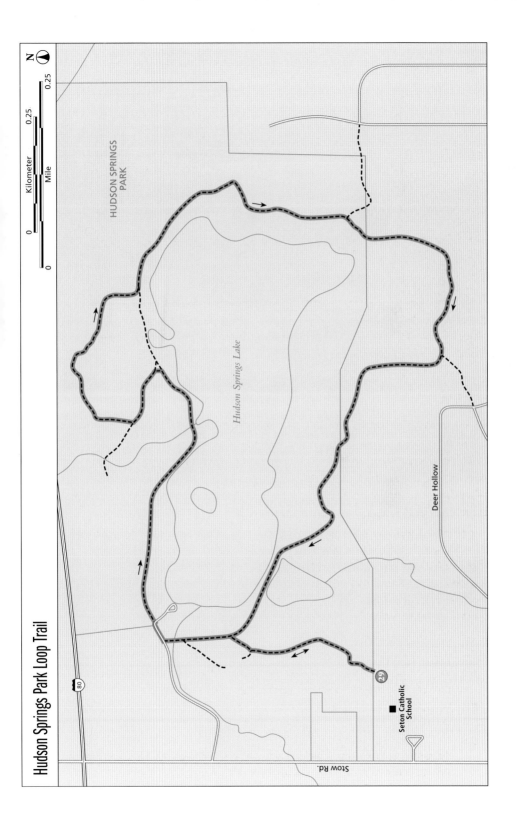

Kilometer
0   0.25

Mile
0   0.25

N

HUDSON SPRINGS
PARK

Hudson Springs Lake

Deer Hollow

Stow Rd.

80

29

Seton Catholic
School

Try coming back in the spring to see the Kathy Wolking Flower Bed in full bloom.

0.8 Now you'll reconnect with the yellow trail you started on, staying on the combined red and yellow trail for the remainder of the hike. Continue hiking southeast around the lake.

1.1 Turn right (south) to continue downhill alongside the lake. After the descent, you'll pass a sign announcing you've reached the midpoint of the hike.

1.4 Keep straight, bearing right (northwest) back toward the lake. A red arrow on a stump will help guide the way.

1.6 Approach an overlook of the Hudson Springs Lake on your right (north). It's a very short hike worth the detour to snap a few pictures.

2.2 Arrive back at the parking lot to end your hike.

Hike Information

Local Information

Downtown 140; (330) 655-2940; www.downtown140.com
Merchants of Hudson; www.merchantsofhudson.com

Hike Tours

Cleveland Hiking Club; www.clevelandhikingclub.org
NEOHiking; www.meetup.com/NEOHiking

30 Gorge Trail, Gorge Metro Park

The Gorge Trail provides access to the stunning Mary Campbell Cave before taking on a more rugged character. The primitive Class D Trail passes through incredible rock formations that will excite and impress anyone regardless of how poorly geology class went in high school. Finish with an easy hike along the Cuyahoga River and an overlook of the deafening Ohio Edison Dam.

Start: Main entrance on Front Street
Distance: 1.8 miles
Approximate hiking time: 45 minutes
Difficulty: Easy due to distance, but includes moderate terrain
Trail surface: Rough forested trail
Best season: Year-round
Other trail users: Hikers and runners only
Canine compatibility: On a leash (8-foot max)
Land status: Public
Fees and permits: None for individuals and families; a Special-Use Permit may be required for large/organized hiking groups
Schedule: Daily 6 a.m.–11 p.m.
Maps: www.summitmetroparks.org or the free Metro Parks mobile app

Trail contacts: (330) 867-5511 or www .summitmetroparks.org
Finding the trailhead: Drive south from Cleveland on I-77 for about 6.5 miles to merge onto I-480 East toward Youngstown. In 12.1 miles, keep left to continue on I-271 South for 3.4 miles. Take exit 18A on the left for OH 8 South toward Boston Heights/Akron. Merge onto OH 8 South for 12.5 miles. Take exit 4 for Howe Avenue/Cuyahoga Falls Avenue. Turn right onto East Cuyahoga Falls Avenue in 0.2 mile and a sharp right onto Front Street in another 0.4 mile. Destination will be on the left in 0.3 mile. GPS: N 41 7' 14.4156" / W 81 26' 36.5136"

The Hike

The Gorge Trail may be deceiving at first glimpse. Flat, crushed limestone cuts through the front of Gorge Metro Park as you leisurely stroll up to Mary Campbell Cave. This approximately 0.2-mile hike to the cave actually earns Class B status, which means folks with wheelchairs, walkers, canes, and strollers should have no problem. But after you're finished admiring Mary Campbell Cave and its oddly yet perfectly cut roof, hikers who continue west will find the trail quickly becomes more challenging.

What was originally flat and easy suddenly becomes rugged and littered with exposed roots and rocks. Things only become more interesting after you pass a light waterfall surrounded by lucky stones that would make for a perfect caveman's shower.

You'll then hike over a small bridge and onto rocky terrain that can prove tricky with even the slightest bit of condensation. These rocks become slippery in a hurry.

Farther up the way you'll find an easy bypass. Take it if you're looking for something more akin to the earlier Class B trail. But then you'd be missing out on some truly interesting rock formations that even someone who made fun of geology nerds in high school can appreciate.

The gorge of the Gorge Trail COURTESY OF SUMMIT METROPARKS

Hiking on the "difficult trail," you'll immediately find yourself towered by large boulders with the trail cutting in between. Anyone of size will have to duck and maybe even slightly contort his or her body to make it through tight corners. In fact, a trail marker sits in front of what first looks to be a small cave. Yes, you are supposed to hike through whatever this hole is and into the darkness.

The Gorge Trail post, squeezing in between the giant rock formations towering above
Courtesy of Summit Metroparks

Turns out it's actually not so bad, just a bit of squatting to hike yourself through the rock formations and uphill a bit. But it can definitely make for an awkward moment if you're hiking with a friend who is on the plumper side.

Hiking downhill on the difficult leg of Gorge Trail, you'll come to the other end of the "easy bypass." Careful you don't mistakenly hike right onto it or you'll find

WHOSE CAVE? MARY CAMPBELL'S CAVE!

Most Americans will recognize the names of famous European explorers throughout history, like Ferdinand Magellan or Sir Francis Drake. But who was the first white child to visit the wild frontier of the Western Reserve? Why that was Mary Campbell, of course.

Granted, Miss Campbell was a reluctant explorer. Captured in Pennsylvania by Delaware Indians in 1759, Campbell was taken to the present day cave of her name in Gorge Metro Park to become the first white child to explore unknown territory of the 18th century. She eventually settled with the tribe in a village on the banks of the Cuyahoga River before being released in 1764 after a treaty ended the French and Indian War.

Of course, there is an ongoing debate about the veracity of this story. So perhaps you're better off just enjoying the hike.

yourself back where you've already hiked. Take a sharp right after the downhill to take a series of wooden stairs down to the lower level of the Gorge Trail. Now all you have to do is hike due east once you reach the bottom of the staircase.

Hiking along, you'll start to get some of the best views of the Cuyahoga River south of you, and anyone with a decent pair of ears will notice the growing sound of a pounding waterfall. You'll even catch the occasional glimpse through the trees and brush lining the trail. But just 0.3 mile before you end the hike, you'll come to a perfect overlook of the thundering Ohio Edison Dam, powered by the Cuyahoga River. Simply put, the sound is deafening.

From here, it's just an easy jaunt back to the trailhead. Though you might be wishing the trail were longer—especially the difficult trail—you certainly won't be disappointed with this Metro Parks hike.

Miles and Directions

0.0 Start on gravel trail following the Metro Parks sign toward the Gorge Trail and Mary Campbell Cave, north. You'll quickly come to a split in the trail. Stay right (north) to hike the skinny loop counter-clockwise toward Mary Campbell Cave.

0.2 Ignore a series of wooden stairs to your left. This leads down to the lower portion of the Gorge Trail you'll hike on your return. Continue hiking on the upper level as the trail bends northwest toward the cave.

0.3 Arrive at Mary Campbell Cave. Continue west onto somewhat rocky trail as it runs slightly downhill.

0.6 Hike past an interesting rock formation with a light waterfall. Continue over the wooden bridge onto a mix of dirt and rocky trail. You'll then hike alongside a dilapidated chain link face before arriving at a split for an easy bypass. Stay right (due west) to hike the difficult trail.

Gorge Trail, Gorge Metro Park

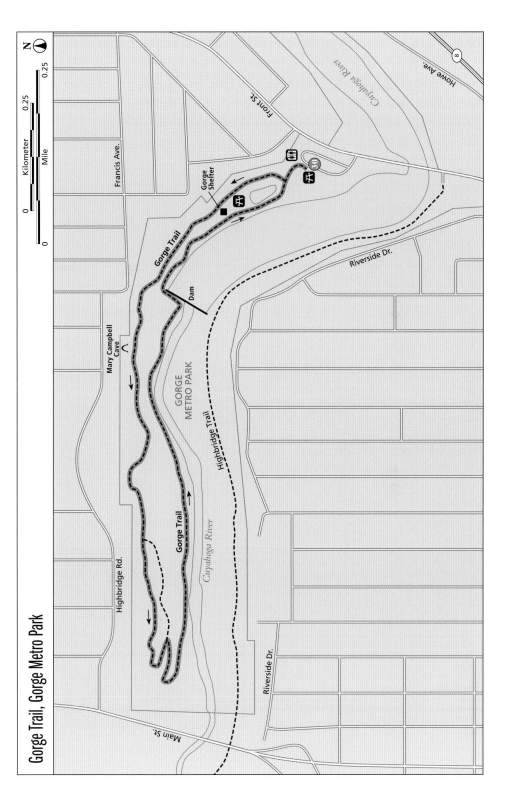

0.9 Take a sharp right (west) after hiking downhill to continue on the difficult trail toward a series of stairs. This will take you to the lower section of the Gorge Trail, turning you east once you reach the bottom. Follow this due east for the remainder of the hike. (Continuing straight at the junction will put you on the easy bypass, hiking back to where you've already been.)

1.4 Stay right (east) to hike downhill with wooden posts lining the trail on your right.

1.5 Arrive at an overlook of the dam. Afterward you'll continue on more wooden stairs that lead you north back to the trail.

1.6 Keep east on the crushed gravel trail.

1.7 The trail becomes paved as you hike by a fishing dock on the Cuyahoga River.

1.8 Arrive back at the trailhead to end your hike.

Hike Information

Local Information

Cuyahoga Falls Riverfront Square District; (330) 928–8230; www.fallsriver squaredistrict.com

31 Adell Durbin Park & Arboretum

Tiny Adell Durbin Park & Arboretum makes up for its size with a gorgeous wild-flower meadow and enjoyable hiking trails that make this Summit County picnic favorite worth the visit.

Start: All three trails begin at the small wooden kiosk located between Campbell Lodge and the Native American statue (west side of parking lot).
Distance: 1 mile
Approximate hiking time: 20 minutes
Difficulty: Easy
Trail surface: Grassy and natural terrain
Best season: Year-round
Other trail users: None
Canine compatibility: Dogs are not permitted.
Land status: Public
Fees and permits: None
Schedule: Park is open daily till dusk.

Maps: www.stow.oh.us
Trail contacts: Stow Parks & Recreation; (330) 689-5100; www.stow.oh.us
Finding the trailhead: From Cleveland, drive south on I-77 for about 6.5 miles. Take exit 156 to merge onto I-480 East for 12.1 miles. Keep left to continue on I-271 South for 3.4 miles. Take exit 18A on the left for OH 8 South for about 10.5 miles. Take the Graham Road exit and turn left onto Graham Road for 1.8 miles. Turn right onto Darrow Road. The destination will be on the right in 0.9 mile. GPS: N 41 9' 19.2378" / W 81 26' 27.6828"

The Hike

Just down the road from Gorge Metro Park, Adell Durbin Park & Arboretum makes for a nice add-on to the Gorge Trail. Or the arboretum is perfectly capable of standing on its own with incredibly beautiful wildflowers and a fun, albeit brief, woodland hike around the property. A small creek winds through the scenic gorge area beneath a comfortable observation deck. And near the wildflower meadow, a series of bluebird houses have been installed, which have re-introduced the scarce bird to the area.

You'll begin from the Campbell Lodge, following yellow trail markers south around the parking lot and toward tennis courts. The trail will squeeze in between the courts and Darrow Road before shooting due west in the arboretum of the park.

Here the trail can seem very undefined. But rest assured you'll continue to find yellow trail markers as you hike west past the Wildflower Meadow. Of course, you'll want to stop at the meadow first to enjoy a panoramic view of seemingly endless wildflowers. It may be tempting to jump in and do your best *Sound Of Music* run, but resist the urge. Instead, continue west where you'll eventually land in the woods for trail hiking.

Because there are few trails and options, you can just as easily make up your own route or wander around at your own pace without backtracking or inconveniencing yourself too much. A simple enough option is to follow the yellow trail as it bends

An overlook of the Adell Durbin Park & Arboretum wildflower meadow early on in the hike

south next to a residential property. This will loop back north where you'll hop on the red trail for the remainder of the hike.

This is the most rugged portion of the hike, but still easily conquerable by most standards. Before long—it is just a mile hike—the red trail will push you back out to Campbell Lodge where you started.

Interestingly enough, Campbell Lodge is named after Homer Campbell, who donated the park to the City of Stow in 1939. But if a lodge is named after him, who holds the honor of having the park naming rights? His mother-in-law, Adell Durbin.

A tip of the hat to Mr. Campbell for setting the son-in-law bar so high.

Miles and Directions

0.0   Start at the western end of the parking lot next to a sign for the Adell Durbin Park & Arboretum. Trail markers will direct you. To begin, follow the Yellow Trail south. The trail will wrap around the southern end of the parking lot and meander farther south in between Darrow Road and tennis courts.

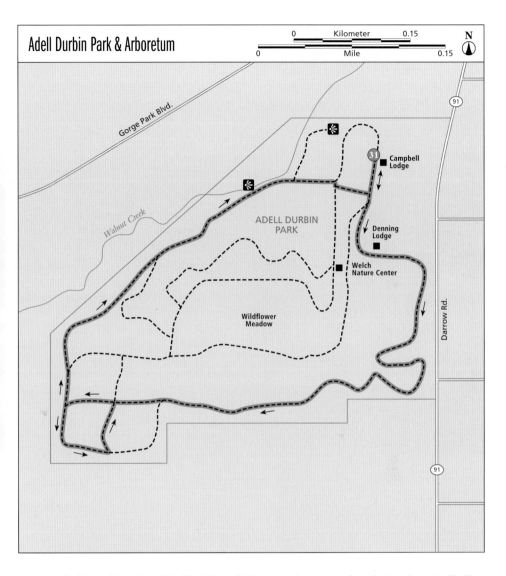

Adell Durbin Park & Arboretum

Gorge Park Blvd.

91

Campbell
Lodge

31

Walnut Creek

ADELL DURBIN
PARK

Denning
Lodge

Welch
Nature Center

Darrow Rd.

Wildflower
Meadow

91

0.1   Turn left (southwest) to hike into a slightly wooded area away from the tennis courts. You'll cross a small bridge and continue to follow the grassy trail west, marked by yellow posts.

0.3   Following the yellow markers across the grassy field, you'll hike into more dense woodland.

0.5   Continue hiking south to complete the brief southern loop. You'll notice a residential complex on your right.

0.6   Turn left (east) onto the Red Trail, following it north as you return to the previous junction where you turned south. When you return, turn right (north) to hike the northern area of Adell Durbin. This is more rugged with an initial uphill climb and the occasional exposed root.

0.7   Keep left (east) to hike downhill slightly on the merged Red/Blue Trail. Turning right will mistakenly take you on the Blue Trail only toward the parking lot.

Totem pole at the start of the trails at Adell Durbin Park

0.9 Take the wooden steps uphill, hiking east. You'll soon come out of the woods. Continuing due east will take you back to the picnic area where you started.

1.0 Return to the Adell Durbin Park & Arboretum parking lot to end your hike.

Hike Information

Local Information

Cuyahoga Falls Riverfront Square District; (330) 928-8230; www.fallsriver squaredistrict.com

GREEN TIP
On the trail eat grains and veggies instead of meat, which has a higher energy cost.

Cuyahoga Valley National Park

O ne of the youngest national parks in the country yet one of the most popular, with 2,474,220 yearly visitors on average between 2008 and 2012, Cuyahoga Valley National Park reclaims the rural landscape along the Cuyahoga River and covers 20,339 acres between Cleveland and Akron. Due to its size, you'll find everything from bedrock outcroppings and powerful waterfalls to scenic ravines and rugged terrain with hikes along Ohio's rolling hills.

About 400 million years in the making (if you count the rocks), Brandywine Falls is everyone's favorite sight in the Lake Erie Watershed.

32 Tree Farm Loop Trail, Cuyahoga Valley National Park

The Tree Farm Trail is an excellent choice for anyone looking for short mileage with plenty of diversity. Within this hike you'll find a large, serene man-made pond, an expanse of spruce and pines growing on a nearby tree farm, and easy hiking along smooth dirt trails.

Start: At the southern end of Horseshoe Pond. You can hike straight toward a dock for some views and continue west briefly for a picnic pavilion. The Tree Farm Trail begins on your right (east) through tall grasses before the dock.
Distance: 2.75 miles
Approximate hiking time: 1.5 hours
Difficulty: Easy
Trail surface: Natural
Best season: Year-round
Other trail users: Public
Canine compatibility: Leashed
Land status: Public
Fees and permits: None
Schedule: Public
Maps: Cuyahoga Valley National Park; (330) 657-2752; www.nps.gov/cuva

Trail contacts: Cuyahoga Valley National Park; (330) 657-2752; www.nps.gov/cuva
Finding the trailhead: From Cleveland, drive south on I-77 for about 16 miles. Take exit 146 toward I-80 toward Toledo/Youngstown. Just under a mile, keep right at the fork and follow signs for OH 21/Richfield. Turn right onto Brecksville Road for 0.5 mile. Turn left onto Boston Mills Road for just over a mile and right onto Black Road for 1.2 miles. Turn left onto OH 303/Streetsboro Road for another mile. Turn right onto Stine Road for yet another mile and continue onto Major Road in 1.1 miles. Destination will be on your left. GPS: N 41 14' 0.5418" / W 81 34' 9.354"

The Hike

The Tree Farm Trail is a perfect hike if you're looking for something that isn't strenuous, but stretches through different habitats. Within this hike you'll get scenic views of the man-made Horseshoe Pond (an aerial view makes it clear how the pond got its name), dense woodland trail, and panoramic views of the surrounding pine and spruce tree farm. Seeing this particular view during the winter with a healthy dusting of snow will put even the grumpiest of scrooges into the holiday spirit.

The trail begins right off the parking lot. Mr. Magoo himself couldn't miss it. In fact, it's the only trail in the area, so Mr. Magoo could easily navigate this hike too.

Straight ahead you'll find a dock with some impressive views of Horseshoe Pond. You might see folks fishing or others canoeing off in the distance. Follow the trail west for a picnic pavilion. Otherwise, the loop starts and ends before the dock. You'll see a V-shape cut in the grass that serves as the trailhead. There's no compelling reason to choose hiking either clockwise or counter-clockwise. Your decision point is whether or not you want the best view of Horseshoe Pond in the beginning or end.

Tree Farm Trail Rachel Faber

If you're impatient, hike clockwise where a grassy, dirt trail will guide you north alongside the eastern end of the pond. Take it in for a moment before looking for a trail marker on the northeastern corner of the pond that directs you into the woods.

Now you'll be hiking in relatively dense forested area with natural terrain. All kinds of animals call these parts home. Chipmunks, squirrels, rabbits, and even owls have made themselves known. If you see or hear a barred owl, resist the urge to ask how many licks it takes to get to the center of a Tootsie Pop. It's a dated reference that will only age you to younger hikers.

Continuing, the trail meanders west before charging back east where you'll exit the woods for a grassy hike along a wide-open field covered in spruce and pine trees. Off in the distance you can see Heritage Farms due east. Soon the trail will turn southeast and you'll reenter the woods for the remainder of the hike.

You won't find much difficult about the remaining trail, which is flat and easy. Though to be honest, the entirety of this hike is an easy stroll. In fact, some might even combine this hike with one of the other many Cuyahoga Valley National Park hikes nearby for more mileage.

Again, there's no junction or offshoot from the Tree Farm Trail. This is a hike where you can let your thoughts wander without paying much attention to where

Tree Farm Loop Trail, Cuyahoga Valley National Park

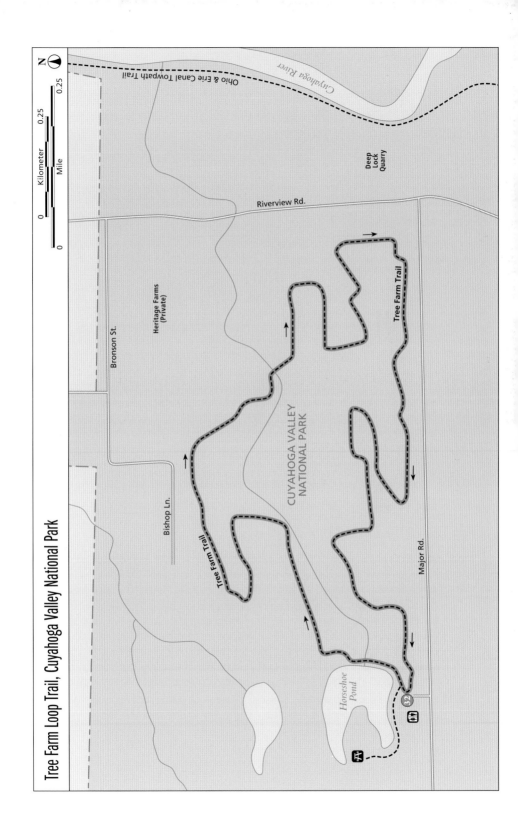

N

0   0.25   Kilometer   0.25
0   Mile

Ohio & Erie Canal Towpath Trail

Cuyahoga River

Deep Lock Quarry

Riverview Rd.

Bronson St.

Heritage Farms (Private)

Bishop Ln.

Tree Farm Trail

Tree Farm Trail

Tree Farm Trail

CUYAHOGA VALLEY NATIONAL PARK

Major Rd.

Horseshoe Pond

3.2

The view around Horseshoe Pond

you are. Continue hiking along the natural surface and you'll soon reemerge to the southeast corner of Horseshoe Pond.

Miles and Directions

0.0 Start at the northwestern edge of the parking lot, hiking on paved trail north toward Horseshoe Pond. Follow the path to the left (west) once you're alongside the pond to take a short out-and-back leg for a west-to-east view of the pond. When you're done, return toward the trailhead, turning left (east) onto grassy trail just before the parking lot. Stay to the left (northeast) to hike back toward the eastern edge of the pond. As you hike around the pond, you'll be guided into the woods near the northeastern corner of the pond. At this point you'll continue to hike northeast, with the trail eventually winding due north toward a wide open field of trees. Being the lone trail, you will not stray from this route for the entirety of the 2.75-mile hike. There are no junctions and the trail is very well marked.

2.75 Hiking west, the trail will wind you back right to where you started your trek alongside the parking lot.

33 Oak Hill to Plateau Trail, Cuyahoga Valley National Park

Right off the highway, yet as remote a feeling as you'll get on a hike. Surrounded by tall pines, you'll feel like you're lost in the Carolinas or Smokies, light years away from the city. Sandy, dirt trails take you over predominantly flat terrain for a serene hike that brings special meaning to getting "lost in the woods."

Start: Oak Hill Trailhead parking lot
Distance: 4.5 miles
Approximate hiking time: 2 hours
Difficulty: Easy to moderate
Trail surface: Natural, dirt
Best season: Year-round
Other trail users: None
Canine compatibility: Dogs must be on a leash no longer than 6 feet.
Land status: National park
Fees and permits: None
Schedule: Public

Maps: Cuyahoga Valley National Park / Boston Store Visitor Center; (330) 657-2752; www .nps.gov/cuva
Trail contacts: Cuyahoga Valley National Park / Boston Store Visitor Center; (330) 657-2752; www.nps.gov/cuva
Finding the trailhead: Drive south from Cleveland on I-77 for 20.5 miles. Take exit 143 for OH 176 and drive 0.3 miles to turn left onto Wheatley Road for 2.8 miles. Turn left onto Oak Hill Road. Destination will be on the right in 1.1 miles. GPS: N 41 13' 10.9554" / W 81 34' 33.9162"

The Hike

Something about this hike makes you feel like you're in the Smokies rather than Northeast Ohio with the crisp air and smell of pine trees surrounding you throughout. The remote feeling you'll experience is rather surreal considering a major interstate is just a short drive away. But there's no need to ask questions, just enjoy it.

You'll find the Oak Hill / Plateau Trailhead in the northeastern corner of the parking lot. The trail splits off early on, and you'll want to follow the Oak Hill Trail toward Sylvan Pond to the right, hiking east. Flat and smooth, there's nothing particularly challenging about the trail. Still, you'll find it's indescribably beautiful. Perhaps it's indescribable because it's a surprising beauty. After all, there's no noteworthy waterfall or powerful river flowing through (though the Cuyahoga River is nearby to the east). But there is certainly something special about these trails. The fun is discovering it for yourself.

Before long the trail will guide you out of the forest to an expanse where you'll find Sylvan Pond. Fishermen are welcome as are sizeable water snakes (watch your step!). Oak Hill continues around the northern end of the pond, meandering south where you'll briefly reconnect with the Plateau Trail. But you'll stay on Oak Hill until a later junction that directs you south to Meadowedge Pond—also welcoming of fishermen. This 0.6-mile leg of the Plateau Trail acts as a mini-loop of sorts, returning you

Oak Hill to Plateau Trail DJ REISER

to an early Oak Hill junction. You'll backtrack for just 0.1 mile where the Plateau Trail splits from Oak Hill for the remainder of the hike. Take this junction east.

As its name would indicate, the Plateau Trail treks across flat terrain. The mostly natural, dirt trail crawls through dense woodlands with towering pines. Again, there's nothing particularly important to note, no natural wonders or landmarks of historical interest. This is simply a beautiful, serene hike. It's the kind of hike that can calm the mind of even the most caffeinated king of cubicles.

Only two junctions will come up for the remainder of the Plateau Trail. One will come within the first mile that leads to the Valley Picnic Area—nothing worth going off track for. And in just over 0.5 mile you'll find a 0.2-mile junction that leads back to Sylvan Pond. You can take this if you need to bail out early for any reason. Otherwise, you'll continue for another 1.5 miles until you reach your initial split where you first took Oak Hill. Backtrack the last 0.1 mile back to the parking lot to end your hike.

Hopefully by the end you'll understand what has been difficult to articulate about this hike. This is a hike worthy of the trite expression "hidden gem." That might make you roll your eyes upon first reading, but hike the Oak Hill and Plateau Trails and perhaps you'll understand.

Oak Hill to Plateau Trail, Cuyahoga Valley National Park

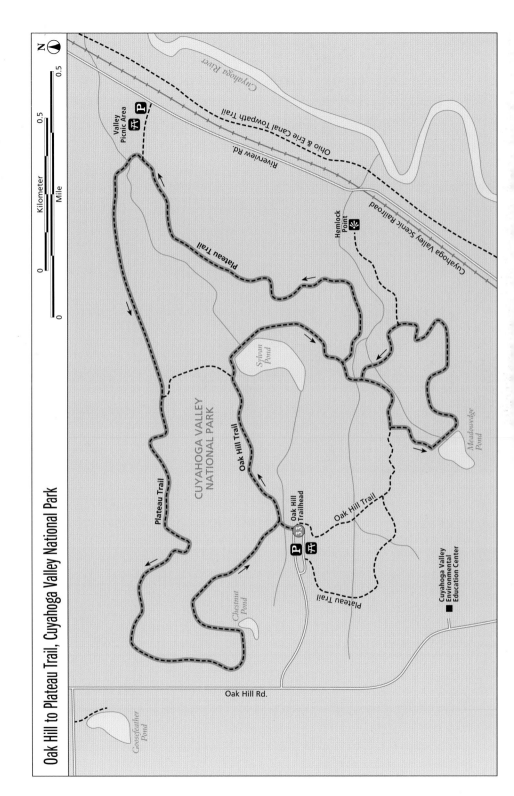

Well-maintained trail heading into the thick of the park

Miles and Directions

0.0 Start hiking north on the Oak Hill / Plateau trailhead at the northeastern corner of the parking lot. In about 100 feet just past a short boardwalk bridge, bear right (east) to continue on the Oak Hill Trail. **Option:** Stay to the left, hiking north to begin the 4.9-mile Plateau Trail.

0.4 Turn right (east) toward Sylvan Pond. **Option:** Turn left (north) to take the Plateau Trail connector. This will take you to the northern portion of the Plateau Trail.

0.7 You'll hike to a junction. Continue straight (west) toward the Oak Hill trailhead.

0.8 Stay straight at another junction heading south, slightly southwest to continue on the Oak Hill Trail for 0.1 mile.

0.9 At this fork in the road, turn left (south) toward Meadowedge Pond onto the Plateau Trail. **Option:** Stay straight heading west to continue on the combined Oak Hill and Plateau Trail, leading back to the parking lot.

1.0 Turn left (southeast) to hike alongside Meadowedge Pond. At the southeastern end of the pond, you'll turn left (east) back into the woods, still on the Plateau Trail.

1.5 Here you'll turn left (west) away from Hemlock Ravine, continuing toward the junction you encountered at 0.8. **Option:** Turn right (east) for a 0.2-mile out-and-back hike to Hemlock Point.

1.6 Return to the 0.8-mile junction, turning right (north) to go back over the wooden bridge and following signs for the Plateau Trail. Soon you'll come to the familiar 0.7-mile junction. This time, turn right (east) for the Plateau Trail, which you'll hike along for approximately the next 3 miles.

2.4 Turn left (west) to continue on the Plateau Trail. **Option:** Turning right (east) will take you to the Valley Picnic Area in about 200 yards.

2.9 Continue straight (west) toward Chestnut Pond. **Option:** Turn left (south) for the Plateau Trail connector back toward Sylvan Pond for a shorter hike.

4.2 You'll return to the first junction you approached at the beginning of the hike with the combined Plateau and Oak Hill Trail. Bear right, heading south over the bridge for the last stretch before the end.

4.5 Arrive at the trailhead and parking lot where you began.

34 Red Lock to Old Carriage Trail, Cuyahoga Valley National Park

Experience Northeast Ohio's famous Ohio & Erie Canal Towpath Trail—a former canal route converted to crushed limestone trail for hikers, runners, and cyclists. Off the Towpath Trail sits the windy and historic Old Carriage Trail. Hike along the Cuyahoga Valley wall and three bridges that stretch across the ravines below before returning to the Towpath in 3 miles for an easy return stretch back to Red Lock. Be sure to check Cuyahoga Valley National Park's website to ensure the bridges are open before setting off on this hike.

Start: At the Red Lock parking lot
Distance: 5 miles
Approximate hiking time: 2 hours
Difficulty: Easy on the Towpath Trail; moderate on Old Carriage Trail
Trail surface: Towpath trail is crushed limestone; Old Carriage Trail is dirt.
Best season: Year-round
Other trail users: None
Canine compatibility: Dogs must be on a leash no longer than 6 feet.
Land status: National park
Fees and permits: None
Schedule: Year-round
Maps: Cuyahoga Valley National Park / Boston Store Visitor Center; (330) 657-2752; www.nps.gov/cuva

Closures: www.nps.gov/cuva/learn/news/closures.htm
Trail contacts: Cuyahoga Valley National Park / Boston Store Visitor Center; (330) 657-2752; www.nps.gov/cuva
Finding the trailhead: Drive south on I-77 for 15 miles. Take exit 147 for Miller Road. Turn left onto Miller Road and right onto Brecksville Road in less than a mile. Take the second left onto Snowville Road for 2.8 miles. Turn left onto Riverview Road and a quick right onto Vaughn Road. Continue onto West Highland Road and the destination will be on the left. GPS: N 41 17' 22.6572" / W 81 33' 50.2884"

The Hike

Cuyahoga Valley National Park's Red Lock trailhead is a favorite starting point for Northeast Ohio hikers with the Ohio & Erie Canal Towpath Trail cutting through. The Towpath Trail is more enjoyable for runners or cyclists than hikers, because the trail's easy grade over smooth terrain provides little challenge or interest for the latter. Still, the Towpath Trail is a true bragging right of Northeast Ohio and worth at least one visit for any hiker. The 0.7-mile leg to Old Carriage is the perfect amount of time to get a taste of this historic trail.

From Red Lock you'll hike north on the Towpath Trail with the Cuyahoga River winding alongside to your left where you might spot ducks, turtles, snakes, or even a chipmunk dashing by in a blurry, spastic way that only a chipmunk knows how. Large sycamore and cottonwood trees line the way for your brief trek to the Old Carriage

Red Lock to Old Carriage Trail Sun Simenc

Trailhead where you'll turn east to hike on a bridge of Goose Pond Weir. This initial leg of Old Carriage, 0.6 miles worth, is open to cyclists and continues east away from the trail to connect with the Metro Parks, Serving Summit County Bike & Hike Trail 0.7 mile away. Asphalt connector leads to the beginning of Old Carriage's rugged dirt trail where only hikers are allowed.

The first thing you'll notice hiking on the meandering Old Carriage Trail is the incised ravine that plunges below. The ground is steep along the trail, so careful you don't find yourself tumbling below. Along the way you'll hike over three industrial-looking bridges with wood paneling. These bridges are of considerable length for a hiker. But considering they're keeping you safe from the fall below, you'll be thankful for them. At the time of this writing, the bridges were closed until further notice for repair. It's suggested you call in advance to ensure the bridges are open.

Unsurprising for a trail with a name like "Old Carriage," there's a bit of history around the hike. A late-19th, early-20th-century Shaker Heights businessman named Wentworth Marshall purchased 1,000 acres in Sagamore Hills for a summer getaway farm. When he wasn't raising livestock, experimenting with trees, and inviting impoverished Cleveland youths to camp, Marshall was busy creating a system of carriage roads. As context clues would hint, those "old carriage trails" of Mr. Marshall's are part of today's Cuyahoga Valley National Park trail system.

The trail wanders around for about 3 miles before rejoining the Towpath Trail just 0.4 mile from where you first left the Towpath Trail. From here you'll simply head

Mixed-use cyclist, trail runner, and hiker portion of the trail (Ohio and Erie Canal Towpath)

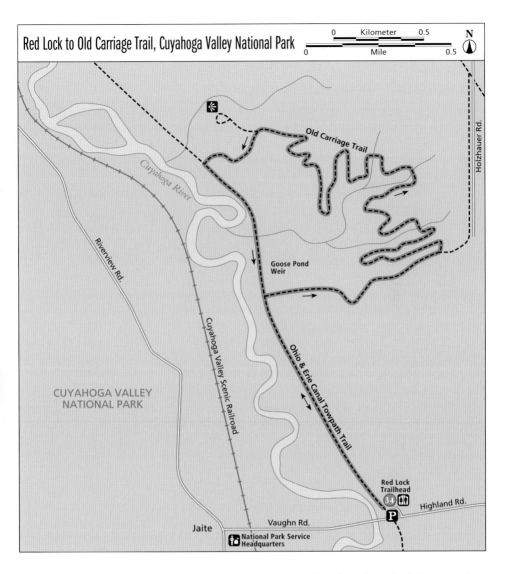

Red Lock to Old Carriage Trail, Cuyahoga Valley National Park

Old Carriage Trail

Cuyahoga River

Riverview Rd.

Cuyahoga Valley Scenic Railroad

Holzhauer Rd.

Goose Pond Weir

Ohio & Erie Canal Towpath Trail

CUYAHOGA VALLEY NATIONAL PARK

Red Lock Trailhead
34

Highland Rd.

P

Jaite

Vaughn Rd.

National Park Service Headquarters

back south for a straight shot to the Red Lock trailhead, ending the hike just a hair over 5 miles.

Be sure to enjoy the views of the Cuyahoga River on your return. The river seems more prominent hiking south for some reason, offering terrific sights as the crooked river winds alongside you. Some might even want to pause for a moment to "take it all in," as the expression goes. You certainly won't be rushed. A handful of hikers, runners, and cyclists may pass you by, but this is a rather remote corner of the Towpath Trail compared to the critical mass you'd find in downtown Peninsula. For the time being, this is your Towpath Trail. And because nobody is around, nobody can tell you otherwise.

Miles and Directions

0.0 Start at the Red Lock Trailhead across the street from Brandywine Ski Resort. Begin the hike on the Ohio & Erie Canal Towpath Trail, heading north.

0.7 Turn right (east) to begin hiking the Old Carriage Trail.

1.3 Now you'll want to turn left (north) away from the Metro Parks, Serving Summit County Bike and Hike Trail. Stay on this trail until the overlook, which will come just before you reconnect with the Towpath Trail.

1.8 Cross the Rocky Run Bridge over the ravine. You'll have a brief uphill hike at the other end before the trail levels off (bridge closed).

2.3 Take the Twin Oaks Bridge over another ravine. Continue the Old Carriage Trail after crossing (bridge closed).

2.5 Here you'll hike across the Hemlock Bridge (bridge closed).

3.4 Stay to the right to go slightly uphill for a brief hike to the overlook. When you return, take a hard right (south) to finish the remainder of the Old Carriage Trail and return to the Towpath Trail.

3.8 Return to the Towpath Trail. Turn left (south), and continue hiking for about a mile on the Towpath until you return to the Red Lock Trailhead and parking lot.

5.0 Arrive at trailhead and parking lot.

Hike Information

Camping

Primitive camping; www.nps.gov/cuva/planyourvisit/lodging.htm

35 Riding Run to Perkins Bridle Trails and Furnace Run Trail, Cuyahoga Valley National Park

Valley Trail runs under the Everett Road Covered Bridge before beginning the forested hike of Riding Run over rolling hills and through a couple of creeks. This leads to Perkins Trail for hiking on similarly flat, natural terrain before returning back perfectly to the bridge. Looking for more miles? The Furnace Run trailhead conveniently sits across the street from your parking lot, leading to a nice view of the Furnace Run tributary and blooming bluebells in the spring.

Start: Everett Road Covered Bridge
Distance: 7.1 miles total
Approximate hiking time: 2.5 hours
Difficulty: Moderate with difficult climbs
Trail surface: Natural terrain
Best season: Year-round
Other trail users: Horses
Canine compatibility: Dogs are allowed on a leash no longer than 6 feet.
Land status: National park
Fees and permits: None
Schedule: Year-round

Maps: Cuyahoga Valley National Park / Boston Store Visitor Center; (330) 657-2752; www .nps.gov/cuva
Trail contacts: Cuyahoga Valley National Park / Boston Store Visitor Center; (330) 657-2752; www.nps.gov/cuva
Finding the trailhead: Drive south from Cleveland on I-77 for 19.8 miles. Take exit 143 for OH 176 toward I-271 North for 0.3 mile. Turn left onto Wheatley Road for 2.9 miles, and then a slight left onto Everett Road. The destination will be on the right in 0.1 mile. GPS: 41 12' 14.9826" / W 81 34' 51.4416"

The Hike

This hike begins on crushed gravel Valley Trail off a small, remote parking lot in Cuyahoga Valley National Park. Driving in you'll see the Everett Road Covered Bridge, which you'll be hiking underneath within the first 0.1 mile. You'll continue hiking parallel to Everett Road, following the trail as it bends north alongside a small stream. Before Wheatley Road, Riding Run Trail will turn west into the woods. The trail here is your basic dirt, natural surface that flows nicely through relatively dense forest. Hiking along, you'll notice these trails serve as bridle trails too. Meaning you might have to watch your step, lest you get a foot-full of the remnants of a horse's dietary intake.

The forested portion of Riding Run Trail will last for about 2.2 miles before you reach the Perkins Trail junction. If you need to bail out, you can finish the loop in about 1.2 miles, returning to the Everett Road junction where you first entered the woods. Otherwise, turn south onto the Perkins Trail. You'll find a 0.1-mile-long bypass in about 0.3 mile that you can also take to bail out early. But to get the

EVERETT ROAD COVERED BRIDGE

As you might have guessed, there's historical significance to the Everett Road Covered Bridge you've been hiking through. The bridge crosses the Furnace Run tributary and is the only remaining tributary in Summit County. But flashback a couple centuries ago and it was just one in over 2,000 across the Buckeye State, which was the nation's leader in covered-bridge construction.

Covered bridges such as Everett Road were vital in the era's transportation system. Farmers specifically used the bridge for access to the nearby Ohio & Erie Canal to ship their goods north to Cleveland.

The story goes that Cuyahoga Valley farmers John Gilson and his wife needed to cross Furnace Run on a winter night in 1877. Winter storms rendered a ford they would have used defunct, forcing the duo to pass around the ford. Tragically, Mrs. Gilson fell into the stream. Mr. Gilson was next with his horse dragging the poor man into even deeper waters. Mrs. Gilson was rescued, but her husband's fate was far more grisly with his body discovered 4 days later.

Rumor has it that the covered bridge was built in response to this story. Others say the bridge actually predates the tragedy, making one wonder how the Gilsons struggled so much to cross Furnace Run. Whichever story you choose to believe, the Everett Road Covered Bridge continues to stand today, after surviving major storm damage twice throughout the past century.

complete experience, continue hiking south for a mile. This will get you to the opposite end of the bypass, but with the more adventurous route. Now all you have is another 0.8 mile before you're back at the Everett Road Covered Bridge, hiking the Valley Trail the last 0.1 mile back to your car.

Overall it's a nice, moderately difficult hike thanks to the occasional climb and minor stream crossing. Nothing that will have you on your back by the end of the day, but you'll by no means coast through this one if you're out of shape.

Now if you've been eating your Wheaties, you might be looking to add another couple of miles to your hike. Luckily you'll notice a trailhead on the north side of Everett Road, right across from your parking lot. This is the Furnace Run Trail, a lollipop hike that will add another 2 miles to your day when all is said and done. But these 2 miles are hardly a breeze. You'll begin with steep uphill climbs that might leave you wishing you conquered this lollipop before the bridle trails.

The hike leads due north before turning you west to cross Oak Hill Road, which takes you to the loop portion of the hike. At the western end of the loop, you'll find a less than 0.1 mile out-and-back leg that takes you to some scenic views of

These two photos show the diversity of the hike's trails. D.J. REISER

Furnace Run Trail TED TOTH

the Furnace Run tributary. Come in the spring and you'll find a field of bluebells blooming.

When you're finished, simply finish your loop and backtrack the handle of the Furnace Run lollipop to end your day's hiking. You can now leave knowing you've personally discovered yet another gem of one of the most popular national parks in the country.

Miles and Directions

Riding Run to Perkins Loop Trail

0.0 Start hiking out of the western end of the parking lot onto the Valley Trail toward the Everett Road Covered Bridge, which you should see just down the trail.

0.1 You'll come to a very small loop. Staying to your left (south) will take you to some plaques with park history. When you're done, continue hiking west under the Everett Road Covered Bridge. After emerging from the covered bridge, you'll approach a post with directions for Riding Run and Perkins Trails. This is where you'll return near the end of the hike. For now, continue straight (west) alongside the Furnace Run tributary and Everett Road.

0.4 Continue hiking alongside Everett Road, turning right (north) with the bend in the road until you reach a post for Riding Run Trail just before Wheatley Road. You'll be ushered across Everett Road (west) and into the woods to hike Riding Run.

0.7 After crossing Everett Road, you'll hike to a Riding Run Trail junction. Turn right (north) to hike the northernmost leg of the Riding Run Trail. **Option:** Turn left for a shorter, 1.2-mile hike to the Perkins Trail.

Riding Run to Perkins Bridle Trails and Furnace Run Trail, Cuyahoga Valley National Park

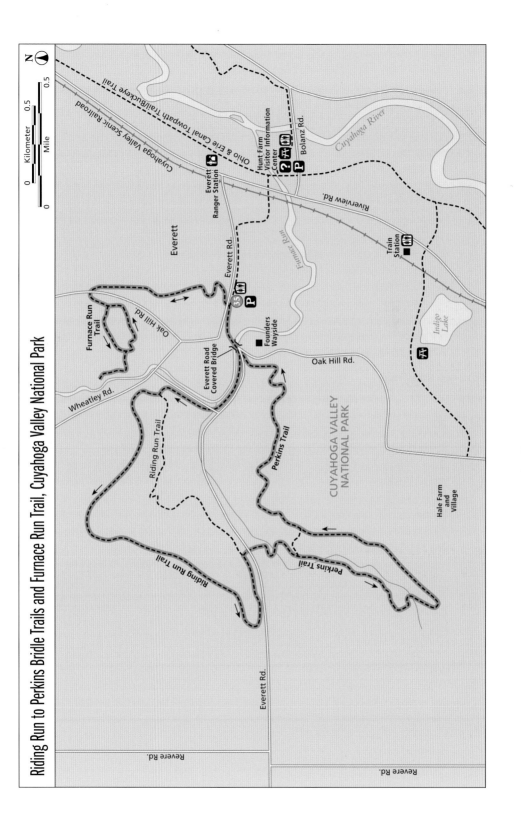

2.0 Turn left (east) to hike alongside Everett Road toward the beginning of your Perkins Trail hike.

2.3 Approach the Perkins Trail junction. Turn right (south) down a small slope and cross Everett Road to complete Perkins Trail. **Option:** Continue straight (northeast) to skip Perkins Trail and finish the 4-mile Riding Run Trail.

2.6 Continue straight (south) at this Perkins Trail junction to finish the entire 2.75-mile trail. **Option:** Turn left (east) for a 0.1-mile connector that shortens the Perkins Trail by about a mile as you head back to the Everett Road Covered Bridge.

2.7 Cross an approximately 30-foot-wide creek, and continue hiking the Perkins Trail on the southern side of the stream.

3.1 Hike across another creek crossing heading due south. You'll see the trail continues on the other side for an uphill climb.

3.8 Continue straight (north) toward Everett Road Covered Bridge, ignoring the 0.1-mile connector you passed at 2.6.

4.7 The trail will push you back out to a familiar portion of Everett Road, directing you east to hike again underneath Everett Road Covered Bridge.

5.0 Return to the parking lot to end the Riding Run to Perkins Trail portion. **Option:** Extend your hike by completing the approximately 2-mile Furnace Run Trail, beginning on the northern side of Everett Road across from your parking lot.

Furnace Run Trail

0.0 Start the trail on the northern side of Everett Road, across the street from your parking lot. You'll begin with an uphill climb, and take the wooden steps to continue uphill in less than 0.1 mile.

0.6 Stay to the left (west) to cross Oak Hill Road toward the loop portion of the trail.

0.7 Arrive at the loop of the Furnace Run Trail. Hike the 0.5 mile clockwise by staying to the left (south).

1.0 You'll come to a junction for a very short out-and-back leg that leads to the Furnace Run tributary. Turn left (west) for the brief excursion that's less than 0.1 mile. When you reach the end of the trail, noted by an END OF TRAIL sign, you'll turn back to this junction. **Option:** Stay straight hiking north to skip the out-and-back.

1.1 Return to the junction where you started the out-and-back. Turn left (north) to finish the loop.

1.4 Arrive at the junction where you began the short loop. Turn left (north) to head back toward Oak Hill Road and backtrack to the beginning of the trail.

2.1 End your hike at Everett Road, crossing the street to return to your parking lot.

Hike Information

Camping

Primitive camping; www.nps.gov/cuva/planyourvisit/lodging.htm

Other Resources

National Park Service; www.nps.gov

36 Stanford to Brandywine Gorge Trail, Cuyahoga Valley National Park

The Stanford Trail is a relaxing and unchallenging stroll compared to the occasionally steep climbs of the Brandywine Gorge Trail. Both, however, offer memorable, picturesque views of rural Northeast Ohio. First, you'll be guided toward the historic Stanford House before hiking your way back toward the breathtaking and powerful Brandywine Falls, perhaps Ohio's most noteworthy waterfall. A scenic overlook at the end of the hike allows for idyllic nature photography.

Start: Stanford trailhead at the northwestern end of the Brandywine Falls parking lot
Distance: 4.4 miles
Approximate hiking time: 2 hours
Difficulty: Moderate with steep climbs near the end
Trail surface: Paved, forested, occasionally grassy
Best season: Year-round
Other trail users: Public
Canine compatibility: Dogs must be on a leash no longer than 6 feet.
Land status: National park
Fees and permits: None
Schedule: Brandywine Falls Area parking lot is closed from dusk to morning; open 7 a.m. to 11 p.m. or dusk.
Maps: Cuyahoga Valley National Park / Boston Store Visitor Center; (330) 657-2752; www.nps.gov/cuva

Trail contacts: Cuyahoga Valley National Park / Boston Store Visitor Center; (330) 657-2752; www.nps.gov/cuva
Finding the trailhead: Drive south on I-77 for 15 miles. Take exit 147 for Miller Road toward OH 21. Turn left onto Miller Road for approximately 0.6 mile before turning right onto Brecksville Road briefly, and taking the second left onto Snowville Road. Continue for about 2.8 miles, turning left onto Riverview Road, then 0.25 mile right onto Vaughn Road, which quickly turns into West Highland Road. Finish by continuing for another 1.4 miles on West Highland Road, turning right onto Brandywine Road for about another mile. The entrance and parking lot will be on your right. GPS: N 41 16' 36.0078" / W 81 32' 24.1506"

The Hike

Easy and unassuming at first on light gravel trail, this hike takes you through one of the most historic corners of rural Northeast Ohio.

Before long you're ushered into the woods where the trail becomes slightly rougher with exposed roots scattered throughout, though you're ultimately unchallenged thus far. Signs reminding you where you are and how far you've gone or need to go are frequent. In fact, it's safe to say this is one of the best-marked trails in the region, making it easy for even the shortest of attention spans to keep on track.

Staying on Stanford, the trail eventually becomes grassy and opens up to a large field as you approach the bulky Stanford House, which also serves as a hostel and

Northeast Ohio's most popular natural tourist attraction doesn't slow down for winter.

campground. Near the parking lot you'll notice a handful of primitive campsites you'll use when you do the overnight Buckeye Trail hike. Primitive campsites are available from Memorial Day weekend through October.

Across from the house is the famous Ohio & Erie Canal Towpath Trail, which you can explore by bike as far south as New Philadelphia. But for the sake of this hike, you'll turn around and backtrack to the Averill Pond junction. You'll quickly notice that everything's a bit more difficult this time around, with gradual climbs all the way back to the junction.

At the junction, you'll continue straight toward the pond for about 0.3 mile. Of course you can skip it and continue back toward Brandywine Falls if you're growing a bit tired, though the trip to the pond adds little more than 0.5 mile to your entire hike. A bench sits alongside the quiet pond and is a great spot to stop for a snack to cure a growling stomach.

With your hunger cured, you'll continue to backtrack to the junction where you originally left the Brandywine Gorge Trail, and this time take it around back toward the parking lot and Brandywine Falls where you began. You'll know you're getting close to the falls as the sound of plummeting water becomes louder and more frequent. Think *Jaws* theme music with beautiful falls at the crescendo instead of immediate death.

WHAT HAPPENED TO THE VILLAGE AT BRANDYWINE FALLS?

Brandywine Falls wasn't always just a gathering point for admirers of nature's work. The 65-foot falls once powered the tiny and historic village of Brandywine, Ohio.

In 1814, local George Wallace began a trend of building mills at the top of the falls, leading to grist and woolen mills. Behind the thrust of Brandywine Falls, the village became one of the earliest emerging communities in the Cuyahoga Valley. Sadly, a majority of the town was lost due to the construction of nearby I-271, solidifying Brandywine's unfortunate standing as one of the earliest victims of the American highway system.

Fortunately, however, the asphalt monster was unable to swallow the entire village whole. The James Wallace house, built by the son of the aforementioned George Wallace, remains as the Inn at Brandywine Falls—a bed-and-breakfast draped in historic Ohio decor and ambiance with six rooms for visitors. Innkeepers Katie and George Hoy welcome guests to enjoy the former Wallace home's living room, library, dining rooms, porches, and, of course, the surrounding Cuyahoga Valley National Park grounds. Most recently a small, unassuming barn behind the main house of the property was renovated and made into an "elegantly rustic suite."

As you near the end, you'll come to a steep, somewhat rocky climb with the falls pounding on your right. Pause at any moment for a view that would have Ansel Adams scrambling for his camera. But watch your step! It's a doozy of a fall you're not likely to hop back up from.

Finally at the top of the climb, you'll reach the paved Metro Parks, Serving Summit County Bike & Hike Trail. Take this past the historic Inn at Brandywine Falls and over the Brandywine Falls Bridge. You'll come to a VIEWING AREA sign that points you down a collection of wooden stairs reminiscent of M. C. Escher's *House of Stairs*. Take these down for an up close and personal view of Northeast Ohio's most popular natural waterfall. When you're done, climb back up the stairs, and you'll be ushered back out to the parking lot to end your hike.

Miles and Directions

0.0 At the northwest end of the parking lot, you'll hike down some steps for the Stanford and Brandywine Gorge trailheads. You'll want to turn left (west) onto the flat gravel to begin the Stanford Trail.

0.2 The trail will turn into a paved path, and you'll come to a sign indicating to stay left (southwest) for the Stanford House, the terminus of the Stanford Trail, in 1.2 miles.

0.3 You'll approach a very steep downhill with wooden steps to assist your descent. At the bottom you'll come to a junction with Brandywine Falls to the right (north) and the Stanford

Frozen Averill Pond

Trail continuing to the left. Turn left (south) to continue toward the Stanford House, remaining on this well-marked trail until you reach the house.

0.8 Here sits a sign for a short trail to Averill Pond and back. Ignore it for now, continuing west toward the Stanford House. But you'll return here when you backtrack, and then visit the pond.

1.4 You'll cross a wooden bridge over a quiet stream, opening to a large grassy field with the Boston Mills Ski Resort sitting in the backdrop. Shortly thereafter, you'll see the Stanford House and surrounding campground. Hike to the parking lot. Less than a quarter mile away is the Ohio & Erie Canal Towpath Trail if you continue west. You can extend your hike plenty by hopping on the towpath, but you'll need to backtrack to Averill Pond at some point anyhow. Once you're ready, turn back east to begin your backtrack hike to the northeast.

2.4 Return to the Averill Pond junction. Continue straight past the sign, heading north for a brief hike to the pond.

2.5 Arrive at Averill Pond. When you're ready, return to the junction south, and turn left (east) to continue backtracking on the Stanford Trail toward the Brandywine Gorge Trail.

Stanford to Brandywine Gorge Trail, Cuyahoga Valley National Park

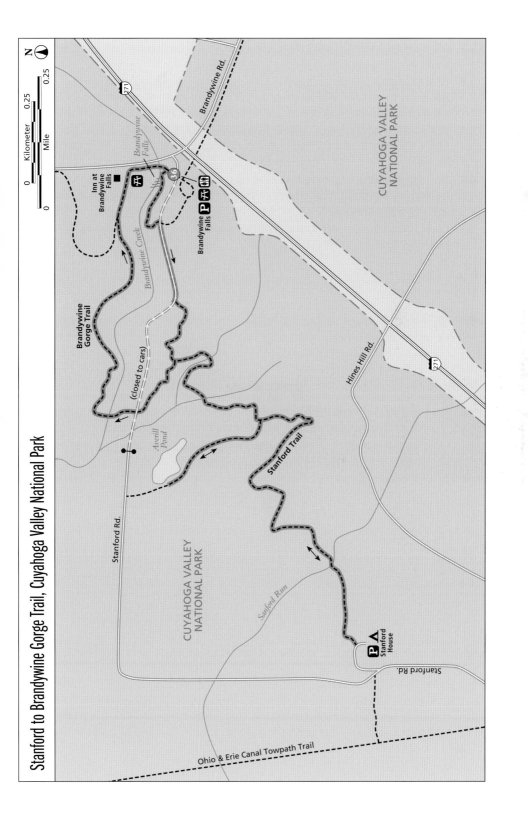

N

Kilometer   0   0.25

Mile   0   0.25

71

Brandywine Rd.

Brandywine Falls

Inn at Brandywine Falls

36

Brandywine Falls

Brandywine Gorge Trail

(closed to cars)

Brandywine Creek

Averill Pond

Stanford Rd.

Stanford Trail

CUYAHOGA VALLEY NATIONAL PARK

Hines Hill Rd.

71

Stanford Run

CUYAHOGA VALLEY NATIONAL PARK

Stanford Rd.

Stanford House

Ohio & Erie Canal Towpath Trail

3.3 Return to Brandywine Gorge and Stanford Trail junction. Turn left (north) to start your trek toward the Brandywine Falls.

3.5 You'll approach a 100-foot or so long wooden bridge that crosses over a stream that's flowing much faster than anything you've seen thus far. The sound will only get louder as you get closer to Brandywine Falls.

4.0 Here you'll find the Metro Parks, Serving Summit County Bike & Hike Trail paved trail. Turn right (east) toward the parking lot, and you'll begin to see Brandywine Falls peeking out of the south.

4.2 Turn right (northwest) off the bike trail toward the falls, following the sign for the Falls Viewing Area. This will lead to some stairs, which in turn lead to a platform viewing area for the best view of Brandywine Falls.

4.4 Return from the wooden stairs to the Stanford Trail junction you first took, adjacent to the parking lot where you started.

Hike Information

Camping

Primitive camping; www.nps.gov

GREEN TIP
If you're toting food, leave the packaging at home. Repack your provisions in zip-lock bags that you can reuse and that can double as garbage bags on the way out of the woods.

37 Cross Country to Lake to Salt Run Trail, Virginia Kendall Unit

A delightful mixture of flat, gravel trail near scenic Kendall Lake surrounded by the dirt trails of the Cross Country and Salt Run Trail loops connected by the rolling Kendall Hills gives hikers a little bit of everything in this hearty hike in the southern Virginia Kendall Unit.

Start: At the southeastern corner of the parking lot on Lake Trail
Distance: 6.5 miles
Approximate hiking time: 4.5 hours
Difficulty: Easy to moderate to difficult due to occasional steep climbs and rough terrain
Trail surface: Gravel and dirt
Best season: Year-round
Other trail users: None
Canine compatibility: Dogs must be on a leash no longer than 6 feet
Land status: National park
Fees and permits: None
Schedule: The entrance to Kendall Lake Shelter is closed from dusk to morning opening.

Maps: Cuyahoga Valley National Park / Boston Store Visitor Center; (330) 657-2752; www.nps.gov/cuva
Trail contacts: Cuyahoga Valley National Park / Boston Store Visitor Center; (330) 657-2752; www.nps.gov/cuva
Finding the trailhead: Drive south on I-77 for 7.1 miles. Take exit 156 to merge onto I-480 East for 12.1 miles. Keep left to continue on I-271 South for 3.4 miles. Take exit 18A on the left for OH 8 South. In 1.4 miles, merge onto OH 8 South for 4 miles. Take exit 12 for OH 303. In 0.3 mile, merge onto Akron Cleveland Road/State Road for 0.9 mile. Turn right onto Kendall Park Road for 1.1 miles. Destination is on the left. GPS: N 41 13' 2.4132" / W 81 31' 29.1786"

The Hike

You'll begin on the Lake Trail from the southeastern corner of the parking lot with Kendall Lake to your side, surrounded by a mixture of cherry, hickory, and woodland maple trees as you make your way into the woods on the wide dirt trails of the Cross Country Trail. True to its name, this trail is a favorite of cross-country skiers in the winter, but is still a worthy addition for hikers in the other three seasons of the year.

Much like the entirety of the Virginia Kendall Unit, you'll approach a mixture of plant life, specifically goldenrods, ironweed, and milkweed. The latter is an important source of food for the monarch butterflies who migrate to Central America sometime in the early fall. Now that you know that tiny butterflies migrate from here to Central America thousands of miles away, there will be no complaining tolerated on any of these hikes!

Not to be outdone, the animals are just as diverse as the plant life with barred owls and swimming beavers making themselves known at various times of the day. Hiking around dusk is your best bet for catching these critters out in their habitat.

Kendall Lake is Cuyahoga Valley National Park's largest at 12 acres and is a popular fishing and canoeing spot.

As you continue along the Cross Country Trail toward its eastern end, the trail will begin to wind south through mowed meadows and open fields before looping you back west toward Kendall Lake where you'll be treated to panoramic views of the Kendall Hills. Time willing, there are short connector trails you can take to hike along the hills. But for our purposes, we're going to continue back toward the southern end of Kendall Lake. Coincidentally, this is actually quite close to where you started your hike, affording you the option to bail or end early by simply finishing the Cross Country Trail, hiking northeast. By itself, the Cross Country Trail is approximately 2.3 miles. If you have a bit more gas in the tank, we'll leave the Cross Country Trail to hike the southern portion of the Lake Trail to connect to the much more windy and rigorous Salt Run Trail.

As you begin the Salt Run Trail, you'll quickly be ushered back into dense woodlands away from Kendall Lake. The dirt trails here are more narrow and rough with occasional root exposure, particularly in the western end where you start to turn around to hike back toward the lake. Given the trail's loop configuration, you can hike either clockwise or counter-clockwise. Like other longer trails in North-east Ohio, there is a connector trail about halfway or two-thirds of the way into the hike that offers you the opportunity to shorten your hike if you feel your legs

VIRGINIA KENDALL UNIT

The land that makes up the Virginia Kendall Unit has been a land of recreation for thousands of years, dating back to the region's first inhabitants.

Native Americans first lived among the rock outcroppings here, using the nearby woods and streams for food and water. When it comes to American history, the Virginia Kendall Unit first made a name for itself during the Great Depression when it was the site of a major public works project. Upon his death in 1927, Cleveland businessman Hayward Kendall (name sound familiar?) willed 390 acres to the State of Ohio for a park, which was named in honor of his late mother. Remember that the next time socks sound like a good idea for a holiday present.

Today, this recreation attraction serves as a natural refuge from the hustle and bustle of everyday life in the cities of Cleveland and Akron.

becoming perilously heavier. Being the Bear Grylls–esque adventurers we are, we skip the connector to complete the entire loop. When you're finished, you'll return to the familiar junction in the southwest corner of Kendall Lake where you began Salt Run Trail.

From here, you'll simply continue to follow the remainder of the Lake Trail that circles Kendall Lake until it combines once again with the Cross Country Trail in the east. This will guide you (briefly) back along the very same wide dirt trails you started on to finish your hike.

Miles and Directions

0.0 Start at the southern end of the parking lot near Kendall Lake. You'll find signs pointing to the three trails you'll be hiking today: Lake, Cross Country, and Salt Run Trails. Hike past the sign heading northeast. Continue hiking until you come to a junction for the Cross Country and Lake Trails. Turn right (east) for the Lake Trail. Immediately afterward, you'll come to another junction for the Lake Trail and Kendall Lake Shelter. Turn left (northeast) to stay on the Lake Trail, hiking away from Kendall Lake.

0.1 You'll come to another junction. Turn left (north) away from the tunnel to hike uphill. At the top of the hill will be yet another junction. This time the Lake Shelter is to the right and the Lake Trail to the left. Turn right (east) for the 2.3-mile Cross Country Trail.

0.9 Here you'll hike out of the woods onto a grassy field with a picnic table. Follow signs that continue the Cross Country Trail heading south before cutting back north slightly and finally back south as you hike along the border between the woods and field.

1.4 Hike back into the woods heading west back toward Kendall Lake to complete the southern portion of this loop.

2.1 You'll come out of the woods onto a downhill, grassy trail. You can see Kendall Lake ahead to the north. Continue hiking toward the lake.

Cross Country to Lake to Salt Run Trail, Virginia Kendall Unit

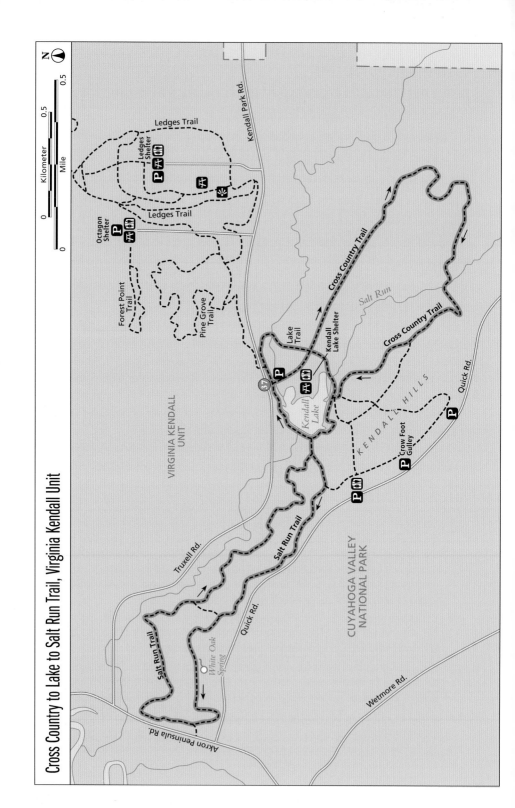

N

Kilometer   0   0.5
Mile   0   0.5

Ledges Trail

Ledges Shelter

Ledges Trail

Octagon Shelter

Kendall Park Rd.

Forest Point Trail

Pine Grove Trail

VIRGINIA KENDALL UNIT

Cross Country Trail

Salt Run

Cross Country Trail

Lake Trail

Kendall Lake Shelter

Kendall Lake

37

KENDALL HILLS

Crow Foot Gulley

Quick Rd.

CUYAHOGA VALLEY NATIONAL PARK

Truxell Rd.

Quick Rd.

Salt Run Trail

White Oak Spring

Salt Run Trail

Akron Peninsula Rd.

Wetmore Rd.

A modest climb up the smooth dirt trail

2.3   Now you'll be alongside the southern portion of Kendall Lake and will need to turn left (west) to leave the Cross Country Trail for the Lake Trail. **Option:** Turn right (east) to finish the Cross Country Trail and end your hike early.

2.5   Stay straight alongside Kendall Lake to continue toward the Kendall Lake Shelter heading north. Shortly thereafter as the Lake Trail starts to wrap alongside the lake to the north, you'll take the Salt Run Trail junction to the left (west) into the woods. As you enter the woods, you'll come to another junction. Stay to the left (southwest) to hike the loop clockwise. You'll return on the right at the end of the loop as you head back to the Lake Trail later on.

3.0 Turn right (north) when you get to Quick Road. You'll hike down a few steps and stay on a dirt trail that descends slightly.

3.4 Stay to the left to continue on the longer portion of the Salt Run Trail. You'll stay on this trail for the rest of the loop until you return to the Lake Trail. **Option:** Turn right (east) to take a short cut to the northern portion of the trail. At the northern end, you'll turn right (southeast) to head back to the Lake Trail.

5.6 You'll return to the junction where you started the Salt Run Trail. Turn left (east) back toward Kendall Lake to pick up the remainder of the Lake Trail. At the Lake Trail junction, you'll take another (left) to hike back toward the parking lot.

6.0 Cross the park's driveway entrance to continue hiking alongside Kendall Park Road heading east. **Option:** You can also turn right (south) at the driveway to return to your car, skipping the last 0.5 mile.

6.3 Now you're back at a junction you faced at the beginning of your hike. Turn right (west) to hike downhill toward Kendall Lake and the parking lot.

6.5 You'll come out of the woods where you began, and end your hike at the parking lot.

Hike Information

Local Information
Cuyahoga Valley National Park/ Boston Store Visitor Center; (330) 657-2752; www.nps.gov/cuva

Hike Tours
Cleveland Hiking Club; www.clevelandhikingclub.org
NEOHiking; www.meetup.com/NEOHiking

Camping
Primitive camping; www.nps.gov/cuva/planyourvisit/lodging.htm

Other Resources
NEONaturalist; www.neonaturalist.com

38 Ledges Area Hike, Virginia Kendall Unit

The Ledges Area of the Virginia Kendall Unit consists of rough terrain with rocks acting as literal stepping-stones throughout. Tiny Haskell Run loops through Happy Days Lodge and serves as a connection to the mostly dense, flat yet scenic Boston Run Trail. Returning to the Ledges via Haskell Run, you'll hike along ridges surrounded by picnic tables and scenic views of the surrounding Cuyahoga Valley. A connector trail to the nearby Pine Grove Loop Trail offers an opportunity for more mileage. Feeling like a warrior? Pine Grove connects to the Kendall Lake trails (Hike 37) for another 6.5 miles of hiking possibilities.

Start: At the Octagon Shelter
Distance: 11.8 miles
Approximate hiking time: 4.5 hours
Difficulty: Difficult due to length
Trail surface: Natural
Best season: Year-round
Other trail users: None
Canine compatibility: Dogs allowed on leash
Land status: National park
Fees and permits: None
Schedule: Morning until dusk year-round
Maps: Cuyahoga Valley National Park / Boston Store Visitor Center; (330) 657-2752; www .nps.gov/cuva

Trail contacts: Cuyahoga Valley National Park / Boston Store Visitor Center; (330) 657-2752; www.nps.gov/cuva
Finding the trailhead: Drive south on I-77 for 7.1 miles. Take exit 156 to merge onto I-480 East for 12.1 miles. Keep left to continue on I-271 South for 3.4 miles. Take exit 18A on the left for OH 8 South. In 1.4 miles, merge onto OH 8 South for 4 miles. Take exit 12 for OH 303. In 0.3 mile, merge onto Akron Cleveland Road/State Road for 0.9 mile. Turn right onto Kendall Park Road for 1.1 miles. Continue onto Truxell Road for 0.2 mile. Destination is on the left. GPS: N 41 13' 33.6757" / W 81 30' 49.3308"

The Hike

The Ledges Trail is *the* definition of a "find." In a region that is underappreciated, the Ledges Trail has the ability to show outsiders and locals alike why living in Cleveland is amazing. In fact, this trail alone proves Clevelanders are actually spoiled, especially when it comes to green getaways available right in our backyard.

From the eastern end of the Octagon Shelter parking lot, you'll find several paths converge. This is as good a spot as any to begin your trek north on the Ledges Trail. And it won't take long to realize you're someplace special. "This is awesome," you're probably thinking as you do a 360 to take in your surroundings.

Thousands of years of nature doing its work have gone into producing the geological shape and splendor of the Ledges Area. You hardly need to be a rock-nerd or even a nature enthusiast to appreciate the diversity of this area.

Large, jagged boulders tower over you on all sides as you hike through the rocky terrain. It's easy to daydream, wondering who might have lived in this area hundreds

Hiking alongside the ledges COURTESY OF CUYAHOGA VALLEY NATIONAL PARK

or thousands of years ago. Tiny caves will make themselves evident throughout the trail. Maybe someone used to call this "home."

Surprisingly, the Ledges Trail is actually quite brief at only 1.75 miles total despite its seeming enormity. In fact, you'll arrive at the Haskell Run junction in just 0.5 mile. The Haskell Run Trail acts mostly as a connector to the 3.5-mile Boston Run Loop Trail through Happy Days Lodge.

When you come out to the lodge area, you'll find the grass cut into a V-shape. The trail here isn't really marked with the expanse of flat greenery ahead of you acting as a front lawn for the lodge. But you'll see a driveway for the lodge straight ahead. Hike there where you'll find a sign directing you to Boston Run via a pedestrian tunnel that runs underneath OH 303. At the other end you'll emerge to a parking lot specifically for Boston Run. Simply hike through it where you'll find a gravel path connecting you to the loop. Take the first left into the woods to hike Boston Run clockwise.

Boston Run is quite the opposite of the Ledges Trail, which makes this area and hike all the more exciting and satisfying. Contrary to the rocky Ledges Trail, Boston

Run is composed of mostly flat dirt trail as it meanders around various ridges and ravines. Beeches, oaks, maples, and tuliptrees populate the area.

When finished with the loop, you'll simply backtrack through the parking lot and pedestrian tunnel to return to Happy Days Lodge. The trail technically takes you back to the aforementioned V-cut grass, but you can just as easily follow the driveway behind the lodge to find the eastern end of the Haskell Run Trail. Take this until you return to an earlier junction where you left the Ledges Trail. Now you'll follow the signs to hike southeast along the second half of your Ledges Trail hike.

This leg takes you up high along—wait for it—the ledges, offering beautiful panoramic views of the surrounding Cuyahoga Valley alongside a number of picnic areas. Ice Box Cave will greet you shortly, but is unfortunately closed off due to the spreading of white-nosed syndrome—Batman's kryptonite, so to speak.

You'll finish the Ledges Trail where you started the hike. If you're looking to add a couple more miles, follow signs along a connector trail to hike southwest toward the Pine Grove Loop Trail. This will take you across the Octagon Shelter driveway you drove in on.

A shallow ravine slides underneath a wooden bridge.

Ledges Area Hike, Virginia Kendall Unit

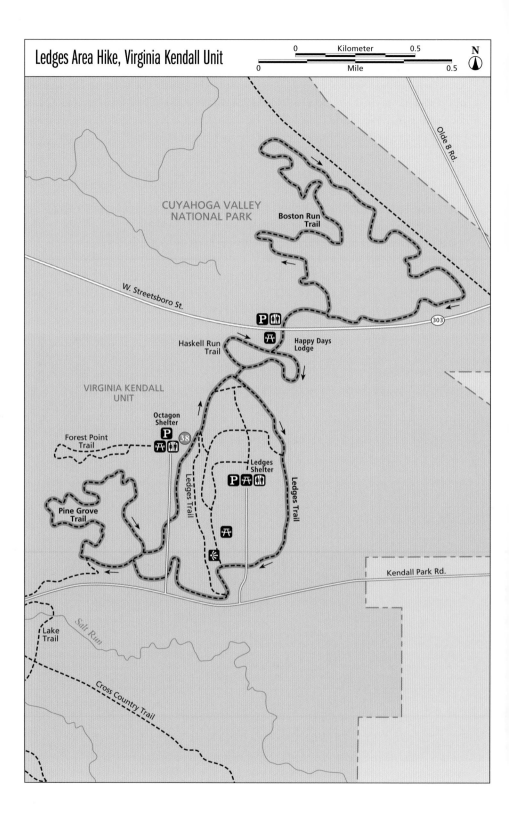

0   Kilometer   0.5

0   Mile   0.5

N

Olde 8 Rd.

CUYAHOGA VALLEY
NATIONAL PARK

Boston Run
Trail

W. Streetsboro St.

303

Haskell Run
Trail

Happy Days
Lodge

VIRGINIA KENDALL
UNIT

Octagon
Shelter

38

Forest Point
Trail

Ledges
Shelter

Ledges Trail

Ledges Trail

Pine Grove
Trail

Kendall Park Rd.

Lake
Trail

Salt Run

Cross Country Trail

Pine Grove itself is an easy hike that serves as an excellent excuse to add more miles to your hike. Early on in the hike, however, you'll find a connector trail that leads to Kendall Lake (Hike 37). Though separated in the book, it is possible to connect the entirety of the Virginia Kendall Unit's trails without much backtracking. But the hikes north of Kendall Park Road will be plenty for most, so finish the loop and use the connector trail to backtrack to your original trailhead.

Miles and Directions

0.0 Start at the Octagon Shelter. You'll find a trailhead at the eastern end of the parking lot with three options. Turn left (north) onto the Ledges Trail toward Haskell Run Trail. You'll continue on this trail, hiking north, until you reach the Haskell Run junction.

0.2 Stay straight (north) past a sign directing toward the Happy Days Lodge, which is off the Haskell Run Trail.

0.5 Arrive at the Haskell Run Trail junction. We're going to hike this clockwise, so turn left to hike northwest.

0.7 After climbing some stairs, you'll come to a grassy field in front of the Happy Days Lodge. Stay left to hike in front of the lodge and turn onto the parking lot driveway. Near here you'll find a pedestrian bridge tunnel that takes you underneath Streetsboro Street to get you to the other side where you'll find another parking lot attached to the Boston Run trailhead.

1.0 You'll find the Boston Run trailhead at the northeastern end of the parking lot with the typical CUYAHOGA VALLEY NATIONAL PARK sign. Hike this trail east toward the woods, taking the first left to hike this loop trail clockwise.

1.2 Take the first left (north) to hike downhill into the woods.

2.5 You'll arrive at a junction where you can take a connector for a shorter loop trail. But we're going to turn left (west) to continue hiking our way north to conquer the entire loop trail.

3.3 Pass the loop connector we skipped earlier. Continue hiking south on your trail back toward the trailhead.

5.1 Come back out of the woods, turning right (west) alongside Streetsboro Street on the same path you took to start the Boston Run Trail. Backtrack through the pedestrian tunnel all the way back to the grassy plain in front of the Happy Days Lodge. This time you're going to hike behind the lodge where you'll find yet another Cuyahoga Valley National Park trailhead to hike the eastern portion of the Haskell Run Trail.

5.9 Follow the Haskell Run Trail heading south.

6.3 Return to the Haskell Run Trail junction you've already visited. Continue straight, hiking uphill.

6.4 Arrive back at the Ledges Trail you left earlier. Keep to the left to hike the eastern portion of this loop trail.

6.9 Now you're at the Ice Box Cave. At the time of writing this, the cave is closed due to bats suffering from white-nosed syndrome. When you're done admiring the sights, continue hiking south on the Ledges Trail.

7.0 Ignore the Ledges Shelter junction and continue toward the overlook, hiking south.

7.8 Cross the driveway toward Ledges Shelter as you continue hiking west.

7.9 Arrive at the overlook. When you're done, follow signs to continue hiking north along the southern portion of the Ledges Trail.

8.6 Continue straight (northeast) past a Ledges Shelter junction.

8.7 Turn left (west) to follow signs toward the Octagon Shelter.

8.8 Take a right (northeast) after hiking downhill. You'll hike alongside some ledges on your right before going down some stairs where you'll arrive at another trail marker. Take a sharp left (north) to take you to familiar territory. Shortly after that turn, you'll approach the trailhead where you started your hike. You have the option of ending your hike now, but we're going to continue straight (south) toward the Pine Grove Loop Trail to add a little more mileage to your hike.

9.2 Cross the driveway that leads to the Octagon Shelter, heading west where you'll pick up the trail again.

9.4 Arrive at the junction to begin the Pine Grove Loop Trail. Turn left (south) to hike the loop clockwise.

9.5 You'll come to a junction for the overlook you've already seen. Ignore it and turn right (west) to continue on the loop.

9.7 Here you'll arrive at the junction for Kendall Lake. Superheroes are welcome to combine both hikes for something close to 20 miles of hiking. But we've included them separately in the book. For now, continue on the Pine Grove Loop Trail.

11.3 Finish the Pine Grove Loop Trail, and turn left heading northwest to backtrack toward your initial trailhead.

11.8 End your hike at the Octagon Shelter trailhead.

39 Wetmore to Dickerson Run to Langes Run Trail, Cuyahoga Valley National Park

The Wetmore area consists entirely of bridle trails with plenty of mileage available for a significant hike without having to spend hours backtracking. Follow the windy and rolling trails through Wetmore before using tiny Dickerson Run to connect with Langes Run for a final, simple hike back home.

Start: At the Wetmore Trailhead
Distance: 9 miles
Approximate hiking time: 3 hours
Difficulty: Moderate
Trail surface: Crushed gravel bridle trail and natural surface
Best season: Year-round
Other trail users: None
Canine compatibility: Dogs must be on a leash no longer than 6 feet
Land status: National park
Fees and permits: None
Schedule: 24 hours
Maps: Cuyahoga Valley National Park / Boston Store Visitor Center; (330) 657-2752; www .nps.gov/cuva

Trail contacts: Cuyahoga Valley National Park / Boston Store Visitor Center; (330) 657-2752; www.nps.gov/cuva
Finding the trailhead: Drive south from Cleveland on I-77 for about 20 miles. Take exit 143 for OH 176. Turn left onto Wheatley Road for 3 miles. Slight left onto Everett Road for just over 0.5 mile and then turn left onto Riverview Road. Take the first left onto Bolanz Road for 0.4 mile and left onto Akron Peninsula Road for 1.4 miles. Turn right onto Wetmore Road and the destination will be on the right in 1.4 miles. N 41 12' 44.3952" / W 81 32' 43.4724"

The Hike

The Wetmore Bridle Trails parking lot sits alongside a nondescript leg of Wetmore Road. Signs will wave you down, guiding you toward the small, gravel-covered parking lot. You might even catch a horse trailer as another indicator you've arrived. Whether it's spotting a live horse or the *remnants* of one, you'll soon see horses love the bridle trail.

After parking you'll find CUYAHOGA VALLEY NATIONAL PARK signage at the southeastern corner. You'll hike past this onto gravel trail between fence posts and woods to start your trek north on Valley Trail that will quickly merge with the Wetmore Trail. Within a couple tenths of a mile you'll come to a junction where you have the option of hiking the loop clockwise or counter-clockwise. Hiking clockwise affords you a more logical hike without any backtracking, so follow the combined Wetmore and Valley Trail west as the trail bends north. In another 0.2 mile, the Valley Trail will split to the left and you'll continue hiking east on Wetmore.

Horses love the bridle trails near the Wetmore Trailhead. In related news, watch out for road apples.

Early on you'll notice why Wetmore is ultimately a bridle trail. The trail is wide enough to accommodate a horse, yet the terrain isn't overly smooth to bore you to tears. It's rather enjoyable if you're in a relaxed state of mind.

Continuing around the trail for about 2 miles, you'll arrive at the Tabletop Trail, which travels to a Dickerson Run and Langes Run junction. Tabletop runs at 0.6 mile as does the leg of Wetmore to the same junction. For simplicity's sake, stick to the Wetmore Trail. In fact, you'll hike northwest past the four-way junction toward the northwestern trailhead of Dickerson Run in another mile.

Keep a sharp eye out for Dickerson Run. It's an easy trail to miss. Once you're on it, you'll be enveloped into far more dense surroundings with ravines and narrow paths slicing through. You'll hike this mile-long trail back to the previously mentioned four-way junction. This time you'll take a sharp right for Langes Run to hike the southern and western areas of the Wetmore Bridle Trails.

Heading onto the Bridle Trail

Langes Run will trek across Wetmore Road after about 1 mile. You'll continue west for another 1.5 miles along similar, easy trail before reconnecting with the Valley Trail, which comes from the Everett Towpath Trail junction and runs north through where you started your hike.

The trail comes out to a small grassy plain straddled between the woods you've just emerged from and Peninsula Road to the west. You'll simply hike along the western edge of the woods, following the now-grassy trail before cutting back through the woods. Here you'll hike a turnaround that will direct the remaining trail southeast before bending northeast to Wetmore Road. From here you can see that you've emerged across the street from your parking lot. Cross the street to end the hike.

Miles and Directions

0.0 Start at the Wetmore trailhead marked at the southeastern corner of the parking lot next to a map of Cuyahoga Valley National Park. Begin hiking north on this combination of the Valley and Wetmore Trails.

Wetmore to Dickerson Run to Langes Run Trail, Cuyahoga Valley National Park

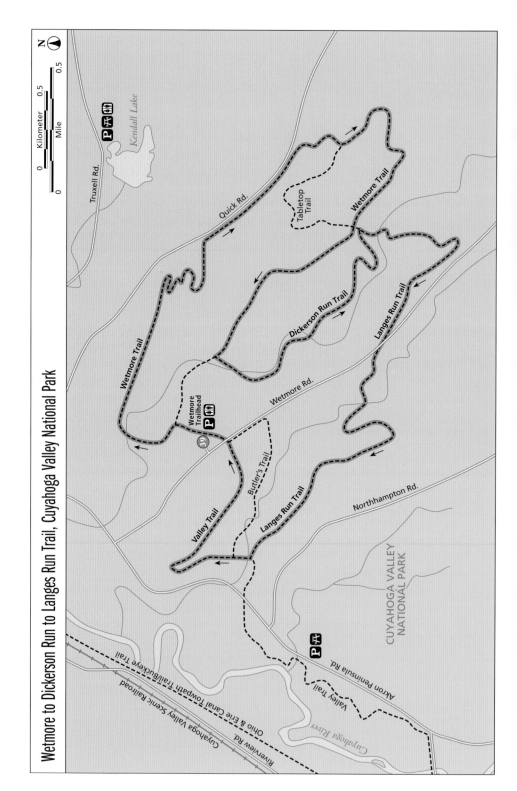

0.2 Stay to the left (west) to continue on the combined Valley and Wetmore Trails for another 0.2 mile. **Option:** Turn right (east) to hike 0.3 mile to the Dickerson Run Trail or complete the Wetmore Trail counter-clockwise.

0.4 Turn right (east) at this junction to leave the Valley Trail and continue on Wetmore. **Option:** Stay to the left to continue hiking north on the Valley Trail.

1.8 Continuing straight clearly leads to Quick Road. Instead, turn right (southeast) to continue hiking on the Wetmore Trail alongside the road.

2.5 You'll leave the woods for a brief excursion through a meadow before bending right back into the woods to continue the hike. On your right (west) you'll see the 0.6-mile Tabletop Trail.

3.4 Arrive at a trail junction for Wetmore, Dickerson Run, and Langes Run. You're going to ignore the junction, continuing northwest on the Wetmore Trail for another mile until you reach the northeastern end of the Dickerson Run Trail. **Option:** Turn left (south) to start the 1-mile Dickerson Run Trail now, hiking back toward the parking lot, or to skip a mile of the Wetmore Trail to begin the Langes Run Trail.

4.4 Turn left (south) to leave the Wetmore Trail and begin the Dickerson Run Trail. **Option:** Continue straight (northwest) to finish the Wetmore Trail in 0.5 mile and end your hike early.

5.5 Here you'll arrive near the Langes Run junction you ignored earlier to continue on Wetmore. This time take a hard right (south) to begin the 3.5-mile Langes Run Trail. **Option:** Turn left (north) to head slightly uphill toward where you already hiked the Wetmore Trail. If you need to bail out, you can either take this back to the parking lot or backtrack on Dickerson Run.

6.5 Cross Wetmore Road and follow the Bridle crossing sign to continue hiking west on Langes Run.

8.0 You'll come out to a small, grassy plain with approximately 12-foot-high wooden posts with green trail markers. Keep these to your left and you'll shortly be directed to the combined Valley and Langes Run Trails. Turn right onto the combined trail (north) to finish the last mile of your hike. **Option:** When you reach the Valley and Langes Run junction, you can turn left (west) for an approximately 1.7-mile hike to the Hunt Farm Visitor Information Center.

9.0 Cross Wetmore Road heading north, and you'll hike into the driveway of your parking lot to end your hike.

Hike Information

Camping

Primitive camping; www.nps.gov/cuva/planyourvisit/lodging.htm

GREEN TIP

Carry a reusable water container that you fill at the tap. Bottled water is expensive; lots of petroleum is used to make the plastic bottles; and they're a disposal nightmare.

Hiking past one of the countless blue blazes you'll find along the Buckeye Trail

Buckeye Trail

Welcome (finally) to the blue blazes, otherwise known as your guide along the state's most famous hike—the Buckeye Trail. Sure, you've seen these blue blazes intermittently during other hikes in the book, but now it's time to get closer to this wonderful trail. Now it's time to really get to know the Buckeye Trail over a day and a half of hiking, ending with a ride home on the commanding and simply awesome Cuyahoga Valley Scenic Railroad.

Blue Hen Falls in Cuyahoga Valley National Park

40 Buckeye Trail to Peninsula Cuyahoga Valley Scenic Railroad Station

The longest hike in *Best Hikes Cleveland* takes you 13.5 miles on Ohio's most famous trail along various reservations alongside the Ohio-Erie Canal en route to the Stanford House camping grounds for an overnight. The next morning, finish with a fast 5.5-mile hike to the lovely and quaint town of Peninsula where you'll take the magnificent Cuyahoga Valley Scenic Railroad back home.

Start: At the Cuyahoga Valley Scenic Railroad Brecksville Station
Distance: 19 miles
Approximate hiking time: 8 hours
Difficulty: Difficult due to backpack weight and mostly rugged terrain
Trail surface: Mostly rugged natural trail
Best season: Year-round
Other trail users: Runners
Canine compatibility: Dogs allowed on leash
Land status: Public
Fees and permits: None
Schedule: Cuyahoga Valley National Park is open twenty-four hours a day unless otherwise noted in this book and on its official website.

This hike does not go through any portions that close, but, of course, it's advised to make it to your overnight spot before sundown.
Maps: Available from Buckeye Trail Association
Trail contacts: Buckeye Trail Association; www.buckeyetrail.org
Finding the trailhead: From Cleveland, drive south on I-77 toward Akron for about 14 miles. Take exit 149A to merge onto OH 82 East/East Royalton Road toward Brecksville. Continue to follow OH 82 for 3.5 miles. Turn right onto Riverview Road and left onto Valley Parkway in just 0.2 mile. In another 0.2 mile, your destination will be on your left. GPS: N 41 19' 7.5396" / W 81 35' 16.9146"

The Hike

The Buckeye Trail is a statewide network that meanders throughout many of Northeast Ohio's parks before extending its reach west to Toledo and south to Cincinnati. The Buckeye Trail easily features some of the most rugged terrain in Northeast Ohio. You might have noticed in other hikes when the Buckeye Trail snuck into your hike. Today, it's all Buckeye Trail.

Beginning from the Brecksville station of the Cuyahoga Valley Scenic Railroad, you'll hike west on the paved all-purpose trail briefly before meandering south on Riverview Road, where you'll finally be pushed into the woods. At last, let the backpacking begin.

Your initial trek will take you southwest toward the eastern end of Cleveland Metroparks' Brecksville Reservation. But no matter what reservation or park you stumble upon, you can rest assured that the trail will always be marked by the blue blazes. In fact, you shouldn't be hiking this trail if you're not confident in your ability to follow blue paint. The trail is well marked, and it would be insulting to your

Yours truly in his happy place early on in the Buckeye Trail, crossing one of the overnight hike's many stone-hopping stream crossings

intelligence to note every single minor trail junction. Realistically speaking, this is one of the easier trails to follow.

By now you've no doubt noticed that the Buckeye Trail is at its most rugged when it's running solo. Some of the most enjoyable portions of this hike are early on as you complete your westernmost half-loop to Brecksville and back east to eventually hike south alongside Riverview Road. It's very serene. Only someone with bat ears could hear the traffic running by.

Continue hiking through the rolling hills and various shale-covered stream crossings, passing Snowville Road and Columbia Road along the way to Blue Hen Falls near Boston Mills Road. Blue Hen is a small waterfall at just about 15 feet tall. The more scenic Buttermilk Falls runs just downstream, but is unfortunately a bit out of the way. Make a mental note to come back.

The trail soon thereafter crosses Boston Mills Road, continuing alongside briefly before offering one last woodland hike and dumping you into the middle of Boston

GRANDMA OF THE BUCKEYE TRAIL

Thank you, thank you, *thank* you to Mr. Merrill. One might call this man the godfather of the Buckeye Trail for his 1958 *Columbus Dispatch* article calling for a hiking trail to connect Cincinnati to Lake Erie. This energized people, and quickly a base of support (including Merrill) met to discuss possibilities. A year later, the Buckeye Trail Association was born with the first 20 miles receiving dedication in Hocking County.

The trail network grew over the next 20 years, completing in 1980 at Deer Lick Cave in Cleveland Metroparks' Brecksville Reservation within the borders of Cuyahoga Valley National Park. At this point the trail covered 1,444 miles. For context's sake, the Appalachian Trail is 2,179 miles. Not bad for Ohio, considering this network is housed entirely in one state whereas the white blazes of the AT span across fourteen states.

Speaking of the AT, the two trails have a special woman in common. Ohio's hiking great-grandmother, Emma Gatewood, was the first woman to through-hike the Appalachian Trail in 1953 at the age of 67. As if that wasn't enough, she conquered the trail again and a third time in sections. Perhaps raising eleven children on farms along the Ohio River was all the training she needed.

Naturally, Grandma Gatewood was among the thirty-four BTA leaders and founders who dedicated the first stretch of Buckeye Trail on September 19, 1959.

center. Just after crossing the Towpath Trail, you'll leave the Buckeye Trail for a Valley Trail hike under a mile to get to your campsite at the Stanford House. It's fairly unremarkable trail at this point. But after 13 miles, it's a relaxing godsend. By the time you reach the Stanford House, you'll be ready to collapse. Goodnight, backpacking friends.

Rise and shine! It's time for a 5.5-mile hike to finish the trip. Use the backtrack to Boston Mills Road as an opportunity to reboot. Here's hoping you're recharged by the time you cross Boston Mills south.

You might be confused with what to do after crossing Boston Mills Road, but you'll see blue blazes once again as you hike toward the Boston Store Visitor Center parking lot. The Boston to Peninsula section starts with a fairly taxing uphill climb, especially after hiking 13.5 miles the day before. Soon you'll complete a small mini-loop that crosses Boston Mills Road and takes you right back onto the trail. It's a potentially dangerous section that you'll be forced to cross. Just tap into what you learned in grade school, look both ways, and haul ass across the street to continue the trail on the other side.

Day two starts with the constant hum of traffic. But once you hike past I-271, I-80, and Boston Mills Road, the trail will become more remote and surprisingly

An old brick road heading into town

serene. The fresh air off the towering pines couldn't come at a better time as you near the end of your overnight journey.

About a mile or so near the end you'll come out of the Pine Lane Trailhead parking lot onto a brick-covered access road. At first you may think you've lost the trail, but you'll notice blue blazes painted on the road as you continue hiking west.

Considering this trail traverses the entire state, there are ways to make it longer. You can follow the Towpath further south from Peninsula, or rejoin the Valley Trail at Pine Lane before reaching Peninsula. If you're really feeling adventurous, consult your map. Better yet, have a chat with the Buckeye Trail Association if you're that anxious to take on something more challenging. For now, finish hiking west into Peninsula where the train tracks beckon. Grab some breakfast at Fisher's Cafe & Pub before hopping on the Cuyahoga Valley Scenic Railroad home. Soon you'll discover that what took you 19 miles and an overnight camp is less than 30 minutes and a couple of train stops on the railroad. But a backpacker knows that you do it for the experience. And there's nothing in Ohio like the Buckeye Trail.

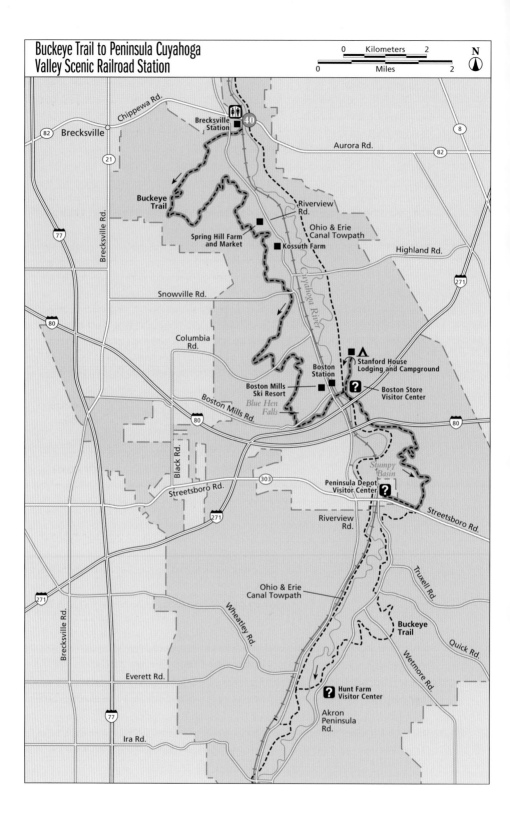

Buckeye Trail to Peninsula Cuyahoga Valley Scenic Railroad Station

Kilometers
0 — 2
Miles
0 — 2

N

Chippewa Rd.

82 Brecksville

Brecksville Station
40

Aurora Rd.

8

21

82

Buckeye Trail

Brecksville Rd.

77

Riverview Rd.

Spring Hill Farm and Market

Kossuth Farm

Ohio & Erie Canal Towpath

Highland Rd.

271

Cuyahoga River

Snowville Rd.

80

Columbia Rd.

Stanford House Lodging and Campground

Boston Station

Boston Mills Ski Resort

Boston Store Visitor Center

Blue Hen Falls

Boston Mills Rd.

80

Black Rd.

80

Stumpy Basin

Streetsboro Rd.

303

Peninsula Depot Visitor Center

271

Riverview Rd.

Streetsboro Rd.

Truxell Rd.

271

Ohio & Erie Canal Towpath

Buckeye Trail

Quick Rd.

Brecksville Rd.

Wheatley Rd.

Wetmore Rd.

Everett Rd.

Hunt Farm Visitor Center

77

Akron Peninsula Rd.

Ira Rd.

Miles and Directions

0.0 Start at the Brecksville Station of the Cuyahoga Valley Scenic Railroad. Next to the railroad crossing, you'll find a tree marked with the blue blazes standing next to a paved path guiding you west to start your hike.

0.1 Turn left (south) to cross Valley Parkway (may be Chippewa Creek Drive on some maps) and follow the blue blazes through a small grassy field.

0.2 Now cross Riverview Road on your right (west) over a guardrail. It may seem like an odd way to continue the hike early on, but you'll see the blue blazes continuing just across the street after hiking over a bridge. Turn right (west) to follow the blue blazes into the woods and toward the eastern edge of Cleveland Metroparks' Brecksville Reservation, which is outlined by the Buckeye Trail.

1.1 Here you'll be merged onto paved trail within the Brecksville Reservation. Continue following the blue blazes, hiking on the all-purpose trail. In less than 0.1 mile, you'll turn right (west) onto a small dirt path to cross Valley Parkway. You'll see a Buckeye Trail post on the other side.

1.8 Turn left (south) to again cross Valley Parkway. You'll see your Buckeye Trail marker across the street next to another all-purpose trail. This junction is one of the few, if not only, potentially confusing junctions in that the Buckeye Trail does continue west if you do not turn. But this will take you out toward Medina County, far from your campsite. So it's best if you keep your eyes open for this crossing. Continue hiking south on this trail, winding alongside Cleveland Metro Parkway.

2.6 You'll come out of the woods onto Ottawa Point Driveway. Hike across it heading northeast very briefly. You'll see the blue blazes of the Buckeye Trail not even 20 feet away, which you'll follow along on the crushed gravel driveway.

2.8 Arrive at the parking lot for the gravel trail you've been hiking on. Continue hiking straight past the fence posts, heading past a grassy field for the northeast corner of the woods where you'll continue the Buckeye Trail.

3.8 Cross a small stream alongside (at the time) fading blue blazes to continue your hike south.

3.9 Merge onto the Bridle Trail very briefly. You'll come to a junction where you'll turn left (east) to continue on the Buckeye Trail.

5.5 You'll see a bird house to your left above what looks like hiking trail, but you'll want to turn right (south) to continue following the blue blazes.

7.0 Arrive at the north side of Snowville Road and turn left (east) to hike briefly alongside the road. You'll continue for about 100 feet or less when you have to cross Snowville Road, hiking south. Make sure there's no traffic and turn right (southwest) to cross into the woods on the other side where you'll see markers for the continuation of the Buckeye Trail. Follow this trail southwest as it winds through rolling hills for the next 2 miles.

9.0 Now you'll cross Columbia Road hiking south, continuing the trail downhill back into the woods on the opposite side next to a wooden post noting Boston is 3.3 miles away. Follow the trail east as it winds to the northeast.

11.0 You'll come to a junction for Blue Hen Falls. Turn left (east) for a short out-and-back to the falls. Return to this junction after the falls to continue hiking south on the Buckeye Trail. From here you have about 1.6 miles left until Boston.

Waiting for the train in Peninsula

11.5 Cross the street heading south into a dirt, overflow parking lot, and follow along the eastern edge of the parking lot where you'll quickly find a Buckeye marker guiding you into the woods, hiking east.

11.7 You'll come out of the woods to hike east alongside Boston Mills Road with a blue blaze on a nearby telephone pole. As you continue, you'll pass a Summit County Engineer's station on your right (south). Just after you pass it, you'll find a post for the Buckeye Trail that guides you south, away from Boston Mills Road. Continue following this trail as it wraps to the east for less than a mile hike to Riverview Road.

12.5 Arrive at Riverview Road where you'll want to cross to continue east, hiking alongside Boston Mills Road to the historic heart of Boston surrounded by train tracks. You'll continue past these tracks, still hiking east as you pass a Trail Mix store run by the Conservancy for Cuyahoga Valley National Park. Also, stop in CVNP Boston Store Visitor Center.

12.8 Turn left (north) onto the Valley Bridle Trail alongside Stanford Road. You'll hike on this grassy trail for the next approximately 0.6 mile to your final destination for the day.

13.5 Turn right (east) onto a driveway for the Stanford House where you'll camp, (rooms are also available) ending your hike for the day. In the morning, backtrack Boston Mills Road. Cross the road hiking south toward the Boston Store Visitor Center parking lot, following signs for the Valley Bridle Trail. This will take you south around the parking lot onto paved trail, hiking underneath I-271.

14.3 Passing a sign for the Buckeye Trail, you'll continue hiking south toward a post directing you left (east).

14.4 Turn left (east) using a series of exposed roots as steps. Following the blue blazes, now very prominent, you'll follow the trail through pines as it winds east and southeast between Boston Mills Road and the I-80 turnpike.

15.5 Cross Boston Mills Road, hiking north. The Buckeye Trail continues on the other side.

15.8 The Buckeye Trail will again run into Boston Mills Road. This time you'll have to turn left (south) on the road, cross it to the west, and continue the trail in the woods on the other side.

16.3 You'll see signs for Hudson Parks, letting you know you've taken the Buckeye Trail into new territory. Additionally you'll notice Hudson Parks has marked trees white for their own path. Nevertheless, you'll continue to follow the blue blazes by turning right (west).

18.2 Arrive at the Pine Lane Trailhead parking lot. Signs will direct you west along the parking lot, which leads to an old access road. You're going to follow this brick-covered road with blue blazes due west until it pushes you back into the woods in about 0.1 mile.

18.7 The trail will turn into Dell Road, which in turn will dump you out onto OH 303 or Main Street. Cross south and continue hiking west toward downtown Peninsula. You can see train tracks out in the distance. This is the Peninsula station where you'll end your hike. Continue hiking west until you reach the station.

19.0 End your hike at the Peninsula station of the Cuyahoga Valley Scenic Railroad. Grab some eats in town and then hop on the train home!

Hike Information

Camping
Stanford House; (330) 657-2909

Restaurants
Fisher's Cafe & Pub; (330) 657-2651; www.fisherscafe.com

Organizations
The Buckeye Trail Association; www.buckeyetrail.org

Hike Index

Summit County

Adam Run Loop Trail, Hampton Hills Metro Park, 155

Adell Durbin Park & Arboretum, 175

Dogwood to Mingo Trail Loop, Sand Run Metro Park, 160

Gorge Trail, Gorge Metro Park, 169

Hudson Springs Park Loop Trail, 165

Cuyahoga Valley National Park

Cross Country to Lake to Salt Run Trail, Virginia Kendall Unit, 207

Ledges Area Hike, Virginia Kendall Unit, 213

Oak Hill to Plateau Trail, Cuyahoga Valley National Park, 185

Red Lock to Old Carriage Trail, Cuyahoga Valley National Park, 190

Riding Run to Perkins Bridle Trails and Furnace Run Trail, Cuyahoga Valley National Park, 195

Stanford to Brandywine Gorge Trail, Cuyahoga Valley National Park, 201

Tree Farm Loop Trail, Cuyahoga Valley National Park, 181

Wetmore to Dickerson Run to Langes Run Trail, Cuyahoga Valley National Park, 219

Buckeye Trail

Buckeye Trail to Peninsula Cuyahoga Valley Scenic Railroad Station, 226

About the Author

Joe Baur is a writer, filmmaker, and author of several books, including three with Falcon Guides and most recently, *Talking Tico: (Mis)adventures of a Gringo in and Around Costa Rica* about his time living in Central America. He first became interested in the great outdoors when Grandpa Bud took him, his brother Dave, and cousins to the nearby Lake Metroparks Farmpark. He vaguely recalls milking a cow and it being a generally weird experience. Nonetheless, his father continued to push staying active outside with occasional trips to the Holden Arboretum, which naturally led to an obsession with hiking, backpacking, and finding new ways to go off the beaten path. Originally from Northeast Ohio, Joe is now based in Düsseldorf, Germany, where his weekends are often spent riding the train, hiking a trail, and drinking a beer. Life is good.

You can catch up with Joe at both joebaur.com and WithoutAPath.com.